A Gospel for the Poor

A Gospel for the Poor

Global Social Christianity
and the Latin American Evangelical Left

David C. Kirkpatrick

PENN

UNIVERSITY OF PENNSYLVANIA PRESS

PHILADELPHIA

Published by
University of Pennsylvania Press
Philadelphia, Pennsylvania 19104-4112
www.upenn.edu/pennpress

Printed in the United States of America
on acid-free paper

1 3 5 7 9 10 8 6 4 2

Library of Congress Cataloging-in-Publication Data
Names: Kirkpatrick, David C., author.
Title: A gospel for the poor : global social Christianity and the Latin
    American evangelical left / David C. Kirkpatrick.
Description: 1st edition. | Philadelphia : University of Pennsylvania Press, [2019] |
    Includes bibliographical references and index.
Identifiers: LCCN 2018046938 | ISBN 9780812250947 (hardcover)
Subjects: LCSH: Evangelicalism—Latin America—History—20th century. |
    Liberalism (Religion)—Protestant churches—History—20th century. |
    Social gospel—Latin America—History—20th century. | Church and social
    problems—Protestant churches—History—20th century. | Christianity and
    politics—Latin America—History—20th century. | Latin America—Church
    history—20th century.
Classification: LCC BR1642.L29 K57 2019 | DDC 278/.082—dc23
LC record available at https://lccn.loc.gov/2018046938

For Anna

CONTENTS

ABBREVIATIONS

ATE   Evangelical Theological Association, Asociación Teológica Evangélica

BGCA   Billy Graham Center Archives, Wheaton, Illinois

BGEA   Billy Graham Evangelistic Association

CELA   Latin American Evangelical Conference, Conferencia Evangélica Latinoamericana

CELAM   Latin American Episcopal Council, Consejo Episcopal Latinoamericano

CEPAL   Economic Commission for Latin America, Comisión Económico para América Latina

CICOP   Catholic Inter-American Cooperation Program

CLADE   Latin American Congress on Evangelization, Congreso Latinoamericano de Evangelización

EBTS   Eastern Baptist Theological Seminary

EFMA   Evangelical Foreign Missions Association

ETS   Evangelical Theological Society

EUSA   Evangelical Union of South America

FTL   Latin American Theological Fraternity, Fraternidad Teológica Latinoamericana

FTS   Fuller Theological Seminary

IAMS   International Association for Mission Studies

IFES   International Fellowship of Evangelical Students

INFEMIT   International Fellowship of Evangelical Mission Theologians

ISAL   Church and Society in Latin America, Iglesia y Sociedad en América Latina

ISEDET   Instituto Superior Evangélico de Estudios Teológicos

IVCF   InterVarsity Christian Fellowship

IVF   InterVarsity Fellowship

LAM   Latin America Mission

MEB	Base Education Movement, Movimento de Educaçao de Base
OMSC	Overseas Ministries Study Center
PTS	Palmer Theological Seminary
SBL	Seminario Bíblico Latinoamericano
SCM	Student Christian Movement
TEDS	Trinity Evangelical Divinity School
UCCF	Universities and Colleges Christian Fellowship
UNAM	Universidad Nacional Autónoma de México
WCC	World Council of Churches
WCASA	Wheaton College Archives and Special Collections
WEF	World Evangelical Fellowship
WSCF	World Student Christian Federation

Toward a Gospel for the Poor

"Young people [ask] questions regarding the Christian attitude towards a Marxist regime, while the pastors [discuss] the length of the skirts that girls are wearing in church. A social ethic—we have none."[1] In August 1972, Ecuadorian evangelical René Padilla wrote a personal letter to one of the key architects of postwar evangelicalism in the United States, theologian Carl F. H. Henry. For Padilla, the social retreat of evangelicals was "much more dangerous" than tobacco, alcohol, and dance—traditional taboos of fundamentalist missionaries from the United States and many Latin American evangelical pastors.[2] At the time, many Protestant evangelical pastors in Latin America preached naked moralism and saving individual souls from a damned world while overlooking their pressing sociopolitical context. Latin American Protestant evangelicalism is an unlikely location for social Christianity and has been widely overlooked by observers precisely because it often mirrored fundamentalism in the United States.

Carl Henry likewise decried the social retreat of fundamentalists from the ails of a postwar American culture in his brief but influential study, *The Uneasy Conscience of Modern Fundamentalism* (1947).[3] Henry presented U.S. culture as morally vacuous and beckoned fundamentalists to fill the void with evangelical theological and political materials. *Uneasy Conscience* became a blueprint for rebranding fundamentalism as "neo-evangelicalism" and a rallying cry for postwar evangelical activism in the United States. At the time of Padilla's letter, however, Henry was planning a forty-day trip to eight Latin American countries under the auspices of the Latin American Theological Fraternity (Fraternidad Teológica Latinoamericana or FTL).[4] Given Henry's reputation as a leading evangelical expert in social ethics, one might expect Latin American evangelicals to request Henry's assistance in developing a new brand of evangelical social Christianity. Instead, in the same letter, Padilla sharply warned Henry to avoid the topic completely precisely because he was an American.[5] Much had changed in the preceding decades, and leaders from the Global South were rising to take their place at the table of theological and political discourse. In fact, a nascent Evangelical Left in Latin America was *already* developing a brand of social Christianity, flavored by the political and social ferment of the global Cold War.[6]

Pressing conversation regarding the relationship between social action and the Christian faith was neither new nor unexpected. An entire generation of Latin American theologians insisted that the church should center on the poor—in Pope Francis's words, to build "a Church which is poor and for the poor."[7] Their response was profoundly shaped by their Cold War context. The intense ideological struggle of the global Cold War—the undeclared war between the United States and the Soviet Union that dominated international affairs roughly between 1945 and 1991—was an extension of European colonialism and the proving ground of ideologies forged in Moscow and Washington.[8] Both sides attempted to determine the destiny of the Developing World often through means of economic coercion, political assassinations, and propping up repressive military regimes.[9] From within this sociopolitical ferment, a generation of religious elites—both Catholic and Protestant—sought to mold new theologies to fit the Latin American reality.

The Cold War was the seedbed of social Christianity. While Latin America has been widely credited with inspiring Catholic social teaching, especially theologies of liberation, this same context has been widely overlooked in the story of Protestant evangelicalism. Latin American evangelicals shared the sociopolitical context while negotiating a unique path as a religious minority community in an overwhelmingly Catholic continent. They drew from personal biographies filled with anti-Protestant acts of violence, oppression, and discrimination, in addition to pervasive inequality and repressive military governments. This was, according to Padilla, "part and parcel of life for non-Roman Catholic Christians and others in pre–Second Vatican Council days" in Latin America.[10] On this divergent road, an embryonic progressive coalition of evangelicals began to develop a social Christianity that would challenge evangelical political and theological loyalties around the world.

These developments in Latin America coincided with a brief political moment for an Evangelical Left in the United States.[11] *Newsweek* magazine christened 1976 "The Year of the Evangelical" as the American public elected its first "born-again president." Yet, this evangelical was not a conservative but a progressive and not a Republican but a southern Baptist Democrat—Jimmy Carter.[12] For American evangelicalism, this was largely political prologue, the first act in a drama dominated by the Republican Party and the so-called Religious Right. Around the globe, however, an increasingly diverse cast of characters began to revise the evangelical script. To put it succinctly: the political and theological moment of the Evangelical Left was neither brief nor driven primarily by American actors. In particular, an emerging Latin American Evangelical Left was busy marketing social Christianity to a younger, emerging generation of global evangelical activists—including many in the United States.[13] In the late 1960s and early 1970s, this Latin American negotiation of power, politics, and theologies presented the most formidable challenge to American management of expansive sectors of global Christianity. As Latin Americans shifted, they pulled many globally conscious evangelicals with them. Latin American leadership here was far from accidental; they drew unique inspiration from their story as a religious minority community.

Protestantism in Latin America

The identity of Latin American Protestantism was forged at the intersection of Catholic hegemony, systemic violence, and American missionary oversight. Indeed, their story is one marked by migration, missions, and negotiation. Prior to World War I, Protestant communities were mainly the product of early nineteenth-century immigration.[14] As the nineteenth century progressed, two realities converged in the fields of politics and religion: the independence of Latin American nations from the colonial powers of Spain and Portugal and the legacy of the Second Great Awakening in the United States, a Protestant revival movement that flourished from the 1790s to the 1830s. Those factors inspired new missionary initiatives from the North and an influx of Protestant missionaries from the United States into Latin America.[15]

After Ecuadorian independence in 1822, for example, the liberal reforms of President José Eloy Alfaro Delgado opened the door to a wider foreign missionary presence.[16] At the end of the nineteenth century and into the first part of the twentieth century, every Protestant missionary in Ecuador was from the United States.[17] During the first Alfaro presidency (1895–1901), the Gospel Mission Union was established in 1896 and the Christian and Missionary Alliance in 1897—Protestant denominations from the United

States that compose 40 percent of Ecuadorian Protestants today.[18] In 1906 (during Alfaro's second presidency), the Ecuadorian government established a new constitution, which, at least on paper, separated church and state and placed wider restrictions on Catholic clerical influence in areas such as education.[19] It is no coincidence that the years 1900–1912 saw the establishment of influential missions such as those described above and also the American Bible Society (la Sociedad Bíblica Americana) and Evangelical Mission Union (Unión Misionera Evangélica).[20] Yet, none of these missions could boast an indigenous church membership roll of more than 100 by 1910.[21]

At the turn of the twentieth century, wider trends in migration began to reshape the internal structure of Latin American life. In 1960, one political scientist observed the tail end of these migration patterns, saying, "There is no Latin American country in which there has been a trend away from urbanization; everywhere the impressive fact has been the movement toward the city, the swelling of urban populations."[22] In the 1930 Mexican census, for example, Mexico City, the capital, contained nearly 961,000 inhabitants.[23] By the next census a decade later, the city had nearly doubled in population to almost 1.5 million inhabitants.[24] After World War II, Protestantism began to gain a foothold in Latin America as urbanization provided a new social context for religious life.[25] Protestant churches found acceptance at the margins of this new urban environment, growing in places that traditional Roman Catholic structures largely struggled to reach—due in part to pervasive priest shortages in the region.

The growth of Protestant churches also coincided with the increasing involvement of U.S. foreign policy in Latin America during the Cold War era. In some cases, Latin American military dictatorships were friendlier to Protestants than to Catholics, as the Catholic hierarchy held power and influence while increasingly siding with the poor.[26] By implication, many Latin American Protestants were seen as foreigners in their own land, labeled "gringos" and Yankees.[27] Many Roman Catholic priests and authorities also viewed Protestant evangelistic efforts toward so-called nominal Roman Catholics as imposing on their religious turf. Priests and religious leaders sometimes played into these fears by stoking up mobs for violence against Protestants.[28]

Until the 1960s, nearly 90 percent of Latin Americans self-identified as Catholic.[29] Today, nearly 20 percent of Latin Americans self-identify as Protestant. Put another way, only one in ten Latin Americans alive today was raised Protestant, while nearly one in five now self-identifies as such.[30] The visibility and influence that Protestants experience today were a distant thought during the first half of the twentieth century. As a marginalized religious minority community, the Protestant path into the present day was one marked by discrimination and violence.

For much of their history, Latin American Protestant evangelical communities were often dependent on North American money, personnel, and theological methods. The intersection of imported political and theological influence from the North and sociopolitical tumult in the South created a third path for the emergence of new, holistic Christianities. Young Latin American evangelicals, notably Ecuadorian René Padilla, Peruvian Samuel Escobar, Peruvian Pedro Arana, and Puerto Rican Orlando Costas, began to search for theological materials with which they could address a revolutionary situation. Rather than rejecting the evangelical theology they received from North Americans, they sought to strip it of its white, middle-class American packaging—to formulate a "gospel for the poor," the marginalized, and the suffering.

The repudiation of forms of Christian theology fashioned in the United States was more than a theological statement—it was a reflection of broad Latin American antipathy toward U.S. foreign policy in the region and of Latin American Protestant evangelical sensitivity to being associated with certain colleagues in the North. Like many members of the Evangelical Left in the United States, Latin American evangelical elites became increasingly discontent with the conservative political loyalties of evangelicals and the perceived excesses of the political left. Indeed, they found critical continuity with so-called radical evangelicals in the United States such as Jim Wallis and his *Post-American* (later *Sojourners*) magazine, Anabaptist ethicists Ron Sider and John Howard Yoder, professor-activist Tony Campolo, and Brian McLaren and the Emerging Church Movement, all of whom protested U.S. imperialism and the captivity of American Christianity to free-market capitalism. Progressive Latin Americans also converted conservative power-brokers to their brand of social Christianity. Important here is the travel diary of Anglican evangelical statesman John Stott found in Lambeth Palace Library in London, which chronicles the friendship and influence of an embryonic Latin American Evangelical Left. After his public conversion to social Christianity (described below), Stott provided a stamp of approval and strategic bridge to a wider global evangelical community. The *New York*

Times put this clearly in 2011: "If evangelicals could elect a pope, [John] Stott is the person they would likely choose."[31]

The renaissance of evangelical social Christianity ushered in a brief moment of progressive political activism and a lasting era of global evangelical relief organizations that command billion-dollar budgets. These organizations became a constant presence in evangelical churches and homes, for example, through pictures of "sponsored children" stuck to refrigerator doors. Indeed, today, a sizable portion of global evangelicalism embraces the pursuit of justice alongside the evangelical offer of salvation. This coincided with an emerging "evangelical internationalism" that has deeply influenced foreign policy in the United States. In this way, our story cuts across conservative and liberal divides—both in terms of Christian forms and political allegiances. The intellectual scaffolding was built not in the American public square but in an unlikely and overlooked context of Latin America. The framework and language developed by a germinal Latin American Evangelical Left has been adopted and borrowed around the world, shifting mission priorities and political loyalties. This represents a surprising and stark reversal within the evangelical world—from widespread fears over the "Social Gospel" to a wide embrace of social Christianity.

Evangelicals and Social Christianity

Adherents of social Christianity, while representing a diverse and eclectic tradition, shared a broad conviction. As historian Heath Carter clarified, for adherents, the concept of sin "infects not only individuals but also systems and structures; that salvation is not only personal but also societal." This widened definition of "sin" and "salvation" then presented clear implications for Christian mission: the struggle for justice is essential, rather than optional.[32] Social Christianity is perhaps most well known in the Social Gospel Movement that arose in the late nineteenth and early twentieth centuries on both sides of the Atlantic. Members of the Latin American Evangelical Left shared varying, disparate, and complex affinities with progressive theological movements like the Social Gospel Movement.

The expression "social gospel" was first articulated in both Britain and the United States in the late 1880s.[33] B. F. Westcott, bishop of Durham and former Regius Professor of Divinity at Cambridge University, utilized the term in his work *Social Aspects of Christianity*, which derived from a series of sermons preached at Westminster Abbey in 1886.[34] The General Baptist minister John Clifford also used the term two years later at his Baptist Union presidential address.[35] Prior to the twentieth century, a dynamic partnership between evangelism and social action was widely accepted and even assumed within evangelical Protestant discourse, though the theological rationale for action on social questions was often of an undeveloped or instrumental kind. As the century turned, the nineteenth-century evangelical consensus on social action split into two identifiable communities. One side became twentieth-century fundamentalists, who reacted against "modernizing" tendencies—what has been widely regarded as the "great reversal" of social theological emphases. The other side progressively broadened their Christianity by developing a theology of social transformation based on the theological motif of the kingdom of God.[36] The so-called Social Gospel became increasingly contested as the rise of modernism challenged evangelical leaders, especially in North America, regarding approaches to the study of the Bible and the authority of science. Fundamentalists, in reacting against these perceived excesses, swung toward a greater focus on evangelization rather than social action in an attempt to stop the drift.

Many have followed this narrative.[37] This "great reversal," however, is largely a theoretical construct that has been read back into the historical narrative by those who see it as a retrograde development. Although the concept has its validity and a degree of explanatory power, it does not fit the full range of evangelical experience at any period and therefore is shorthand for careful, nuanced investigation. The spectrum has always been broader and more complex than a monochrome reversal as previous tradition would imply. For example, the narrative of a "great reversal" often overlooks the fact that many African American Christian leaders continued to maintain a robust understanding of social action in Christian mission right through the twentieth century. African American pastors such as the Baptist Gardner Taylor often spoke of the social dimensions of the gospel, as did Taylor during his forty-two-year tenure as pastor of Concord Baptist Church of Christ (CBCC) in New York City, which began in 1948.[38] This "great reversal" narrative also fails to account for the tendency of American women missionaries to develop more holistic understandings of Christian mission during the nineteenth and early twentieth centuries, as well.[39]

Nevertheless, the relationship between evangelism and social action in Christian mission has been an interpretive crux for Protestant evangelicals in the twentieth century. The controversial nature of social Christianity within evangelical circles can only be understood against the background of the theological landscape of the postwar period. In the late nineteenth and early twentieth centuries, evangelical social action was largely justified theologically, either through the removal of "obstacles to the progress of the gospel" or through the elimination of social sins that contravened divine commands.[40] In terms of theological methodology, this fitted squarely within a "two-mandate approach," which predominated in evangelical theological circles prior to the 1970s.[41] This method bifurcated Christian mission into a primary, spiritual mandate and a subordinate social mandate. This did not mean, however, that evangelicals were averse to social action. On the contrary, missionaries around the world created hospitals and schools, and they lobbied for the rights of the poor—particularly children and women. The language or theology that justified these actions, however, was largely removing barriers to personal, spiritual conversion.

By the 1940s, many fundamentalist leaders in the United States became increasingly restless with the state of fundamentalism and its perceived lack of influence on and engagement with postwar American culture. Thus, even while many Protestant evangelicals began to speak in more explicitly social theological terms, the conversation often concerned "implications of the gospel" rather than the content of the message itself (as Padilla, Costas, and others would later suggest).[42] As Christianity grew in Africa, Asia, and Latin America, the issue became increasingly controversial in the late 1960s and early 1970s; mission leaders from these traditional "mission fields" spoke back to "sending countries" in what has often been called a global reflex. This took place both at public gatherings and in personal correspondence. Until the 1960s, little momentum was made in developing a more satisfactory conservative Protestant discourse on social Christianity. However, beginning in 1966, a series of congresses dramatically accelerated the conversation on both sides of the Atlantic.

The Berlin Congress on World Evangelization in 1966 (Berlin 1966) can trace its origins to a taxi conversation between Billy Graham and Carl F. H. Henry.[43] Their goal, found in the official conference papers, echoed the epochal missionary conferences in New York in 1900 and Edinburgh in 1910: "Our goal is nothing short of the evangelization of the human race in this generation."[44] The map for carrying out this worldwide evangelization project, however, was written by the exclusively white, American, male planning and executive committee.[45] Evangelical leaders at Berlin were also emphatic about the dimensions of evangelization: "Evangelism is the proclamation of the Gospel of the crucified and risen Christ."[46] The congress then outlined the "task" of Christian missionaries through four verbs: to proclaim, to invite to discipleship, to baptize, and to teach. Evangelical Anglican clergyman John Stott's plenary address also set out to "re-examine our marching orders."[47] Stott argued, "The commission of the Church . . . is not to reform society, but to preach the Gospel . . . the primary task of the members of Christ's Church is to be Gospel heralds, not social reformers."[48] As if to not be misunderstood, Stott emphatically repeated, "Again, the commission of the Church is not to heal the sick, but to preach the Gospel."[49] Peruvian Samuel Escobar attended Berlin 1966 and later extolled Stott's teaching there.[50]

The congress had been unambiguous with regard to the mission of the church, affirming the primacy and urgency of evangelization. When Graham began to plan for a follow-up to Berlin 1966, there was little indication that the next congress on evangelization would challenge this widely held assumption of the primacy of evangelism.[51] Yet, across the Atlantic, a group of young evangelical Anglicans in Britain was beginning to press for an increased emphasis on social concern in Christian mission.

The National Evangelical Anglican Congress at Keele in 1967 has been called "the chief landmark in a post-war evangelical renaissance."[52] The congress was a gathering of several generations of evangelical Anglican leaders, with the younger leaders pushing for greater emphasis on social action and sensitivity to issues arising from local contexts.[53] At Keele, John Stott played an instrumental role in reconciling the older and younger generations—foreshadowing his later role at the Lausanne Congress of 1974. After disagreement and debate, the result of the congress was a significant statement on the role of social action in Christian mission. Particularly notable was a section titled "The Scope of Mission": "Evangelism and compassionate service belong together in the mission of God."[54] Stott in particular was prescient in recognizing the social conscience of a new generation of evangelical leadership and the need to create room for their thinking. He was also beginning to reexamine his own understanding of the relationship between evangelism and social action.[55]

Yet, Stott's experience at the Keele Congress cannot fully explain his later "conversion" to holistic Christian mission. In the years that followed the Keele Congress, Stott was increasingly influenced by a wider conversation within global evangelical Protestantism, one driven by concerns from leadership in the developing world and on university campuses around the world. The sensitivity of Stott and many leaders of the Evangelical Left to a younger generation of evangelical thinkers (who were increasingly nonwhite and non-Western) meant they were especially impacted by these trends from the Global South. These waves of change crested at an expansive global gathering of evangelical leaders called the International Congress on World Evangelization in Lausanne, Switzerland—or simply Lausanne 1974.

A growing body of literature has also begun to note the importance of the Lausanne Congress in 1974. A recent academic biography of Billy Graham called the congress "extraordinarily influential."[56] One historian chose two events as "turnings points" in the history of Christianity in the second half of the twentieth century: the Second Vatican Council of the Catholic Church and Lausanne 1974.[57] Careful attention to unstudied personal papers, bilingual interviews, and archival materials from five countries reveals there is much more to this story than has been told.

The Lausanne Congress was perhaps most influential because, for the first time, leaders from the Global South gained a place at the table of global evangelical leadership—bringing their local, while nascent, brands of social Christianity with them. While Berlin 1966 was planned and run exclusively by Americans, Billy Graham himself demanded that "national representatives of the younger churches" be given a place at the table of Lausanne 1974.[58] As a result, Lausanne amplified the voices of an emerging, increasingly diverse evangelicalism, which often included calls for the inclusion of social Christianity.[59] Lausanne's loudest and most controversial voices came from Latin Americans, whose proximity to the United States and fraught history with aggressive Cold War foreign policy positioned them to challenge an often-paternalistic evangelical context.

In 1974, *Time* magazine called the Billy Graham–funded Lausanne Congress "a formidable forum, possibly the widest-ranging meeting of Christians ever held" with nearly 2,500 Protestant Evangelical leaders from over 150 countries and 135 denominations.[60] At Lausanne, "America's Pastor" Billy Graham sowed seeds for world evangelization and nearly reaped a civil war instead. In particular, René Padilla and Samuel Escobar channeled the Cold War context in what proved to be the most controversial of plenary speeches at Lausanne. Padilla rejected the equation of Christian orthodoxy with political conservatism and the exportation of the "American Way of Life" to Africa, Asia, and Latin America in his plenary speech at the global evangelical Lausanne Congress. In one instance, he declared, "American culture Christianity integrate[s] racial and class segregation into its strategy for world evangelization."[61] Peruvian Samuel Escobar followed the young Ecuadorian and struck a similar chord. Escobar, for his part, implicated this missionary-exported Christianity in siding with the ruling class and called for evangelicals to avoid the social quietism of their fundamentalist forebears.[62] In John Stott's words, Escobar had "put the cat among the pigeons."[63]

The Language of Evangelical Social Christianity

These debates surrounding social Christianity cut to the heart of the Christian message and mission. Padilla argued for a wider definition: "A comprehensive mission corresponds to a comprehensive view of salvation. Salvation is wholeness. *Salvation is total humanization.* Salvation is eternal life—the life of the kingdom of God—life that begins here and now . . . and touches all aspects of man's being."[64] When Padilla and Escobar suggested that the gospel had social dimensions, this worried many evangelical leaders (including many from the Global South) who feared that evangelicals were drifting toward emphases characteristic of the Ecumenical Movement and the World Council of Churches (WCC), such as those that had marked the WCC Uppsala assembly in 1968.[65] Since Padilla delivered his Lausanne speech in Spanish, what he actually said was not "comprehensive mission" but "*misión integral.*"

What has become known as "integral mission" is an understanding of Christian mission that posits that social action and evangelism are essential and indivisible components of Christian mission—indeed, that both are central aspects *within* the Christian gospel. Put more clearly, integral mission synthesizes the pursuit of justice with the offer of salvation. *Misión integral* pushed evangelicals to move beyond *implication* language to include social action *within* the gospel message itself. Padilla's use of the term derives from his homemade *pan integral*, or whole-wheat bread. The Spanish word *integral* brings connotations of whole wheat, comprehensive, total, and complete, as well as of integrity. It contains nuances of the English word "holistic" yet Spanish contains the word *holístico*, and thus the phrase "holistic mission" is insufficient.[66] Key members of the Evangelical Left have utilized the English gloss "integral mission," and thus both *misión integral* and "integral mission" are used here to describe the primary language for the social Christianity within an emerging Latin American Evangelical Left.

Figure 1. René Padilla making *pan integral*
in his Buenos Aires home, 2013. Photo by author.

Today, the language of integral mission has become a catchall phrase for
social Christianity within global evangelicalism. Indeed, prominent members of the American Evangelical Left have utilized this language as their
theological framework for social Christianity—including political activist Jim
Wallis, Emerging Church leader Brian McLaren, and even conservative establishment figures such as British Anglican John Stott.[67] "Integral mission"
is also utilized as the official phrase and model by nearly 600 mission and
relief agencies—including World Vision, Compassion International, Food for
the Hungry, International Justice Mission, and World Relief. Thus, as we seek
to trace the origins, development, and global diffusion of ideas from the Latin
American Evangelical Left, this phrase "integral mission" serves as an important marker.

Defining the Latin American Evangelical Left

In the early 1970s, there emerged in various parts of the Protestant world an embryonic but discernible progressive coalition that united around a particular brand of evangelical social Christianity. They often shared in common a suspicion of American imperialism and exportation of theological materials and methods, as well. Key thinkers were often embedded within global evangelical organizations and educational institutions that were sympathetic to their progressive leanings (InterVarsity Christian Fellowship and the International Fellowship of Evangelical Students, Eastern Baptist Theological Seminary, and later the Lausanne Movement, for example). While moving primarily within global organizations, Latin Americans also created their own organizations to develop and spread their ideas—particularly the Latin American Theological Fraternity (FTL) and the International Fellowship of Evangelical Mission Theologians (INFEMIT).

Progressive Latin American evangelicals defined themselves primarily against two perceived ideological excesses: Marxist-inflected theologies of liberation and the conservative political loyalties of the Religious Right. Thus, the emerging coalition of the Latin American Evangelical Left refers primarily to a political orientation rather than a theological one—theologically conservative and evangelical while pushing boundaries on socially progressive ideas. This linguistic designation should not be used to mask its diversity, however. The emerging progressive evangelical coalition in Latin America was as diverse as the denominations and organizations that they represented, similar to a wide spectrum between a so-called Religious Right. The glue that held together this emerging coalition of progressive evangelicals was their brand of social Christianity, which they began to call *misión integral*. At the same time, many of the most vocal critics of social Christianity in the 1970s were conservative Latin American evangelicals.[68] Many indeed rejected *misión integral*, which underlines the need for historians of Latin American Christianity to use precise language that avoids blanket categories such as "Latin American evangelicals."

A Gospel for the Poor sits at the intersection of an emerging body of literature on the Evangelical Left and meager scholarship on the history of Latin American Christianity. This brief historical survey raises a few crucial questions. Why did many evangelicals in the North greet the Evangelical Left as family rather than foe in contrast to their reaction to the so-called Social Gospel of the late nineteenth and early twentieth centuries? Put more clearly, why is the Evangelical Left even considered *evangelical*? What role did Latin Americans—and the revolutionary ferment of the Cold War—play in constructing the Evangelical Left as a foil to the American Religious Right? Similarly, how did evangelical social Christianity gain widespread acceptance across a broad religious spectrum today? While many have noted the influence of the Evangelical Left and even the Lausanne Movement, the full story and key Latin American background remain untold. Where Latin American influence has been acknowledged, the main players are often presented as a monolith. Instead, we must ask, who was the primary mind behind Latin American evangelical social Christianity (integral mission)? This question has also become increasingly important due to recent important monographs that have highlighted Peruvian Samuel Escobar to a greater extent than Ecuadorian René Padilla or treated progressive Latin American Evangelicals as politically and theologically homogeneous.[69] Similarly, crucial questions include, to what extent was *misión integral* simply an evangelical Protestant response to Catholic theologies of liberation? Overall, how might paying careful attention to bilingual interviews, unstudied personal papers, and far-flung archival documents refocus the story of the Evangelical Left and provide a revised picture of the movement?

In attempting to answer these questions, this book begins not at the centers of power or with evangelical elites in the United States but with the unlikely and overlooked influence of progressive Latin American evangelicals. This story aims to be both descriptive and prescriptive. The increasing importance of Latinos within evangelicalism is both the reality of the story and the intentional lens of this book. A global perspective is *necessary* for the study of postwar evangelicalism. Here, transnational conversations provoked the rise of progressive evangelical politics, the explosion of Christian mission and relief organizations, and the infusion of social justice into the very mission of evangelicals around the world, including in foreign policy prescriptions. Evangelicals across a broad spectrum of denominations and affiliations have widened their understanding of the Christian gospel to include social dimensions—a renaissance of evangelical social Christianity. This is the story of how an emerging generation of progressive Latin Americans developed, branded, and exported their version of social Christianity to a changing coalition of global evangelicalism.

CHAPTER 1

A New Style of Evangelicalism
from Latin America

"American culture Christianity infuses racial and class segregation into its strategy for world evangelization."[1] After René Padilla's fiery plenary speech at the Lausanne Congress of 1974, one American leader arose—visibly unnerved—to confront him on the platform: "How can you say *that* when you graduated from Wheaton [College]?"[2] In Padilla's recollection, the astonished leader was struck by the discordance of his thoroughly evangelical education and critical diagnosis of world missions, that the "American way of life" had poisoned the gospel message around the world. In a 2013 interview in Buenos Aires, Padilla declined to name the "very important leader"—someone "very, very related with Wheaton College."[3] The most probable leader given his presence on the platform would be Wheaton president Hudson Armerding (1965–1982). Yet, one might also speculate none other than Billy Graham, given his prominence as a Wheaton alumnus and presence on the platform at Lausanne, as well.[4] Regardless, Padilla recalled responding, "Precisely there [at Wheaton] I learned to do critical thinking."[5] American managerial control was placed on watch.

This brief anecdote sheds light on three key historical details. First, it reveals that many Western leaders were unaware of the revolutionary ferment brewing to the South. At the time, many Americans were unaware of, or simply chose to ignore, the growing voices and discourse from "Third World" thinkers. These voices, however, became harder to ignore, especially for mission leaders in international organizations such the InterVarsity Christian Fellowship–USA and the Billy Graham Evangelistic Association (BGEA). Few could deny these increasingly influential voices after the First International Congress on World Evangelization (Lausanne 1974), due to the prominence

Figure 2. René Padilla giving a plenary speech at the Lausanne Congress,
July 1974. Courtesy of the Billy Graham Evangelistic Association.
Used with permission. All rights reserved.

of African, Asian, and Latin American leaders at the congress and on its platform, as well.

This conflict, second, was a window into the future of evangelicalism—
one filled with tension, disagreement, and negotiation on the place of social
Christianity in evangelical discourse. But third, it reveals an organizational
reality for many evangelicals in the postwar period: the close proximity of
liberal and conservative leaders and corresponding negotiation over the
boundaries of evangelicalism. Indeed, the nascent Latin American Evangelical Left often negotiated the acceptance of social Christianity while many
conservatives guarded the boundaries of traditional evangelical theological
and political loyalties. This negotiation took place not *outside* the gate of
global evangelicalism but *within* its very structures. The growing awareness
and acceptance of diverse voices inadvertently opened the door to a wider
understanding of Christian mission particularly from Latin Americans.

The Latin American evangelical language of a "gospel for the poor"—and
not simply the American middle class—was forged within the heat of liberal
versus conservative battles that erupted in the late 1960s and 1970s. Minority

voices became amplified in the West as emerging postcolonial discourse called for greater attention to the social location of knowledge. In the field of religion, postcolonialists called for the acknowledgment of the contextuality of all knowledge—that every idea is tied to its local context. For theologians, this meant there was no longer "theology" but rather "theologies": North American theology, Latino/a theology, African theology, and European theology, for example. Armed with these ideas, theologians from the developing world began to challenge traditionally held assumptions regarding propositional truth and rote formulae for the evangelization and discipleship of Christians.[6] They also decried imported or prepackaged answers to their local questions, challenging long-held evangelical Protestant traditions.[7]

Thus, the presence of Samuel Escobar and René Padilla on the platform at the Lausanne Congress of 1974 was simultaneously a symbol of emerging evangelical leadership from the Global South and a symbol of protest. Their controversial plenary speeches marked the emergence of a generation of young evangelicals who brought their experience in contexts of oppression, violence, and sociopolitical unrest into discussions of the contemporary problems of the day. In doing so, they helped usher in the evangelical *rediscovery* of social Christianity. In the coming decades, progressive Latin American evangelicals insisted on the noninterference of Western missionary leaders and the relentless independence of theology from the Global South. Lausanne is simply one example of many where Latin Americans dictated the terms upon which this theological independence took place. As Latin American evangelical theologians *shifted* to postcolonial ideological sympathies, they pulled many global evangelicals with them.

Early Opposition and Latin American Inclusion

In July 1974, Catharine Feser Padilla gathered her children around a world atlas in their home in the barrio of Florida Este, Buenos Aires. Her daughter, Ruth Padilla DeBorst, recalled, "The tone of her voice had a certain unaccustomed urgency: 'Today, when he gives his talk here, in Lausanne, Switzerland'—pointing to the city on the map—'Papi will say some things that not everyone is going to want to hear. Let's pray for him and for the people listening to him.'"[8] Neither Samuel Escobar nor René Padilla entered the Lausanne Congress with naive optimism. At the time, both were staff members with global evangelical parachurch ministries—Escobar as general director of the InterVarsity Christian Fellowship in Canada (1972–1975) and Padilla as general secretary of the International Fellowship of Evangelical Students (IFES) in Latin America. IFES is the worldwide representative body that arose out of the InterVarsity Fellowship (IVF), later known as the Universities and Colleges Christian Fellowship (UCCF) in Britain and InterVarsity Christian Fellowship–USA (IVCF). Behind the inception of IFES was the Australian evangelical leader C. Stacey Woods, the founding general secretary of IVCF in the United States (which would quickly become its largest and primary source of financial backing) and the first general secretary of IFES.[9] Woods was uniquely positioned as an Australian to mediate the growing tension between British, American, and Scandinavian approaches to ministry and organizational leadership.[10] Yet, previously unstudied personal correspondence reveals that Woods opposed Escobar and Padilla participating in the Lausanne Congress. Woods destroyed most of his personal papers, but many documents are preserved in those of Latin Americans. Ultimately, both Padilla and Escobar accepted their speaking nominations in opposition to Woods's advice.[11]

In an August 1972 letter, Woods outlined his primary concerns regarding the Lausanne Congress: the presence of Roman Catholic observers and Billy Graham's personal ambition.[12] Regarding the former, Woods wrote sharply, "Just because Roman Catholics in many cases are open to the Gospel, this should not blind us to the unchanging deviltry of the Vatican of its murder, licentiousness and cruelty . . . let us welcome Roman Catholics unreservedly, with open arms, but let us not welcome an implacable curia which has never changed."[13] To this pointed critique, he added the persistent violence of Catholics against Protestants in Latin America. Months earlier, Woods had sent a memo to his entire staff warning of Catholic inclusion and clarifying his position on Lausanne 1974.[14] Escobar appeared unconcerned by Catholic inclusion and avoided the topic altogether in his response letters. This was perhaps surprising given the vehement anti-Catholicism among many Latin American evangelical communities.

Stacey Woods worried that Billy Graham would build a metaphorical monument to himself in Lausanne: "Billy Graham always wants that which is official which will have worldly, organizational, institutional recognition and will give him status, I am afraid."[15] As Escobar and Padilla persisted in their desire to participate, Woods expressed optimism at working with Lausanne convener and British Anglican evangelical A. Jack Dain, who was the assistant bishop of the Sydney Anglican diocese (a particularly evangelical diocese).[16] At the same time, Woods warned the young Peruvian Escobar to stand up to American influence: "You will need to stand against the manoeuvres of the Billy Graham Committee members, who more or less tend to ride rough-shod over everybody else. I think you and [IFES staff member Chua] Wee Hian ought to form a team of two as a kind of a spearhead, cutting through the nonsense to something really worthwhile."[17]

In his reply on August 2, 1972, Escobar braced himself for conflict with "evangelical tycoons" and pondered accepting Billy Graham's invitation to join the planning committee.[18] In one final letter, Woods gave the young Peruvian a strong warning: "God has a great future ministry for you although, and remember this, if you are true to this message I'm afraid almost inevitably it will end, or at least involve, suffering."[19] In the end, Escobar accepted Graham's invitation and soon reported back to Woods on the first planning meeting in September 1972: "In my personal talk with Billy Graham, I expressed my concern about a mutilated gospel and the need to clearly distinguish the Christian message from western and eastern ideologies. He expressed his agreement, although I realize he cannot avoid being influenced by the fact that he is a United States citizen with definite political preferences about which some of the people on his team are very vocal."[20] Escobar worried that Lausanne would cheer a "mutilated Gospel," an American middle-class gospel tainted by the "American way of life" and loyalties to conservative politics. Similarly, for Latin American progressive evangelicals, the issue was not simply agreement with facts but the origin of those ideas—the social location of that knowledge.[21] In many cases, the reality of being American was enough to taint belief and render one suspect.

Escobar concluded his letter to Woods by persisting in his inclusion in the congress: "All in all, Stacey, I think that our presence and our contribution in this committee for the next Congress on Evangelism is worth the time, work and patience involved in it."[22] While Escobar was particularly prescient in predicting Lausanne's influence, ironically, Escobar's inclusion in the planning committee blunted his influence on later progressive evangelical development. When the congress opened two years later, Escobar would be largely sidelined by organizational detail. In his absence, René Padilla took a leading role as organizer, agitator, and exponent of *misión integral* themes among a growing and restless sector of global evangelicalism—including many in the emerging American Evangelical Left.

It is tempting to view Padilla's plenary speech as shocking to all involved. Yet, careful attention to unstudied correspondence reveals that Padilla had already registered on the radar of conservative evangelicals due to his battles with American missionaries and his controversial affinity for leftist politics. This raises a critical question: why would Graham and his associates invite Padilla when many viewed him as suspicious, at best, and dangerous, at worst? Later, we will see that the Billy Graham Evangelistic Association had learned its lesson on paternalism and inclusion through a conference debacle south of the Rio Grande. But here, we can posit a different piece: that Padilla was included, in part, for his thoroughly evangelical educational bona fides. Padilla attended Wheaton College from 1953 to 1959, completing his bachelor of arts (BA) in philosophy and master of arts (MA) in theology. He also completed his PhD from 1963 to 1965 under F. F. Bruce, who at the time was probably "the most prominent conservative evangelical biblical scholar of the post-war era."[23] While Bruce was not a significant *theological* influence on Padilla, he gained from Bruce, more than anything, the academic and evangelical credibility that came along with studying "under" him. This would prove crucial for his inclusion at Lausanne and this global platform, especially in the mind of Paul Little, Lausanne program director and InterVarsity-USA staff member.[24] Similarly, John Stott noted in his travel diary in January 1974 that Padilla studied "under F. F. Bruce at Manchester."[25] This entry came just months before the Lausanne Congress, where Stott's relationship with Padilla would prove crucial to the later inclusion of social elements in the Lausanne covenant.[26]

Evangelization, Social Action, or Civil War?

On July 16, 1974, Billy Graham opened the Lausanne Congress in his booming baritone voice, "Here at Lausanne, let's make sure that *Evangelization* is the one task which we are unitedly determined to do" (italics mine).[27] "The world church has floundered" in its task of world evangelization, Graham argued, blaming the "social Gospel" and "preoccupation with social and political problems."[28] Graham was not anti social action; he simply opposed any reorientation of mission priorities away from evangelism. By the third day of the congress, however, it became clear that an emerging, younger generation of leadership from the Global South would no longer accept a Western-planned agenda for the rest of the world. It is worth noting at this juncture that in American evangelical circles, "evangelization" is a synonym for "evangelism," whereas in Roman Catholic circles, it is a synonym for the whole process of mission.[29] Though Lausanne was officially entitled the International Congress for World Evangelization, evangelization in this context meant verbal proclamation.

When Padilla ascended the platform, he quite nearly ushered in an evangelical civil war. On the third day of the congress, René Padilla was slotted as the only plenary address of the day. Padilla began, "I am going to put all the cards on the table with the prayer that God leads us during these days to a clearer understanding of all that he expects of us."[30] Padilla chose to address the audience in Spanish, though he was fluent in English and spoke English at home with his children.[31] He recalled in 2013 that this linguistic choice was meant to teach Western delegates the experience of listening to a translator and to "protest the linguistic imperialism of English."[32] The reason at the time may have been more innocuous: conference organizers asked him to speak in Spanish.[33]

In contrast to Graham, Padilla focused his aim on the perceived dichotomy between social action and evangelism in Christian mission: "Concern for man's reconciliation with God cannot be separated from concern for social justice . . . the mission of the church is indivisible from its life. I refuse, therefore, to drive a wedge between a primary task, namely the proclamation of the Gospel, and a secondary (at best) or even optional (at worst) task of the church."[34] Padilla expanded, "The lack of appreciation of the wider dimensions of the Gospel leads inevitably to a misunderstanding of the mission of the church. The result is an evangelism that regards the individual as a self-contained unit—a Robinson Crusoe to whom God's call is addressed as on an island—whose salvation takes place exclusively in terms of a relationship to God." As a consequence, "It is not seen that the individual does not exist in isolation, and consequently that it is not possible to speak of a salvation with no reference to the world of which he is a part."[35] What was this wider gospel message? As mentioned in the Introduction, Padilla left no doubt regarding his emerging understanding: "A comprehensive mission corresponds to a comprehensive view of salvation. Salvation is wholeness. *Salvation is total humanization.* Salvation is eternal life—the life of the kingdom of God—life that begins here and now . . . and touches all aspects of man's being" (italics mine).[36] Since Padilla delivered this speech in Spanish, what he actually said was not "comprehensive mission" but "*misión integral.*" His speech set off, in Padilla's words, "fiery debate."[37]

In critical continuity with Padilla, Escobar's plenary speech "Evangelism and Man's Search for Freedom, Justice and Fulfillment" called for an embrace of the ethical demands of discipleship and to evangelize in a truly biblical way. Escobar also spoke of the "rediscovery of the social dimensions of the Gospel" while later moving confusingly between the language of *dimensions* and *implications* of the gospel.[38] Clearer, however, was his shared indictment of comfortable, middle-class Christianity: "They condemn all the sins that well-behaved middle class people condemn but say nothing about exploitation, intrigue, and dirty political maneuvering done by great multinational corporations around the world."[39] While his social Christianity was of a different kind than Padilla's, his warning against identifying Christianity with the ruling class struck a similar chord. This echoed his own words from a 1970 plenary address at InterVarsity's Urbana Missions Conference titled "Social Concern and World Evangelism."

Orlando Costas, for his part, wrote two "strategy papers" for Lausanne's scheduled breakout sessions. Though they received significantly less attention than the plenary addresses, Costas's message was no less sharp, identifying the evangelical missionary establishment as "tainted by links to imperialistic culture and vested economic interests."[40] Costas spoke about the Latin America Mission's (LAM's) Evangelism-in-Depth (EID) outreach program as "an effort to mobilize the church of Jesus Christ with all of her resources for a comprehensive witness in the world."[41] In a similar way to Padilla's speech, Costas's EID paper attacked shallow Christianity, calling it a "cancer" for World Christianity.

René Padilla's speech received "the longest round of applause accorded to any speaker up till that time" at the Congress—signaling that his tone found congruence with many voices in the audience.[42] *Time* magazine highlighted Padilla as "one of the meeting's most provocative speeches" among noteworthy "Third World Evangelicals."[43] One observer, John Capon, editor of *Crusade* magazine, wrote that Padilla's paper "really set the congress alight."[44] Another later commentator raved, "The blue touchpaper for evangelical social responsibility this century was lit at the Lausanne Congress in 1974 by two staff workers of the Inter-Varsity Fellowship in Latin America, Rene Padilla and Samuel Escobar. Their papers on evangelism triggered an explosion."[45]

Padilla himself recalled seeing the body language of North American leaders as he gave his speech—arms crossed, frowned faces. "They felt attacked," he said.[46] This contrasted heavily with exuberant greetings from mostly "Third World" leaders after the speech. This North versus South binary, however, is insufficient to capture the diversity at the Lausanne

Congress, contrary to much of the oral history and scholarship surrounding it. Instead, many conservative Latin Americans disagreed with the perspectives of Costas, Escobar, and Padilla, aligning themselves with their conservative U.S. counterparts.[47] Similarly, many of the emerging American Evangelical Left loudly agreed. Overall, those who cheered Costas, Escobar, and Padilla were increasingly identifiable within this growing progressive coalition.

The controversy surrounding Latin American progressive evangelical presentations represented wider growing pains for the global evangelical community that would play out over the next few decades. One thing was clear: the global reflex of traditional "mission fields" was growing louder and harder to ignore. In private correspondence, Billy Graham was concerned enough to order a written report on reactions to Padilla and Escobar's plenary speeches while still at the Lausanne Congress itself.[48] Padilla and Costas's identification of the United States as the source of shallow or imperialistic Christianity in the Global South was also controversial. Yet, the content of their emerging *misión integral*—especially the social *dimensions* of the gospel—was enough to push the Lausanne Congress into crisis.[49]

Radical Discipleship

The diverse tapestry of Lausanne was beginning to fray by Sunday, July 21. Sensing momentum from his and Samuel Escobar's plenary speeches, Padilla, along with now-disgraced American Mennonite ethicist John Howard Yoder, moved to convene likeminded radical and mostly younger evangelical leaders for an ad hoc meeting. Nearly 500 participants (almost one-fifth of delegates) gathered to discuss topics broached in the plenary speeches under the title "radical discipleship." Padilla thought more would have attended if they had more time to plan.[50] This fringe gathering also highlights the increasing influence of Latin American evangelicals. Three of the four speakers were members of the Latin American Theological Fraternity (FTL)—Padilla, Escobar, and Yoder, who was the only American member at the time.

After an opening song on the acoustic guitar, an unidentified moderator began the proceedings by saying, "We're here, as you know, to get down to some 'tin tacks' about the question of radical discipleship, which as you appreciate, is the best way we can sum up the problem of really coming to grips with the social structures of our society, and how we as Christians should be relating to them."[51] Careful attention to the archival audiotapes reveals that the radical discipleship gathering soon took a decidedly leftist political turn as Padilla made seemingly off-the-cuff comments in his speech.

Padilla explicitly doubted the need for American-style democracy and placed hope in a military regime in Peru—certainly confirming the fears of many Western leaders: "And let me tell you this: you may know of a social ferment in Latin America. I believe that as a matter of fact, we are not all that certain that Latin America *can* find a way of democracy. Not sure the American model of democracy is the one we want *anyhow!* (audible mumbling in the crowd)." Padilla immediately sought to clarify his words:

> What I mean is this: there is evidence, very clear evidence, that most of the Latin American countries are moving toward a totalitarian government, a military government, and that the pity of it all is the choice is between a rightist military government and a Marxist government. I may be oversimplying, there may be another choice, I haven't seen much of a hope except perhaps for a model which is being produced in Peru which is a military government and yet a government that is really trying to make basic changes in the structures of society. Some of us still look to that experiment with a bit of hope.[52]

Calling for a political "third way" in Latin America was certainly nothing new. Liberation theologians, such as the Uruguayan Jesuit Juan Luis Segundo, had been calling for alternative solutions for quite some time.[53] Yet, these political discussions had remained "outside the evangelical gate," so to speak. Now, American conservative political loyalties were put on public trial.

Padilla's leftist political loyalties were shocking to many, especially given the explicit anticommunism of many conservative evangelical leaders such as Graham and Campus Crusade for Christ president Bill Bright. Yet, anyone paying attention to Padilla's writings would not have been surprised. Indeed, in *Christianity Today*, the flagship American evangelical magazine, Padilla had implicated the U.S. State Department in the violent overthrow of Chilean President Salvador Allende a few months earlier.[54] Padilla was perceived as anti-American as early as 1966, registering on the radar of conservative evangelicals. For example, Stacey Woods wrote to the general director of the U.S.-based LAM, Horace L. Fenton Jr., "I'm glad René Padilla was with you, and I do hope that he did not prove himself to be anti U.S. I know there are overtones of that, but I believe with care and prayer this can be overcome with all our Latin American leaders."[55] While Fenton reported back to Woods that he did not observe anti-American sentiments in Padilla, Padilla felt the need to write to Charles Troutman of LAM to defend himself.[56] All of this makes it all the more surprising that John Stott and Billy Graham were able to hold the fragile evangelical coalition together.[57]

In his radical discipleship speech, Padilla followed this political statement with his understanding of a wider gospel message: "You see, I have come to see, that as a matter of fact, Jesus Christ came not just to save my soul, but to form a new society and that that society takes shape first of all in the church. *This is* the new society. . . . Can we really really really say that the church today reflects the fullness of the gospel?"[58] Here, Padilla connected language of a "new society," which hearkened to the writings of many Marxist liberation theologians, to a faithful evangelical gospel message. What if a holistic gospel message called for *leftist* politics rather than a so-called religious right?

The questions from the audience honed in on this central aspect of what would later be termed "integral mission": the inclusion of ethics in the gospel message itself, rather than simply an *implication* of it. These questions came specifically from delegates John Chapman and Paul Burnett. Burnett accused Padilla of conflating the "evangel" with "ethics," which he saw as clearly distinct in the New Testament. Here, Padilla appeared to equivocate, allowing for an intellectual distinction between the two but not a practical one.[59] Eventually, questions had to be cut off so that Escobar and Yoder could also speak. More than anything here, Padilla had proved his ideas demanded response from the evangelical community—ideas that found both acceptance and rejection in the following decades.

In contrast, Escobar took a decidedly irenic tone following Padilla. Escobar argued for the necessity of ethics in partnership with preaching the gospel.[60] Escobar's concern was "really evangelizing" in a biblical way. Thus, he concluded, if we are to "evangelize" effectively, we must live out the ethical "implications of following Christ." This diplomatic, moderate tone perhaps cemented Escobar's inclusion in the drafting committee of the Lausanne covenant, in contrast to Padilla's later exclusion. Careful attention to the audio recordings reveals that Escobar should not be viewed as a parallel or coinfluence on the radical discipleship gatherings, as has been written elsewhere.[61] Escobar was not directly involved in the planning of the radical discipleship group, as he was preoccupied with planning committee meetings.[62] Furthermore, Padilla's influence here was more central than current historiography has implied.[63] Rather, Escobar was included by Padilla and provided a cooperative tone to a decidedly combative gathering. He also presented his ideas within the safer, "implication" language that had predominated in evangelical circles to that point.

The now controversial American Anabaptist John Howard Yoder followed Escobar's speech and found critical continuity with Padilla's understanding of ethics as part of the gospel message. Yoder had partnered with Padilla, Escobar, and the FTL in the early 1970s while living and teaching in Buenos Aires—a reality we will explore in Chapter 4. Their influence on Yoder here is doubtful, however. On the contrary, Yoder had been writing on this issue for years, including a 1971 Spanish article for *Certeza* magazine where Yoder spoke of a wider gospel message.[64] It remains unclear if Padilla was directly influenced by increasing Anabaptist Mennonite literature on the topic. In his own recollection of Lausanne, Padilla either consciously ignored or was surprisingly ignorant of Anabaptist emphases such as "simple lifestyle" when he implied his plenary paper provoked evangelicals to pick up the issue.[65] Padilla may well have been practicing a simple lifestyle prior to coming in contact with Anabaptists such as Yoder, but the term's later capital within evangelical communities should be credited to this earlier Anabaptist heritage. The very name "radical discipleship" speaks to Yoder's influence in channeling this Anabaptist emphasis.

Escobar and Padilla undoubtedly left the meeting feeling optimistic, given the overwhelming support of the delegates present. The group then circulated an alternative congress declaration called "A Response to Lausanne." The document argued that the *content* of the gospel was wider than conservative emphases, including "Good News of liberation, of restoration, of wholeness, and of salvation that is personal, social, global and cosmic."[66] While John Stott privately regretted the public discord, he promptly announced he would sign the document and even included it within the official published documents.[67] This diplomatic coup diffused the tension and played a crucial role in maintaining the fragile coalition. We will later see a necessary correlation between Padilla's significance and Stott's evolution on social Christianity through the lens of their intimate relationship.

In many ways, the Lausanne Covenant was a brokered peace accord between increasingly polarized camps, in particular Western missionaries and agencies, as well as a new generation of evangelicals who were increasingly nonwhite and from the Global South.[68] After the congress, Padilla recalled the radical discipleship document as "the strongest statement on the basis for wholistic mission ever formulated by an evangelical conference up to that date. Social involvement had finally been granted full citizenship in evangelical missiology, mainly under the influence of people from the Two-Thirds World."[69] Until his untimely death from stomach cancer in 1987, Costas, for his part, referred to himself primarily as a "radical evangelical" in a nod to his solidarity with an emerging coalition represented there. Padilla also declared the death of the dichotomy between social action and evangelism in Christian mission.[70] Padilla himself was unequivocal decades later with regard to the inclusion of social elements: "The input from Latin America, the radical discipleship document, formal and informal discussions on the social dimension of the Christian mission during the congress, and John Stott's role as chairman of the drafting committee resulted in the inclusion of various important topics related to Christian social responsibility, radical discipleship, and church renewal and unity in the Lausanne Covenant."[71] This space for progressive evangelical themes, however, was contested at every turn—especially within the interpretation of the Lausanne Covenant itself. What exactly did they decide at Lausanne? The answer to this question would largely determine the trajectory of global evangelical discourse.

Latin American Influence on the Interpretation
of Lausanne

At Lausanne 1974, Billy Graham spoke of his hope for resolution within the evangelical community on the relationship between social action and evangelism. In the aftermath, it became clear that Lausanne's answer to the social action question depended on the interpretation of the documents themselves. Graham hoped for a narrower definition of the mission of the church, one that maintained the evangelical distinctive of the primacy of evangelism.[72] Instead, Stott, along with Padilla and other especially young evangelicals, pushed for a wider definition. Most importantly here, careful attention to Stott's travel diary (from Lambeth Palace Library in London) will shed new light on his motivation and the ultimate trajectory of social Christianity within global evangelicalism.

The actual Lausanne Covenant was an intricate balance struck by Stott, Graham, and those on the drafting committee. Stott worried about losing the next generation of evangelical leaders, who were increasingly diverse and often located outside of the Western world. In the same way, he worried about losing the powerful conservative bloc centered in the United States.[73] Padilla and Escobar left no doubt of their reading of the Lausanne documents. Padilla wrote in an FTL Spanish article in 1975, "In notorious fashion, in the first place, the Covenant eliminates the dichotomy between evangelization and social responsibility."[74] Fellow-plenary speaker Escobar also echoed this sentiment.[75] In general, progressive Latin American evangelicals (including Costas) revealed significant optimism regarding the prospects of holistic evangelical mission. Their optimism would soon turn to stark realism.

Initial reports on the congress also lent themselves to a holistic interpretation. American theologian Carl F. H. Henry signaled openness to social aspects *within* the gospel message.[76] Padilla quoted Henry with approval in "El Pacto de Lausana." Various negative responses to the Lausanne Covenant from conservative missiologists also seemed to suggest that the congress marked a victory for the holistic bloc.[77] Yet, other conservatives argued that Lausanne defined "mission" within a narrower definition.[78] Jack Dain wrote to Charles Troutman in August 1974 that most had warmly received the presentations of Escobar and Padilla: "They were both very warmly received by the vast majority of those present but I think they were misunderstood by two sections most of whom came from North America."[79]

Troutman went on to describe the opposition: "First their emphasis was quite wrongly interpreted as a social gospel in spite of this position being totally repudiated. Secondly they were both regarded as being anti American. Unfortunately quite a number of Latins repudiated their stand on matters of culture."[80] Personal correspondence reveals the complexity and divergent responses from evangelical leaders. One letter from Norman B. Rohrer, executive secretary and director of the Evangelical Press Association, even pushed for Padilla's inclusion in the continuation committee: "I feel also that the outspoken nationals such as Rene Padilla and the African bishop who wondered out loud if missionaries should continue to work in his country, should be included in any large-scale planning."[81] Padilla faced intense opposition even within his own organization of IFES. For example, IVF general secretary Oliver Barclay took issue with the heart of Padilla's Lausanne presentation—"the wider dimensions of the gospel." Barclay wrote to Padilla on September 25, 1974, a few months after the congress, warning him of reaction to his paper in the "media" and attempting to rein in the young leader.[82]

The opposing definitions and interpretations of the Lausanne Covenant came to a head at the Lausanne Continuation Committee meeting held in Mexico City from January 20 to 24, 1975. Leaders from the United States and conservative evangelicals from Latin America were the main opposition to the presentations and holistic emphases. Dain's letter also provided a private window into Billy Graham's perspective. Dain wrote, "I think a small number of Americans were genuinely puzzled, others were angry but many, including Billy himself, accepted what was said and realised that it had to be said."[83] Though Padilla was not included in the discussion, his presence was felt through his influence on John Stott.

The nature of the committee foreshadowed conflict, as many "Third World members" encountered issues with visas and travel restrictions. As a result, many arrived late or not at all. In Stott's diary, he wrote, "The planning committee had originally decided to appoint a Continuation Committee of only 25 people, but the Americans had insisted that they must have 10 members (I think in order to be representative and so the non-American members had to be correspondingly increased). In the end this size of the committee grew to 45, and there were 13 Americans present. This was too large a dominant national group." Stott then concluded, "This imbalance was surely a major cause of the troubles we were soon to experience."[84]

Graham initiated the gathering by sharing his conviction regarding evangelism as the primary task of the church. Stott's travel diary records his own initial thoughts: "Having described the two [views on Christian mission], Billy made it clear that he favoured the first [evangelism as primary]. If we accepted the second, he added, 'we'd get off the mandate given us at Lausanne,' as Lausanne had given us in his judgment 'a rather narrow mandate.' So we must 'not get bogged down in other peripheral matters.' This troubled me very much, and I stayed up several hours thinking about it and preparing a rebuttal."[85] Stott was determined to shape the outcome of the gathering. Stott's personal notes confirm Alister Chapman's analysis: "Stott was especially keen to speak out on this point in the absence of friends like Padilla and Escobar, who might forget about Lausanne if evangelism were the only focus."[86]

When the committee appeared to be leaning toward endorsing evangelism as primary, Stott threatened to resign. To Stott's surprise, he was immediately joined by Jack Dain, who echoed his sentiment. Stott recorded, "To my surprise Jack Dain from the chair immediately supported me, saying he too would resign, since he couldn't possibly return to Australia with the narrow concept, for Australian participants were *already* implementing the broader vision."[87]

As a result, Stott and Fuller Theological Seminary Professor Peter Wagner (who agreed with Graham on the narrower vision) withdrew to discuss a compromise.[88] Their decision was to allow each region to decide specifically what they meant by the Lausanne Covenant—which, in Stott's words, "is probably the healthiest and most practical solution." The minutes from the Mexico City meeting reveal an attempt to please both sides—with perhaps a nod to the conservative reading. It read, "The Continuation Committee understands as the Covenant indicates that 'the furtherance of the church's mission' means the encouragement of all God's people to go out into the world as Christ was sent into the world, to give themselves for others in a spirit of sacrificial service, and that in this mission *evangelism is primary*" (italics mine).[89] In recognition of this language, Peter Wagner signaled victory for the traditional camp, while Johnston lamented the accommodation of social action.[90] In a personal letter to Jack Dain, Samuel Escobar later decried a perceived effort by *Christianity Today* to "change the meaning and the direction of Lausanne." Escobar argued, "They won't be able to do it, because in the memory of people and in the way in which it impressed them, I am sure that a good thing of Lausanne was that it was not an American jamboree but rather a world forum of evangelicals."[91]

To the very end of this consultation, Stott channeled the influence of Escobar, Padilla, and other "Third World" delegates. According to Stott's account, many delegates at the Mexico City gathering wanted Graham to be the head of the Lausanne organization at the conclusion of the gathering. Once again, Stott spoke against this: "Fearing that the Third World delegates would be both too polite and too loyal to Billy to oppose this, I felt I had to." According to Stott's diary account soon after, he was widely panned by American critics, who believed him to be embroiled in a power struggle with Graham. Yet, Graham defused the tension by speaking of Stott's loyalty to him in his closing devotional. Stott recalled, "It was a marvellously gracious speech, and sensitive to the situation; it defused the atmosphere and healed the wounds."[92] Stott privately regretted his own quickness to take the mantle of defending Lausanne and "acting as protagonist for the Third World" but was glad of the outcome. Others were more pessimistic. Leighton Ford, Billy Graham's brother-in-law, observed that "'The Spirit of Lausanne' had quickly dissolved."[93]

Within the Lausanne Movement, there continues to be debate with regard to the interpretation of the original covenant. Indeed, consensus remains widely elusive. The Lausanne Covenant was as much a political settlement as a theological one—making space for progressive and conservative strands of an increasingly polarized movement. Seen in this light, the theological stalemate continues within global evangelicalism because there never was a theological consensus to begin with.[94] To be sure, Padilla and Escobar's influence on Stott here did more to avoid a conservative interpretation from spreading than it did to settle the argument once and for all.

Lausanne was simply one example of many where Latin Americans dictated the terms of evangelical discourse. As Latin American evangelical theologians *shifted* to postcolonial ideological sympathies, they pulled many global evangelicals with them. Rather than a wholesale *shift southward* for global evangelicalism, however, this marked the beginning of a multidirectional conversation with a wide variety of interlocutors. The Lausanne Congress thus signaled the refusal of nonwhite and non-Western Christians to accept a Western-planned agenda for the rest of the world, where issues of social justice often remained marginal.[95] This extended attention to personal papers, audiotapes, and unstudied archival materials also invites further interpretation.

The broad welcome given to radical discipleship themes and their inclusion in the Lausanne published documents reveals a groundswell of support that was gathering among evangelical leaders in the Global South—beyond the purview of many Western leaders. Plenary speeches by Escobar and Padilla, as well as the discussion papers of Orlando Costas and the Radical Discipleship Group, broached topics that had previously been marginalized and provided space for other progressive evangelicals to speak. Lausanne gathered evangelicals from across the political spectrum, expanding the reach of progressive evangelical themes. This creation of space also provided significant avenues for more diplomatic leaders such as Samuel Escobar, Pedro Arana, and later Ruth Padilla DeBorst to exert influence in a more irenic way. Thus, we can begin to parse the unique contributions of these progressive Latin Americans rather than present their influence as a monolith. These developments had implications beyond evangelical conciliar discourse. Indeed, the widening of evangelical discourse would fuel the rise of massive evangelical nongovernmental organizations (NGOs), an "evangelical internationalism" in American foreign policy, alongside the contours of a global Evangelical Left.

Though this "other evangelicalism" had already arisen, it remained widely unrecognized in many corners of the West. The next few decades would see massive shifts in both leadership and strategy for Protestant evangelical mission around the world—a reshaping of global evangelicalism. In hindsight, clashes between polarized ideological camps appeared all but inevitable.

The increasingly radical nature of the World Council of Churches and the proximity of conservative and progressive leaders within evangelical Protestant mission organizations set the stage for conflict and negotiation. Certainly, a swell of progressive evangelical action in North America aided Latin American evangelical influence—including the 1973 Chicago Thanksgiving Workshop on Evangelicals and Social Action.[96] Even the *Washington Post* highlighted this momentum and goal: to "launch a religious movement that could shake the political and religious life in America."[97] Yet, this surfacing of social Christianity in the North was much later than developments in the South.

This new style of evangelicalism from Latin America was profoundly shaped by the economic, political, and religious environment of the Cold War. The postwar Latin American context will prove fertile ground for biographies, relationships, and networks that challenged longstanding evangelical political and theological loyalties. In order to understand the rise of the Latin American Evangelical Left at Lausanne, we must take the story earlier into the Global South. Wider intellectual currents flowed into Latin American evangelical movements, filling in key political and theological spaces.

CHAPTER 2

Revolutionary Ferment

"Around 1966 the challenge of Marxism and of leftist nationalists in general had stopped being only ideological and political. . . . Guerrilla warfare as a possibility of attaining power and transforming the world had quickly become an extremely attractive doctrine and practice, especially in the universities. Every question regarding violence and subversion touched, in one way or another, the field of theology and the teaching of the Bible."[1] Samuel Escobar was organically connected to college campuses across Latin America as a traveling secretary with the student ministry IFES. Escobar, alongside Padilla and Arana, ministered at the epicenter of student political agitation within "a continent characterized by revolutionary ferment" as Padilla would later recall.[2] Here, Latin American student workers converted Cold War tension into evangelical power. Seen through this lens, it is neither accidental nor surprising that the most influential voices at Lausanne 1974 came from evangelicals working on college campuses. Transnational student networks flowed into the Lausanne Congress, channeling the voices and protests of a restless generation.

Many are familiar with the Catholic story from this Cold War context—social theologies that were formed within the heat, forging Marxist class analysis, biblical motifs, and European political theologies. This features perhaps most prominently in the work of Peruvian Dominican Gustavo Gutiérrez and theologies of liberation. The prominence of theologies of liberation, however, has obscured the diversity of responses to sociopolitical events that arose in the aftermath of the Cuban Revolution of 1959 and years following. Indeed, many observers have labeled *any* social Christianity from Cold War Latin America as a *version* of liberation theology, a linguistic designation that implies dependency and causation. Widening our lens captures not only the diversity of Latin American social Christianity but also the example and influence of a globally conscious generation. The tide of revolution ebbed and flowed, often through transnational channels emanating from universities. This flow of student radicalism was multidirectional—from 1968's deadly Summer Olympic protests in Mexico City, student riots in Paris and Great Britain, and the Prague Spring in Czechoslovakia to the wider civil rights movement, Vietnam War protests, and Kent State shooting of 1970— to name a few. In Latin America, protests were particularly violent and widespread.

The salience of universities in Latin America was, perhaps principally, due to the political and social clout of college students. University students possessed vast political influence due to both their numbers and the intrinsic power of education itself. In Colombia, for example, 60 percent of the country was illiterate in the late 1960s.[3] Thus, university students were one of the few groups able to engage the political and particularly Marxist literature of the day.[4] Within an overlapping college campus context, the emerging Latin American Evangelical Left was also inspired by stories and influences shared with Catholic liberation theologians. For example, Samuel Escobar's quote above undoubtedly hearkens to the example of Catholic guerrilla priest Camilo Torres. In a 1965 op-ed in the Colombian newspaper La Gaceta (Gazette), Torres pleaded with college students to join the Colombian armed resistance in a Marxist revolution.[5] The following year, however, Torres was dead—killed in his first combat experience, a failed ambush of Colombian government forces. Torres's perceived martyrdom, alongside the death of Argentine doctor Che Guevara the following year, inspired a generation of college students, fueling the fire of discontent with the political, social, and religious status quo.[6] Marxist revolutionaries, however, were not the only voices pleading with college students to join their cause in 1965–1966.

Escobar penned his own letter to students stuck on the sidelines of Latin America's revolutionary arena. In 1966, he wrote "Diálogo entre Cristo y Marx" (Dialogue Between Christ and Marx), which appeared in the IFES Spanish-language magazine Certeza. Escobar rejected Marxism as a superstructure, pushing instead for the conversion of their "Marxist neighbors."[7] He concluded the article with a call to evangelize leftist students using a probing question: "Why haven't you paid careful attention to [Jesus'] message of transformation, of redemption, as a response to the desperate human situation?" For Escobar, theology and revolution were fused by the searing heat of postwar Latin America. Evangelicals not only aimed to produce divergent results from their Catholic counterparts, but their audience also required a distinctive toolkit altogether.

While Escobar's 1966 article revealed their uniquely evangelical *aim*, René Padilla's article from the same year highlights their strikingly divergent *audience*. Padilla penned, "The greatest practical question confronting the Christian student in Latin America today isn't if a Christian girl *is or is not* permitted to wear lipstick, but the course of action one should take in the presence of prevailing social problems and ideologies that pretend to be able to solve them."[8] Padilla wrote to Latin American *evangelical* students rather than to sympathetic Marxists and aimed at the perceived social retreat and pervasive moralism in evangelical churches that they attended. At first blush, his statement bordered on the absurd. In 1966, university students grappled with the pull of revolutionary action, including the compatibility of guerilla warfare with Christian orthodoxy. Yet, as Latin America continued to experience the aftershocks of the Cuban Revolution, Protestant evangelical churches were often more likely to discuss the morality of modern female fashion than political activism.

A growing segment of evangelical college students was being *conscientized* into political awareness. Peruvian evangelical Pedro Arana, who would later succeed Padilla as general secretary for Latin America of the IFES, enrolled in "various summer courses" with his fellow Peruvian, Gustavo Gutiérrez, in Chimbote, Peru.[9] These lectures would later become Gutiérrez's masterwork, *A Theology of Liberation*. In a 2013 interview, Arana recalled, "It was a time of enriching dialogue, discussion, and without always agreeing."[10] In his own retelling, Escobar remembered Arana visiting his home after Gutiérrez's lectures and wrestling together with the content.[11] Across a wide spectrum, Christian thinkers struggled with the relationship between poverty, justice, violence, and their faith—all within an overlapping space. Orlando Costas, as a Puerto Rican, was profoundly shaped by his experience as a minority in the United States and studying in the American South. Yet, Escobar would later locate Costas's affinity for Marxist class analysis with his time spent in "safe" countries and his ignorance of their lived experience in Latin America, especially on college campuses.[12]

Careful attention to this early history reveals the bold insufficiency of treating Latin American social Christianity as a monolith. Uncovering the origins of this Latin American brand of evangelical social Christianity (*misión integral*) and the trajectory of their influence requires a multilayered story: a shared sociopolitical context and a uniquely evangelical experience of violence, oppression, and dependency. The origins are to be found within a cluster of political and social forces that were reshaping postwar Latin America: rural-urban migration, the resulting complications of urbanization, and the rapid expansion of the universities, where Marxist ideas of revolutionary change were of growing appeal to students. A surge in student enrollment at universities was preceded by waves of rural-urban migration, leaving in its wake urban poverty and creating a context that was ripe for radical student idealism.[13]

Progressive Evangelicals and the Rise
of the Latin American University

Latin American evangelicals experienced the daily struggles of the general population with an added twist. After the Cuban Revolution, rather than a Marxist leftist revolution, nearly every Latin American country received repressive military regimes within the next decade.[14] Thus, to be Latin American in the postwar period was to experience unjust governments that favored landowning elites, repressive military regimes, and widespread inequality. Yet, due to the influence of many local Catholic priests, Protestant children were often rejected by local schools, leaving Protestant parents with few educational options beyond missionary schools or homeschooling. One historian has demonstrated that priestly promotion within the Catholic hierarchy was sometimes tied to the success of anti-Protestant campaigns.[15] In addition to systemic discrimination, many Protestants were also recipients of explicit violence. Indeed, this was the case for the two most prominent leaders in the later Latin American Evangelical Left, Samuel Escobar and René Padilla. Orlando Costas's journey growing up in the United States was markedly divergent but no less impactful—especially in terms of political action. These stories, interweaved with crucial developments in Latin American intellectual and social history, provide insight into the unique challenges of being *evangélico* in Latin America. As a result, they clarify the shared and divergent path of evangelicals within an overwhelmingly Catholic Latin America.

When René Padilla (b. 1932) was two-and-a-half years old, his family moved from his birthplace of Quito, Ecuador, to neighboring Colombia in 1934, as his father sought a better market for his tailoring business.[16] The Padilla family was part of a wider Latin American story of massive rural-urban migration in the first half of the twentieth century described above. Colombia was experiencing unprecedented economic growth, especially in the textile industry—numbers that rivaled even Great Britain during the nineteenth century.[17] Bogotá also experienced a population boom that was typical of Latin American cities.[18] Padilla's father Carlos Padilla was, as Padilla put it, a tailor by necessity and an evangelical church planter by choice.[19] Both Padilla's parents became evangelical Christians before he was born, through the influence of René's uncle, Eddie Vuerto, who, according to Padilla, was one of the first evangelical pastors in Ecuador.[20] While economics was the impetus for crossing borders, evangelism drove the Padillas to move often within the city of Bogotá itself.[21]

The Padilla family's evangelical activism did not go unnoticed by some local Roman Catholics. Multiple arson attempts were made on the Padilla household, while dozens of evangelical church buildings and homes were burned down around them. René was unable to attend first grade because the local school rejected Protestant children—a woman from their church taught him at home, instead.[22] When Padilla *was* able to attend school, the challenges only increased. To this day, Padilla bears scars from stones thrown at him as he walked down the streets of Bogotá, as early as age seven.[23]

The Padilla family moved back to Ecuador when he was twelve years old, fleeing religious persecution.[24] Ecuador did not provide the safe haven the Padillas sought, however. Both René and his older brother Washington were later expelled from school—René for not attending a Roman Catholic procession and Washington for arguing with a teacher about the Bible. Twice people came to their house to burn it down but were stopped by police.[25] By the time Padilla was eighteen years old, multiple attempts had been made on his own life, including an assassination attempt while preaching outside his father's new church.[26] Looking back, he simply notes this was part of being a faithful evangelical Christian in Latin America: "You had to identify yourself as an Evangelical Christian, and if you did, you had to pay the consequences."[27]

As an economic migrant and as a member of a religious minority community, René Padilla came of age within a context of violence, oppression, and exclusion. The relationship between suffering and theology was an organic one—though he lacked social theological categories at the time.

Padilla later recalled "longing to understand the meaning of the Christian faith in relation to issues of justice and peace in a society deeply marked by oppression, exploitation, and abuse of power."[28] For Padilla, his "inherited" Protestant evangelical understanding of the gospel, however, provided little answer to the questions posed by the Latin American context. It spoke strongly of an individual, vertical salvation while remaining muted on "social dimensions in the gospel" to address horizontal issues.[29] The question was not *whether* the gospel spoke to a radical Latin American context but *how.*

In personal interviews and autobiographical writings, Samuel Escobar has recounted a similar experience as an evangelical Protestant in Peru in the 1930s and 1940s: "Being part of a minority became a mark of my identity."[30] Indeed, the international evangelical community became a surrogate family to Escobar soon after his birth in Arequipa, Peru, in 1934. As a child, Escobar attended the Evangelical Union of South America (EUSA) missionary elementary school in his hometown, taught by British missionaries and a handful of local Peruvians.[31] In the absence of his father, he was "formed in the Christian faith," especially by the missionaries.[32] The EUSA (now Latin Link) was founded in the aftermath of the epochal Edinburgh 1910 Missionary Conference.[33] Escobar thus came of age at the intersection of evangelical mission and local Latin American life. His later critiques then were formed out of a deeply personal experience.

The same year he matriculated at San Marcos University (1951), Escobar chose to be baptized by the American Southern Baptist missionary M. David Oates. These two events—his university entrance and baptism—marked the diverse, often conflicted, paths of Latin American evangelicals. Latin American Protestant evangelicals like Escobar often negotiated their identities between personal relationships with American missionaries and growing anti-American attitudes around them. Indeed, anti-American sentiment was thick on Latin American university campuses in the 1950s and 1960s. While many of their friends, pastors, teachers, and financial backers were Americans, broad antipathy toward the interventionist foreign policy and paternalistic role of the United States was endemic to the region. While Padilla enrolled at Wheaton College with the help of American missionaries, Escobar's enrollment at Universidad San Marcos represented a sharp departure from Padilla's journey northward to centers of evangelical education in the United States.[34]

The Latin American university presented a crossroads between the widespread popularity of Marxism and how Escobar understood his Christian faith. In 1951, Escobar entered San Marcos University in Lima, where he was struck by not only the popularity but also the relevancy of revolutionary ideas. Escobar recalled being "tempted" as a young man by Marxist social analysis of class and power; it spoke to the yawning gap between the rich and poor in Peru and the obvious hegemony of the ruling class.[35] In a 2013 interview, he spoke of his decision as to whether he wanted to become a "militant Christian."[36] Escobar was also largely self-taught theologically. Indeed, Escobar's childhood experience at the EUSA elementary school would be the extent of his formal *theological* training. Yet, what Padilla and Escobar shared in common became the primary impetus for their shared development of social Christianity—the revolutionary Latin American context centered on growing university campuses. They also shared a rejection of Marxist social scientific analysis in theology and praxis, in marked contrast to their counterparts in liberation theology.

Orlando Costas, as a Puerto Rican American citizen, did not experience a level of violence or sociopolitical upheaval similar to those experienced by his IFES counterparts. Yet, in the United States, Costas gained significant evangelical educational bona fides, including from the fundamentalist Bob Jones Academy in South Carolina (1958–1962) and studies at Trinity Evangelical Divinity School in Chicago and Nyack Missionary College in New York. While Costas was born in Ponce, Puerto Rico, he grew up in Connecticut after his family migrated to the mainland when he was twelve years old.[37] His experience as a Hispanic American represented a shared path of discrimination and marginalization from the majority. In his words, "As a member of a forgotten minority, I experienced the awfulness of ethnic prejudice, the harshness of poverty (in a country where the great majority have over and beyond their needs), and the oppression of an impersonal, culturally alienating educational system."[38] These experiences sharpened Costas's critique against the United States, missionary paternalism, and the importation of ideas into Latin America in particular.

René Padilla and Orlando Costas addressed both their most effusive praise and most biting critiques to their experiences at religious colleges in the United States.[39] Padilla attended Wheaton from 1953 to 1959.[40] During his time away from Latin America, he developed some aspects of his theological methodology at the expense of others. Social questions were in abeyance, as he focused on conservative evangelical emphases of the time, such as the "historical-grammatical approach to hermeneutics," which he learned from Wheaton Professor A. Berkeley Mickelsen.[41] Padilla would later describe this hermeneutical approach as "a good and necessary step, but . . . not enough."[42] Costas described Bob Jones as containing a "racist and triumphalistic anglosaxon subculture" but appreciated gaining a passion for evangelism and preaching.[43]

During this time, Escobar was more closely connected to wider Latin American intellectual trends in the 1950s and early 1960s than were Padilla and Costas. Padilla wrote nothing on the sociopolitical context or social theologies arising from Latin America during this period. While Padilla was living and studying in England from 1963 to 1965, he did not appear to have been aware of the rise of ISAL or of radical trends in Protestant Christian mission (described below). What is most clear from Padilla's time at Wheaton and Manchester, as well as Costas's time at Trinity Evangelical Divinity School (TEDS), is that it grounded them in an intellectually fertile tradition of evangelicalism, which they would eventually draw upon to critique the very institutions that trained them, challenging the foundations of evangelical mission. Their fierce critiques, then, were not simply a Latin American monologue but the result of a global conversation.

In 1959, both Samuel Escobar and René Padilla joined the staff of IFES as traveling secretaries. Padilla graduated from Wheaton in January 1960 in absentia from Latin America, after being appointed an IFES traveling secretary for Latin America, specifically for Venezuela, Colombia, Peru, and Ecuador.[44] The stark contrast and jolting return threw into question his theological categories, particularly those imparted by his education at Wheaton. In his new role at Latin American universities, Padilla immediately perceived the inadequacy of Western Protestant evangelical theology: "In this [university] context I found myself lacking a social ethic. My years of studies in the United States had not prepared me for the sort of theological reflection that was urgently needed in a revolutionary situation!"[45] Later, Escobar noted that Padilla's way of thinking was quite "Anglo-Saxon."[46]

Perhaps ironically, Orlando Costas encountered the inadequacy of his received theology in reverse direction—after returning to the United States *from* Latin American training. After finally graduating in 1966 from the Inter-American University of Puerto Rico, Costas was called to pastor the Evangelical Baptist Church of Milwaukee. Costas began to sharpen the political edge of his theology with Milwaukee's growing Hispanic community and explore sociopolitical engagement in praxis among the poor. Costas called this his "third conversion," where he "discover[ed] the world of the poor and the disenfranchised as a fundamental reference of the Gospel. [He] came to realize that the Christian mission had not only personal, spiritual, and cultural dimensions, but also social, economic, and political ones."[47] Costas's political engagement and social location in the United States would later serve as a significant bridge between the embryonic Latin American and American Evangelical Left.

In stark contrast to the Rust Belt of the United States, the effects of the Cuban Revolution reverberated throughout Latin America, and university students pressed Christian student works for a response to the pull of revolution. Their own discontent with existing approaches to ministry, mixed with student demand for social engagement, resulted in a unique recipe for social theology. Padilla and Escobar encountered a famine of scholarship that was able to address this situation. Escobar recalled, "Years before, when I faced personally the strong challenge of Marxism in university, I found out that the evangelical theological canon was no help in the struggle." Then, "When I asked for help for my intellectual struggles on campus, the best my missionary-pastor could give me was a poorly translated Spanish version of the book *Christian Evidences* by E. Y. Mullins," the notable Southern Baptist theologian and educator.[48] At the same time, the Latin American university context placed them within the quickening tide of revolutionary religious ideas. As traveling secretaries with the International Fellowship of Evangelical Students, Escobar and Padilla found themselves at the center of growing student protests, violence, and pull toward guerilla warfare.

Student Activism Among Demographic Change

The International Fellowship of Evangelical Students was founded in August 1947 at Phillips Brooks House in Harvard University.[49] The IVF, an organization originally based in Britain, had recently expanded into the United States in 1937 under the direction of Woods and the Canadian IVCF. The rise of the evangelical InterVarsity movement can also be seen in contrast to the relative decline of the various national Student Christian Movements (SCMs).[50] The founders of IVF, in particular the chairman

Martyn Lloyd-Jones (1899–1981), viewed the British SCM as incurably liberal and infected by Barthian theology, in particular.[51] Indeed, "The SCM
which had nurtured the older generation of denominational leaders ca-
pitulated in this decade to a form of quasi-Marxist political activism
that relegated prayer and Bible study to the margins, and had no place
for mission in any traditional form."[52] A meeting between IVF and SCM
leadership in London in 1950, which SCM leaders hoped would lead to
cooperation, demonstrated that the opportunity for reconciliation had
long since passed.[53]

In the same decade as it expanded into the United States, Stacey Woods
dreamed of extending the reach of IFES southward. Woods first traveled to
Latin America in April 1937, when he and Charles Troutman, a senior missionary with Latin America Mission (LAM) and a "leading figure" of the
IVCF-USA movement, drove to Mexico together (Woods had an intense fear
of flying).[54] Woods returned to Latin America in 1944 (Mexico, Guatemala,
Nicaragua, Costa Rica, and Colombia) and wrote to the board of IVCF-USA
outlining his desire to see IFES begin work in Latin America.[55] This vision
was further encouraged by donations from students in Canada, who continued to send funds even when no plans existed—just as they did for the United
States years earlier.[56] In February 1945, IVCF-USA staff worker Ed Pentecost
enrolled as a postgraduate student in Hispanic literature at Universidad
Nacional Autónoma de México (UNAM). There, he began to initiate student
Bible studies and meetings, mostly based in his home. At UNAM, he met
various Mexican students who had attended "Campus-in-the-Woods" in the
United States—a "veritable breeding ground" for North American Protestant
evangelical leaders.[57] As IFES began expanding its ministry southward in the
1940s, one of the first observations was Mexico's widespread and violent in-
tolerance of Protestantism.

Antipathy toward Protestant evangelicals only increased as revolutionary movements multiplied.[58] Ed Pentecost immediately noted the revolutionary context and violence surrounding the future IFES chapter at
UNAM: "Probably not six months have gone by in the last fifteen years
when some have not been killed for being Protestants and many more burnt
out of their homes."[59] That same year of 1948, for example, David Ruesga,
founder of the Church of God denomination, estimated that an attack on
Protestants occurred on average once a day.[60] IFES certainly was not alone
in its proximity to political ferment; reports from ecumenical SCM staff
workers reveal striking continuity with those from IFES staff.[61] SCM

staff worker and later general secretary Valdo Gallard of Uruguay began his 1953 travel report with the story of the murder of an evangelical pastor in Guatemala. According to Gallard's account, in late April of that year, a Roman Catholic mob burst into a church, prompted by false rumors that an ex–Roman Catholic priest was performing a Protestant service. The evangelical pastor was murdered at the front of his church.[62] As violence and discrimination against Protestants grew, so did corresponding evangelistic campaigns that targeted largely Roman Catholic communities. For student missions, growth in Protestant converts coincided with an explosion of student population numbers at Latin American universities.

Careful scrutiny of Latin American census data reveals two preliminary conclusions regarding a vast postwar matriculation boom at Latin American universities. The first appears to be a stark, interwar increase of rural-urban migration. The second is a great surge in student enrollment within the universities themselves. Peru recorded similar urban growth to Mexico City (described in the Introduction) during this period. The population of Lima stood at nearly 300,000, according to the November 1931 government census.[63] Less than a decade later, it had nearly doubled, with over 500,000 inhabitants in 1940.[64] This trend continued: Lima's population reached over 800,000 in 1950.[65] These countries were by no means unique within Latin America.[66] The interwar and postwar era in Latin America witnessed an explosion of urban migration, with a rise in economic ambitions as its corollary.

These patterns converged in the Latin American university. For example, UNAM had in 1928 an enrollment of 7,527 students, yet by 1950, this number had ballooned to nearly 25,000. By 1960, the student population in that year had surpassed the aggregate for the entire decade of 1940 to 1950. Indeed, the total number of graduates between 1940 and 1950 numbered only 62,584. But in the year 1960 alone, the university contained over 70,000 students. Today, UNAM has nearly 325,000 students, over 36,000 academic staff, and an endowment of over 2.5 billion U.S. dollars—a vast increase from just 7,000 students nearly a century ago.[67] Mexican universities certainly were not alone in witnessing this phenomenon—indeed, it was universal in Latin America.[68] The most prominent university in Peru, Universidad de San Marcos, contained 1,849 students in 1928, nearly 9,000 by 1955, and 14,000 by 1962.[69]

Burgeoning populations and expanding universities overwhelmed the urban infrastructure. Large-scale industrialization certainly followed this widespread urbanization. However, while countries such as Colombia saw a level of industrial growth in the 1930s similar to that of Great Britain in the nineteenth century, growth tapered off after 1945.[70] Indeed, industrialization and economic growth were unable to keep pace with demand for work. This story of rural-urban migration, the accompanying influx of university students, and declining economic opportunity set the stage for revolutionary action in cities around Latin America.

René Padilla observed this in the mid-1960s and wrote a series of articles expounding his observations.[71] In "La universidad: Lo social, lo spiritual" (The University: Social and Spiritual), Padilla diagnosed Latin America with a "social bottleneck": an abundant desire for upward mobility but a dearth of opportunity to achieve it.[72] Padilla wrote, "The university has become the sore spot where the sickness of the whole organism is made evident."[73] Enrollment at a university was far from a guarantee of socioeconomic improvement: according to Padilla, only about a quarter of those enrolled eventually graduated, and those who did graduate faced meager job prospects.[74]

Most Latin American cities also lacked the structural framework to integrate such an increased population. The rate of urbanization was higher than the rate of industrialization, in some cases as much as twice the rate.[75] To put it another way, "The urban process raised *social* aspiration levels without relieving *economic* pressures."[76] This led to widespread disillusionment, particularly among young people.[77] The importance of political action among university students is better understood when seen in this light. Padilla wrote, "The student strikes (which at times lead to the closing of the university for weeks and even months) . . . are mere manifestations of the problems that afflict the whole society." Thus, according to Padilla, "From this perspective it is possible to explain the importance that politics is given among the students . . . the professional agitator seeks to channel the bitterness of the oppressed into the narrow passages of a violent revolution."[78]

Latin American history contains a long tradition of government toleration of student radicalism.[79] But much had changed in the preceding decade—namely, the Cuban Revolution, a rapid spread of repressive military regimes, and vast rural-urban migration, all of which funneled into the Latin American university context.[80] The sociopolitical environment proved particularly salient for the development of social theologies in the second half of the twentieth century. In this context, Latin American social theologies that challenged the Western theological status quo were often viewed with similar suspicion and fear; trends in migration and urbanization had set the stage for the rise of Protestantism, bringing new ideas and practices that challenged traditional Latin American religion.[81] The intellectual climate of postwar Latin America presented a shared resource for this emerging generation of the Latin American evangelical elites and broader Protestant communities, such as those associated with the World Council of Churches.

War for the Soul of Christian Mission

While many are familiar with the Catholic roots of liberation theology in the work of Gustavo Gutiérrez and others, fewer acknowledge the parallel and overlapping history of mainline and evangelical Protestantism at the edge of the Cuban Revolution. Protestant theologies of liberation flowed through the pipeline of organizations such as the World Council of Churches (WCC), as well as the World Student Christian Federation (WSCF) and its national SCM affiliates.[82] Channels for radical mission ideas were often carved by missionaries themselves as they moved across national, cultural, and linguistic boundaries. For Protestant evangelicals like Costas, Escobar, Padilla, and Arana, these ideas were often much more accessible than those from Catholic thinkers—especially in the work of thinkers like Richard Shaull, José Míguez Bonino, and the World Council of Churches. Protestant cross-pollination in Latin America produced a crop of new social Christian fruit.

In the late 1960s and early 1970s, the embryonic Latin American Evangelical Left exerted considerable energy debating mainline Protestant theologies of liberation—considerably more than they engaged Catholic versions. In the late 1960s, for example, Pedro Arana wrote his master's thesis at Free Church College, Edinburgh, where he discussed the influence of the "theology of revolution" in the work of Richard Shaull.[83] The American Presbyterian missionary to Colombia and Brazil, Richard Shaull, subsequently a professor at Princeton Theological Seminary, exercised immense influence on the rise of Protestant liberation theology through these organizations in Latin America.[84] In the early 1950s, as Shaull transitioned from a ministry in Colombia to Brazil, his thinking also began to shift—a transition signaled in his work *Encounter with Revolution* (1955).[85] He had become convinced that Latin Americans needed to be awoken from their theological slumber to produce their own contextual theologies and to achieve holistic liberation. Shaull's "conversion" to the Latin American context had profound implications for the WCC and the later contours of liberation theology.[86] When the WCC began organizing conferences in the mid-1950s in Latin America, Shaull invited individuals with whom he had worked in the SCM in Latin America—students José Míguez Bonino, Rubem Alves, and Julio de Santa Ana, among others in the first generation of Latin American liberation theologians.[87]

In 1955, the WCC inaugurated a ten-year conference series called "Christian Responsibility Toward Areas of Rapid Social Change." Míguez Bonino, an Argentinian Methodist, had just returned from studies in Europe and the United States. After a preparatory meeting in July 1961, a discussion forum titled "Iglesia y Sociedad en América Latina" (ISAL) was formed through the influence of Míguez Bonino, along with Shaull, Alves, and others.[88] ISAL was geared toward stimulating conversation of a quite radical nature on the growing unrest provoked by socioeconomic stratification in the Latin American context. The SCM groups, under Shaull's leadership, were "ideological incubators" for the future leaders of ISAL and a "veritable pipeline" for the dissemination of WCC sociopolitical themes, which included "concepts clearly related to the theologies of liberation."[89] Thus, "by early 1964, ISAL was arguing that social change in Latin America demanded participation in revolution," and by late the same year, "revolution had become almost a monochord in ISAL publications."[90] For example, Shaull's 1966 plenary speech in El Tabo, Chile, entitled "Social Justice and the Latin Churches," called for the liberation of Latin American theology.[91]

These ideas swirled at the ecumenical seminary Instituto Superior Evangélico de Estudios Teológicos (ISEDET), aided by tailwinds from Argentine José Míguez Bonino, who later taught classes alongside visiting ISEDET professors John Howard Yoder and British evangelical Andrew Kirk. René Padilla was also based in Buenos Aires during these crucial years. Míguez Bonino, together with these strategically placed evangelicals, engaged radical theologies emanating from ISAL and the WCC and negotiated the place of new evangelical Christianities. This took place not through the lens of North American evangelical publications or intellectuals but—once again—at its center of production in Latin America.

Latin America became a battleground for the soul of Christian mission in the 1960s. Historic denominations, especially those associated with the World Council of Churches, increasingly moved away from traditional

Protestant mission emphases. As a crescendo, in 1968, the WCC assembly in Uppsala, Sweden, radically redefined the purpose of mission as "humanization" rather than conversion.[92] These wider shifts rattled foreign missionary structures and altered the framework of Christian work around the world.[93] As historian Mark Laing clarified, "The post-colonial quest to reorganize and restructure missions led to the more fundamental questioning of how mission should be *redefined*."[94] Thus, according to Angel Santiago-Vendrell, "Ecumenical missiology turned to the world as the crucial *locus* for mission."[95] While these shifts within the WCC have been widely viewed as the result of pressure from southern Christians upon traditional Western structures, the reality on the ground, however, was influence of a multidirectional and transnational kind.

The effort to awaken Latin American Christians from their political and religious dependency was a diverse effort of both Protestants and Catholics from the Global South *and* the Global North. Indeed, theologies of liberation were flowing through diverse denominational pipelines that crossed national, linguistic, and denominational boundaries. At the same time, evangelical student workers were experimenting with their own social Christianities, principally through the International Fellowship of Evangelical Students.

Laboratory for Social Christianity

Progressive Latin Americans, wielding their own theological and biographical materials, carved their own paths prior to and contiguous with theologies of liberation. In January 1966, Samuel Escobar and René Padilla developed and presented, in Lima, what was probably the first Latin American–led training course for evangelical university students. In turn, this course was a significant marker on the journey toward developing *misión integral* and sociocontextual theological ideas. Each afternoon, after "discipleship" and evangelism training, the students were sent into poor neighborhoods to partner with local churches in service projects. C. Stacey Woods, IFES general secretary, had initially been skeptical but increasingly deferred to his Latin American staff, allowing them to set the direction and content of student work and thus providing an intellectual freedom that was unconventional within contemporary Protestant evangelical student ministries.[96] Woods was booked as the plenary speaker, and Padilla sent him an advance itinerary for the week. René Padilla's recollection is that Woods approved of the itinerary with one major exception—the student work in poor neighborhoods.

According to Padilla, Woods responded in a letter saying, "What does this have to do with student work?"[97] Padilla remembers his own response as, "Our interest is not just evangelizing students. Our interest is to form disciples *conscientized* of their context."[98] While Padilla's 2013 word choice may import later social categories, his words echoed the contiguous educational method coined by Brazilian educator Paolo Freire. Freire had been carrying out his Movimento de Educaçâo de Base (MEB, Base Education Movement) in Brazil, a massive literary project to "conscientize" the poor into political awareness. (The term "conscientization" came from the Portuguese *conscientização*, meaning "to perceive social, political, and economic contradictions, and to take action against the oppressive elements of reality."[99]) Freire later wrote his influential *Pedagogy of the Oppressed*, where he decried the dependence of the poor on an unjust system—one marked by widespread illiteracy and educational inequality.[100]

Two years prior to the IFES training course in Lima, a military coup d'état had deposed leftist Brazilian president João Goulart, and the military government began targeting perceived threats, which included prominent university intellectuals like Freire, who fled to nearby Chile. Ironically, Freire's exile in Chile served to spread his ideas rather than to contain them.[101] The Chilean priest Sergio Torres recalled the influence of Brazilian exiles in Chile and how Freire spread the concept of conscientization at the University of Santiago.[102] Freire's ideas were adopted not only in the area of education but also in religion—perhaps most prominently in Latin American theologies of liberation. For our story, IFES in Latin America operated with a constant eye toward the changing political and religious situation, which provided ample intellectual exchange. This Lima course was a strategic attempt at awakening evangelical university students to what would later be termed *misión integral*.

Stacey Woods's final response to Padilla and Escobar was a lucid reflection of his leadership style and approach to IFES national movements: "I do not quite understand what you're doing, but you are in charge," Padilla recalled Woods saying. After attending the program and visiting impoverished neighborhoods with the students in 1966, Padilla recalled Stacey Woods pulling him aside and whispering, "René—now I understand."[103] Even if this dialogue was perhaps partially imagined or embellished, the point remains: Padilla and Escobar began shaping the ministry of IFES in Latin America around what they would later call "wider dimensions of the gospel message." In personal interviews and writing, Padilla, Escobar, and their later colleague Pedro Arana highlighted the significant theological freedom Woods provided his staff workers.[104] This nationally focused organizational context, to be further described below, was prescient and even perhaps unique within global evangelical parachurch organizations.

Padilla later recalled the Lima course as "a way of promoting not only evangelization as oral proclamation of the Gospel, but of promoting integral discipleship, including the social dimension of the Gospel."[105] Yet, this full-orbed understanding of *misión integral* is most likely applied retrospectively here. The first time Padilla utilized the phrase "social dimensions of the Gospel" in writing was in 1973, in an article for *Certeza* magazine—the IFES magazine for Latin America.[106] A year earlier, he had used the phrase "dimensions of the gospel."[107] Yet, in June 1966, Padilla was three months removed from having completed his Manchester doctoral dissertation, in which his language reflected the prevalent Protestant evangelical understanding of social theology—social action was an *implication* of the gospel message, not *inherent* to it. Padilla certainly emphasized social action in his thesis by saying, "It cannot be overemphasized that the Gospel has social implications."[108] Yet, he lambasted the attempt to read social transformation into the Bible:

> To the embarrassment of the modern social reformer, in none of the Pauline epistles is there the slightest suggestion that the Church will eventually mould the social structures or that it is incumbent upon her to do so. To hold that . . . is an arbitrary modernisation of his teaching. *The idea that the Church is an agency of "social redemption" to be brought about through the permeation of society by Christian principles is a modern invention; the attempt to justify it by an appeal to Paul or any other Biblical writer is doomed to failure.* (Italics mine)[109]

It is clear, then, that in the mid-1960s, René Padilla's understanding of social ethics reflected mainstream Protestant evangelical theology. Archival documents also reveal that Padilla's doctoral thesis was more than a distant thought in his mind—indeed, it formed the basis of his plenary talk at Lima

1966 titled "The Church and the World." One participant in the course wrote, "In René Padilla's lectures the conclusion of more liberal theological approaches was rejected, i.e. that God's purpose is to change the structures of society . . . the only Biblical approach that of [sic] winning the individual in bringing him deliverance from the Kingdom of Darkness to the Kingdom of Light."[110]

Ultimately, the curriculum content at Lima 1966 emerged from eight years of experience in Latin American universities and mirrored broader trends in Latin American Christianity, such as the Roman Catholic Church's shift toward the poor in the mid-1960s.[111] Unfortunately, the historiographical record has, instead, credited Western leaders with the curriculum, in particular in interpreting it as based upon a training course by Swiss IFES staff worker Hans Bürki in 1965 in Casa Moscia, Switzerland, which Padilla and Escobar attended. Pete Lowman, for example, mistranslated and misquoted Escobar as saying the 1966 Lima course was "something which gave form to all that *we had learnt*" from Bürki and his course. Other historians have followed Lowman's lead, as described in his *The Day of His Power*, which relied heavily on Samuel Escobar's work *La chispa y la llama*.[112] Escobar himself wrote of the 1966 Lima course that "we had begun to articulate something that was very evangelical but also very much our own: something which brought together *our own experience (propia vivencia)*, inside the tradition of the Fellowship."[113] That unique element was social theology, manifested in practical social action among the poor.[114]

Latin American influence at Lausanne 1974 arose from Cold War ferment. The origins of *misión integral* are to be found within a cluster of political and social forces that were reshaping postwar Latin America: rural-urban migration, the resulting complications of urbanization, and the rapid expansion of the universities, where Marxist ideas of revolutionary change were of growing appeal to students. The surge in student enrollment at universities was preceded by waves of rural-urban migration, leaving in its wake urban poverty and creating a context that was ripe for radical student idealism. Traveling secretaries with the global college ministry IFES found themselves at the center of student political agitation, a shared resource with later theologies of liberation. The social origins of *misión integral*, then, are found within a revolutionary university context, grounded in the global evangelical student movement, and developed by Latin American thinkers themselves.

Latin American evangelical social Christianity was not a fusion of liberation theology and social action. Indeed, these social theological themes arose not as a response to developments within the Catholic Church and mainline Protestantism but as a response to the same political and social stimuli that gave rise to theologies of liberation. Their theological toolkit, then, was of an evangelical kind, drawn primarily from their negotiated identities. Indeed, this generation of Latin American evangelicals came of age within a context of violence, oppression, and exclusion often at the hands of a Catholic majority. They were also uniquely positioned between deeply personal relationships with American missionaries and the growing anti-American agitation on university campuses. These biographies fused with developments in the North, such as critical evangelical biblical scholarship that flourished in the 1960s.

The *shared* materials with liberation theology were primarily sociopolitical. While this above account has often been presented within an exclusively Catholic framework, we have already seen the parallel and overlapping history of mainline Protestantism that developed within the same sociopolitical context. Evangelical Protestants shared these sociopolitical contextual resources while carving their own path throughout their contested journey. This was the environment within which the emerging Latin American Evangelical Left began to question the importation of Protestant evangelical theologies into Latin America—a protest that gained a wider hearing at Lausanne.

While evangelical Protestants are often left out of narratives on social Christianity in Latin America in the twentieth century, their story overlaps in surprising and significant ways. Similarly, while northern evangelical leaders were slower to address Cold War Christianities, they were not silent regarding the Marxist penetration of Latin America. Ultimately, it would be Latin Americans themselves who would place their stamp on global evangelical social Christianity and provide an enduring response alongside sympathetic northern leaders.

Crucial questions in this story remain unanswered. If Western leaders in the evangelical establishment were concerned about the spread of communism and liberal trends in mainline Protestant missiology, why were René Padilla and Samuel Escobar chosen as plenary speakers at Lausanne 1974? Similarly, why was Orlando Costas chosen to present two strategy papers, given his growing reputation as a provocateur with leftist leanings?

In other words, why provide a global platform to the emerging Latin American Evangelical Left at all? Answering this question requires a wider cast of characters. Indeed, the answer lies in a complex web of networks that crossed national, theological, political, and linguistic boundaries. The transnational nature of postwar evangelicalism connected northern leaders with emerging trends in Latin America. This critical interface between missionaries from the North and an emerging progressive coalition in the South created friction and fissures that threatened long-established loyalties.

CHAPTER 3

Cold War Christianity

"Some professors at the Latin America Seminary [*sic*] in Costa Rica, one of the oldest evangelical seminaries whose leadership has in recent years been turned over to Latin Americans, *espouse a compromise form of liberation theology,* take a hard line critical of North American mission board influence and support socialism as a preferred economic option and violence as a Christian possibility for social change" (italics mine).[1] With these words, the influential American evangelical Carl F. H. Henry poked a bee's nest of controversy.[2] The flagship evangelical seminary in Latin America, Seminario Bíblico Latinoamericano (SBL), had recently gained independence from American missionary control, the product of fierce negotiation led primarily by Puerto Rican theologian Orlando Costas. In the early 1970s, Latin American faculty defended their hard-won turf and heightened their radar for U.S. incursion. Henry's article struck a nerve between two prevailing sensitivities: the Latin American demand for self-rule and the reality of financial dependency. The seminary still depended heavily on donations from conservative evangelical households in the United States. This situation, however, appeared increasingly unsustainable—rejecting American evangelical opinion while requiring their approval.

News of Henry's letter quickly reached the SBL leadership in Costa Rica as they scrambled to contain the damage. To make matters worse, the EP News Service copied Henry's above paragraph and pasted it separately as a feature. Thus, while the sentence was only a minor part of Henry's three-page report, it became the headline. In response, SBL Rector Ruben Lores protested to editor Norman Rohrer, defending the evangelical bona fides of the SBL: "As an institution fully committed to the Word of God whose professors yearly sign an evangelical statement of faith we protest biased reporting to North American Christians."[3] Five days later, SBL faculty penned their own defiant open letter defending the seminary.[4] They rejected accusations of radical theology but also defended the viability of socialism as a political option: "We recognize that it is difficult for some of our white North American evangelical brethren who live in a relatively free, democratic, and wealthy society to understand how Christians . . . might prefer one of the socialist parties here to the military dictatorships."[5] While financially beholden to conservative American evangelical perception, they remained unwilling to surrender to foreign theological and political control.

Samuel Escobar, then president of the FTL, soon joined their defense. While his letter was characteristically measured, he echoed their protest of perceived American paternalism: "There is a growing weariness of police attitudes from persons and institutions in North America who have made themselves the watchdogs of orthodoxy around the world."[6] In similar fashion elsewhere, Orlando Costas presented American missionaries as overbearing mothers refusing to allow their children to leave the house.[7] These battles were uncontained by regional borders; Latin Americans dragged their local clashes to the global stage.

Latin American rejection of dependency on U.S. leadership, theology, and politics is the background for fractures and fissures that emerged at the Lausanne Congress of 1974. The Latin American Evangelical Left chipped away at the wall of American managerial control by using shared tools—influential postcolonial ideologies drawn from a wide variety of intellectual fields. In particular, theories of dependency provided an indictment of the global status quo and Christian forms that were, according to them, "made in the USA."[8] In this way, Latin American evangelicals joined wider Cold War negotiation in fields of economics, education, religion, and politics.

Theories of Dependency in Evangelical Perspective

After World War II, the Economic Commission for Latin America (Comisión Económico para América Latina or CEPAL) was established with United Nations funding in Santiago, Chile.[9] At the time, economic theories of development predominated, popularized by works such as American economist W. W. Rostow's *The Stages of Economic Growth: A Non-Communist Manifesto*.[10] Rostow's analysis was based on the British economy and laid out five stages of economic development that underdeveloped countries could be expected to follow. Yet, as the export boom of 1940s waned and Latin American dependence on development loans and aid packages increased—especially from the United States—many Latin American economies continued to languish at the lower rungs of the economic ladder. By the mid-1960s, many economists in both North America and Latin America began to question economic theories of development in favor of dependency theory—a theory championed by Argentine economist Raúl Prebisch at the UN-backed CEPAL.[11]

For advocates, dependency theory argued that Latin America did not simply lag behind Western countries in terms of economic development but suffered from an unjust system that channeled resources from peripheral, poor nations to core, wealthy economies. Recent studies have also shed light on the use of development as a "weapon in the ideological combat that was the Cold War" to "secure and extend an American-dominated liberal order."[12] While this modernizing project was not specific only to the United States, in Latin America's case, the United States played an outsized role.[13] Put more broadly, according to historian David Ekbladh, "Modernization is deeply implicated in what has been more aptly described as the establishment of American global hegemony."[14]

Dependency theory created an ideological unity and shared suspicion of Western efforts, funding, and ideology among a politically conscious theological elite in the Global South.[15] What Latin America needed, then, was not *development* within the world economy but *liberation* from the world economic status quo. In historian Brian Stanley's words, "The reality of *dependency* was as unacceptable in *theology* as in *economics*."[16] The rise of theories of dependency also provides crucial clarity to our story here. The situation of dependency was also acute within Protestant evangelical communities. In the first half of the twentieth century, many churches were dependent on the importation of North American money, personnel, and theological methods. This often paternalistic context was certainly not unique to Latin America—dependence and independence in the field of religion is a theme that could be explored in diverse locales. Yet, dependency within Latin American evangelical communities was layered and complex. Ultimately, for Latin American theologians, the path toward theological independence became increasingly clear in the aftermath of the Second Vatican Council of the Catholic Church.

In the late 1960s, Western commentators were just beginning to come to grips with the development, promotion, and newfound prominence of theologies of liberation. The documents of the Second Vatican Council itself, such as *Gaudium et spes*, and Pope Paul VI's encyclical *Populorum progressio* of 1967 had begun to accelerate a wider shift toward the poor, alongside a call for liberation from oppression and dependency.[17] *Populorum progressio* in particular decried the selfish and exploitative components of capitalism. An emerging generation of Catholic elites in Latin America viewed these developments as license and endorsement of their inculturating project. For example, on August 26, 1968, the Latin American Episcopal Conference (CELAM) met in Medellín, Colombia, to develop and apply social Christianity to their sociopolitical context. Their contextualizing tools were drawn from sources as wide as economic theories of dependency, Freire's *conscientization*, and this accelerating tradition of Catholic social Christianity.

Documents released by CELAM bishops provided a blistering indictment of the economic dependency of Latin America, the injustice of the current economic system, and a call for *conscientization* of the masses. At Medellín, the bishops wrote, "Many of our workers, although they have gradually become conscious of the necessity for . . . change, simultaneously experience a situation of dependency on inhuman economic systems and institutions."[18] Thus, "We must awaken the social conscience and communal customs . . . this task of conscientization and social education ought to be integrated into joint pastoral action at various levels."[19] Catholic social thinking at this time drew deeply from wells dug within the field of education (Freire) and economics (theories of dependency), where emerging thinking questioned structural inequality and the dependence of the poor.

Liberation theologians gave a distinctively theological voice to the growing awareness of the chronic dependency of Latin America. To capture the revolutionary ethos, the Brazilian Presbyterian theologian Rubem Alves (1933–2014) wrote his doctoral dissertation entitled "Toward a Theology of Liberation" at Princeton Theological Seminary in 1969—probably the first use of the phrase "theology of liberation."[20] This same year, the Peruvian Dominican priest Gustavo Gutiérrez (who is widely considered the "father of liberation theology") lectured on liberation themes in Lima—lectures that were later published under the title *A Theology of Liberation* (*Teología de liberación*). Gutiérrez provided a searing critique of developmentalism, which he calls "aseptic, giving a false picture of a tragic and conflictual reality" in a chapter titled "Liberation and Development."[21] In the end, "The notion of dependence emerges therefore as a key element in the interpretation of the Latin America reality."[22] It is perhaps unsurprising, then, that the loudest and most salient voices to protest dependency upon American evangelicalism arose from Latin America given a shared Cold War context.

At the Lausanne Congress, many American evangelicals caught their first glimpse of an emerging, younger generation of leaders from the Global South—many who rejected the equation of theological conservatism with political conservatism. Indeed, for many conservative leaders, the fierce rejection of dependency on American leadership, theology, and politics was surprising and even shocking. Carl Henry was not alone in his encounter of Latin American protest during crucial years *preceding* the Lausanne Congress, however. Lausanne's primary catalyst, "America's Pastor" Billy Graham, learned hard lessons from the Latin American rejection of dependency. The emergence of theories of dependency provides crucial background for the reshaping of global evangelicalism.

In 1969, the BGEA planned the boldly titled *First* Latin American Congress on Evangelization (CLADE I) in Bogotá, Colombia, attempting to capitalize on momentum from the evangelical congresses in Berlin (1966) and Keele (1967). The Berlin Congress of 1966 convened in a city divided by communism. The congress was also entirely planned and executed by Americans. Given Graham's famously anticommunist preaching and the recent choice of Berlin, it is less surprising that the BGEA planned a lesser-known congress in Latin America, where the aftershocks of the Cuban Revolution continued to rattle the edifice of religion and politics—90 miles off the coast of Florida. Personal correspondence also reveals wariness over the Marxist penetration of Latin America and the shifts of the WCC away from traditional Protestant missiology.[23] But this conference also produced furious backlash and influential unintended consequences. Our protagonists in the Latin American Evangelical Left were already developing their own strategic networks and evangelical forms of social Christianity within an overlapping context with Catholic developments above. Thus, while most narratives surrounding these events have begun with CLADE I, we must begin earlier with a widely overlooked gathering called the Asociación Teológica Evangélica (ATE, Evangelical Theological Association).

For Graham and key American evangelical leaders, lessons learned in Latin America would shape the planning and execution of the Lausanne Congress in 1974 while widening the space for controversial Latin American voices pressing for change. This would further inform Graham's inclusion of Padilla, Escobar, and Costas, even as they became increasingly controversial. While Graham was beginning to tone down his anticommunist rhetoric, Latin American evangelicals were just beginning to wield the ideologies forged within their restless context.

Asociación Teológica Evangélica
(Evangelical Theological Association)

On March 4, 1969, an eclectic assemblage of progressive evangelicals gathered in Buenos Aires with the shared goal of constructing new forms of social Christianity. The ATE included the Argentine Methodist José Míguez Bonino, British Anglican Instituto Superior Evangélico de Estudios Teológicos (ISEDET) Professor Andrew Kirk, Spanish-born Methodist Plutarco Bonilla, and René Padilla, who was the principal organizer of the gathering. At the first ATE, intellectual freedom and paternalism were fresh in their minds. That year, Bonilla was in the midst of the fierce battle regarding nationalizing the seminary faculty and leadership at SBL. Bonilla was elected as the first Latin American rector that year, accelerating its break from the oversight of U.S.-based Latin America Mission, its founding structure. This SBL story resurfaces later in the chapter as key background here.

At the first ATE gathering, a more subtle rejection of paternalism can be observed, as well. Míguez Bonino's close association with the World Council of Church's Iglesia y Sociedad en América Latina (ISAL) and various strands of liberation theology rendered him suspect to a wide swath of the evangelical community. His presence itself was a form of protest, as his later exclusion from the FTL makes clear. Padilla's invitation to Míguez Bonino and the willingness of other evangelicals to participate with him sent a clear, early message regarding managerial control of Latin American evangelicalism. The founding of the ATE was thus a brief moment of ecumenism prior to the reassertion of northern divisions—both at CLADE and the later FTL. The inclusion of Míguez Bonino in particular made U.S. donors nervous and furthered the perception of Padilla as theologically suspect. At ATE, Andrew Kirk, for his part, was much less controversial—in his words, he "came with an evangelical reputation."[24] Yet, Kirk was also sensitive to the need for local social Christianity, due in part to his collegial relationship with Míguez Bonino and ISEDET colleagues.

René Padilla initiated the ATE because of a perceived "vacuum" in Latin American Christian thought and leadership. Yet, more than a vacuum in leadership, the first gathering of the ATE focused on a void in the gospel itself. At the first meeting, Plutarco Bonilla declared, "The Gospel that we commonly preach in Latin America . . . is an amputated Gospel. We need to return to a recognition that God's intention is to save men, not souls separated from the body." This theme of social Christianity would permeate the early evangelical gathering. In sum, the ATE's press release later read, "The public meetings organized by Asociación Teológica Evangélica during their first year of existence have provoked much interest on the part of a select group of evangélico leaders in the study of a theme of vital importance for the cause of Jesus Christ: the communication of the Gospel in the world today." In a similar way to the Catholic CELAM gathering in Medellín, progressive evangelicals sought to construct a contextualized social Christianity with their own theological tools.[25]

Perhaps most important, the ATE deepened friendships that cut across denominational lines and developed beyond the gaze of conservative evangelical leadership in the North. Similarly, the relationships formed at ATE encouraged both theological reflection and called for Latin American autonomy in organizational and theological leadership. René Padilla in particular was prescient in utilizing personal relationships and networks for the purpose of theological reflection. The timeline here also throws additional light on the backlash against CLADE I. When American evangelicals attempted to delineate the boundaries of theological thought in the region, these progressive leaders bristled at the incursion into their own construction site. The embryonic coalition of the Latin American Evangelical Left was taking shape prior to this infamous congress of 1969 and played a crucial role in establishing strategic networks across the Spanish-speaking world. The formation of the later think tank FTL, in particular, was also aided by organizational developments within Latin America itself and, in particular, the ATE network. As events surrounding the Cold War gripped the headlines in the United States, evangelical Protestants were deeply affected by and quietly reshaping the Latin American religious landscape. Yet, these leaders at the ATE were not, of course, the only one who perceived an intellectual and theological void within Latin American evangelicalism. While Latin

American theologians tested the boundaries of Christian orthodoxy during the Cold War, the Billy Graham Evangelistic Association intervened.

Cold War Fears and Evangelical Boundary Making

A total of 920 delegates gathered in Bogotá, Colombia, from November 21 to 30, 1969, for the First Latin American Congress on Evangelization (Congreso Latinoamericano de Evangelización or CLADE I).[26] The professed goal of the BGEA was not power or paternalistic influence but the "evangelization of the whole of Latin America."[27] The title of the congress publication declared the urgency of their gathering: "Action in Christ for a Continent in Crisis." The "crisis" for progressive Latin American evangelicals, however, was the stubborn continuation of paternalism—that the congress was "made in the USA" with scant contribution from Latin Americans themselves.[28] Compounding the offense for progressive evangelicals was a missionary attempt to define boundaries of social Christianity for Latin America, which we explore below. Referring to paternalism, Padilla later called this "typical of the way in which work was done sometimes in the conservative sector."[29]

CLADE was not, in fact, the first Latin American congress for evangelization. The Latin American Evangelical Conferences (Conferencia Evangélica Latinoamericana or CELA) began in 1949 in Buenos Aires. For many Protestants in the region, CELA I was the first Latin American–led Christian conference, begun without influence or impetus outside of Latin America. The second CELA gathering in 1961 drew influential ecumenical Protestant leaders such as British theologian Lesslie Newbigin, Scottish missionary to Latin America John Mackay, and José Míguez Bonino. Yet, the background of CELA II was a gathering three weeks earlier in Huampaní, Peru, from which the WCC-sponsored ISAL arose (described in Chapter 2). An emerging radical strand of ecumenical theology gained momentum at CELA II and caught the attention of conservative evangelicals. In calling CLADE the first, it was a bold rejection of CELA conferences as not *evangelical* enough and a call to clarify—and guard—boundaries. These theological developments, alongside pervasive anticommunism and persistent Cold War fears, provoked the BGEA to action in Latin America.[30] Soon after Medellín, CLADE sought to cauterize the spreading wound of Marxist thought and improve the prognosis of Latin American evangelicalism.

The organization of plenary speeches and participation was not the only intervention planned by the BGEA. Indeed, the greatest offense for progressive evangelicals was a private distribution of materials at CLADE aimed at blunting the development of social Christianity. At the congress, each participant received a copy of American missionary Peter Wagner's book, *Teología Latinoamericana: Izquierdista o evangélica? La lucha por la fe en una iglesia creciente* (1969, *Latin American Theology: Radical or Evangelical? The Struggle for the Faith in a Young Church*).[31] Wagner was also on the planning committee of CLADE I. Wagner's book was distributed free of charge to every attendee at CLADE I, denoting BGEA's confidence in its contents.[32] Wagner's main purpose was to present the "dangerous" strands of the predominant ecumenical theology, then to "criticize" this theology "from the point of view of the church growth position popularized by Dr. Donald McGavran."[33]

Yet, more than taking on so-called liberal theologians, Wagner attempted to posit a contextual Latin American understanding of Christian mission.[34] Wagner's writing was a particular affront to Padilla and Costas and their fledgling social Christianity. Indeed, the quotation from Bolivian Methodist minister Jorge Pantelís (b. 1938) that Wagner attacked in his introduction read as if Padilla or Costas themselves had written it: "The idea that the Church's evangelization ought to be reduced to the 'salvation of souls,' . . . is simply one of the worst heresies that we have to face in our times."[35] To this, Wagner responded, "His obvious purpose is to discredit the evangelical emphasis on the doctrine of personal salvation" and that it represented "a deep struggle for the faith, with the very life of the church hanging in the balance."[36] Thus, Wagner wholly rejected integral missiological emphases as contrary to Protestant evangelical theology and fatal to the fledgling Latin American Protestant evangelical church.

Wagner's analysis also lacked nuance, lumping more evangelically minded thinkers such as José Míguez Bonino, Emilio Castro, and Justo Gonzalez together with radical/ecumenical theologians like Rubem Alves and Richard Shaull. Wagner did acknowledge there was a "certain spectrum" of theologies and that his analysis "does not apply equally to all those who have associated themselves with the radical left."[37] He also wrote that Míguez Bonino "is considered by many as the dean of Latin American theologians."[38] Yet, Wagner criticized him for social engagement: "[Míguez Bonino] agreed with the liberals in their opposition to 'the narrowing of the Christian faith to the purely individual realm and to the after-death.' He applauded their call for 'an active participation in society, for the abandonment of the pietistic ghetto,

for the proclamation and realization of the social dimension of Christian redemption.'"[39]

Wagner's criticism of Míguez Bonino and Justo Gonzalez, as also, indeed,
the book's central argument, displayed a bold rejection of social emphases
in Christian mission. His final section, "Evangelical Alternatives," highlighted
Latin American writers from his own experience as a missionary and, in
doing so, manifested a limited understanding of existent Latin American
Protestant evangelical writing. For more progressive evangelical thinkers like
Padilla, Wagner's book was just one aspect of a noticeable North American
stamp on CLADE I. Orlando Costas later wrote, "We were offended by the
purpose, content and methodology of the book."[40] As a result, Padilla, Escobar, and SBL faculty members Costas, Plutarco Bonilla, and Rubén Lores
(who led a Bible study at CLADE) planned to write a book in response to
Wagner. Months later, they abandoned this project in favor of later FTL
consultations—though Padilla himself published a scathing article in response.[41]

The speakers at CLADE largely came from stable democracies (Puerto
Rico, Costa Rica, and Hispanic communities in the United States), which,
for progressives, aggravated the foreignness of the congress. Yet, Peruvian plenary speaker Samuel Escobar was a notable exception. Indeed, Escobar's paper
was titled "The Social Responsibility of the Church," which spoke of an
awakening of political conscience among the evangelical community in Latin
America—spurred on by the work of British missionaries, who had helped
them discover the "social dimension of the gospel."[42] Escobar, however, also
affirmed the centrality of evangelization: "The comprehension of evangelization as the central task should not lead us to close our eyes to other urgent
tasks."[43] Escobar continued, "We should affirm that evangelization is *one* of
the tasks of the church, it is not the only task of the church and it does not end
in proclamation."[44] Social structures affected the church and the reception of
the gospel—not to recognize this "disfigures" the gospel and "impoverishes
the Christian life."[45]

To Escobar's surprise, the reception of his paper at CLADE I was overwhelmingly positive.[46] Padilla also recalled, "His paper on 'The Social Responsibility of the Church' provoked a standing ovation and threw into
relief the fact that a significant sector of the evangelical leadership in Latin
America was fertile soil for social concerns from a biblical perspective."[47] In
response, Vergil Gerber, executive secretary of the Evangelical Foreign Missions Association, wrote a glowing personal letter to Escobar on December 4,

1969. He wrote, "How we thank God for top-notch men such as you who are leading the Latin American Church into glorious days of victory ahead." He also asked Escobar to "dedicate this God-given ability to theological works which will have a lasting impact" in Latin America.[48]

Those who cheered social Christianity's advance were certainly disappointed by the absence of Orlando Costas. In addition to his increasing political activism in Milwaukee, two years earlier, Costas had also enrolled as a master of divinity (MDiv) student at Trinity Evangelical Divinity School (TEDS) in Deerfield, Illinois, approximately 60 miles south of Milwaukee. TEDS was known for its academic reputation but also as an increasingly polarized political environment; progressive evangelical student political activism flourished during years of the Vietnam War and civil rights movement. Perhaps most notably, evangelical leftist political activist Jim Wallis founded the *Post-American*, later *Sojourners*, at TEDS two years after CLADE in 1971. At the time, many TEDS faculty were "refugees" from the evangelical civil war at Fuller Theological Seminary a decade earlier.[49] Thus, at TEDS, Costas was formed within a politically engaged, yet theologically conservative evangelical tradition—an environment that revealed the increasingly contentious, generational fault lines between younger and older evangelicals.

A conservative versus liberal lens, however, cannot explain Costas's absence from CLADE. At a cursory glance, one might assume Costas was excluded due to his progressive leanings. Careful attention to personal papers reveals that Costas was, in fact, invited by CLADE organizer Clyde Taylor. After a misunderstanding over funding for his trip, however, Costas chose to attend the WCC-sponsored CELA III conference instead, which took place the same year. Costas's decision was more than dollars and cents. He consistently cultivated influence outside the borders of evangelicalism, especially within ecumenical circles. This type of border crossing certainly labeled Costas with an evangelical question mark, given the contentious history of CELA and CLADE described above. Even in Escobar's words, "He could not always convince all of us, his Latin American colleagues, that we should cross the borders he crossed."[50] In Costas's absence, progressive evangelicals at CLADE still gained the upper hand through the unlikely reception of Samuel Escobar's plenary speech.

After the congress, Escobar reflected on the benefits of CLADE I in a letter to IFES General Secretary Stacey Woods: "From November 21st to 30th we were with Rene at the famous Latin American Congress on Evangelism. The many contacts we made were valuable. My paper about 'Social

Figure 3. Orlando Costas unveiling *El Cristo Roto*, painting by Juan Alvarez
Cuauhtémoc, while members of the Milwaukee Christian Center
board look on. Photo courtesy of the University of Wisconsin–Milwaukee
Libraries, Archive Division.

Responsability [*sic*] of the Church' was well received to my surprise. Apparently the conscience that we must do something here 'while it is the day' is little by little coming to Evangelicals."[51] Escobar's letter highlighted the rising social conscience among evangelical leaders in Latin America and a moment of optimism within this emerging coalition. Stacey Woods also maintained a close connection to his IFES staff workers and was shifting in his own understanding, as well.

Despite the presence of Padilla, Escobar, and SBL faculty member Rubén Lores, the actual declaration issued by CLADE I kept strangely aloof from the sociopolitical context of Latin America—nothing in the text spoke specifically to the Latin American context. This contrasted with the WCC-sponsored CELA III, which not only sought to address the sociopolitical context but also included Roman Catholics and Pentecostals in its gathering.[52]

The main breakthrough of CLADE I was not in its public pronouncements but in its facilitation of networks of evangelical thinkers and in the awareness it created of the need for a truly Latin American–led leadership organization. Though CLADE I had genuine intentions, the most profound impact of the congress was unintended due to the Latin American reaction to the cultural misunderstandings and perceived "prepackaging" of CLADE's purpose and program. Years later, Escobar recalled, "We said, now is the time that we as Latin Americans decide who is *evangélico* in America Latina and what it means to be *evangélico*. And from there came the idea of the Fraternity."[53] Thus, Padilla later wrote, "In light of the purpose of the organizers, CLADE I was a failure as the only concrete result was the unintended formation of what later became the *Fraternidad Teológica Latinoamericana*."[54]

CLADE I produced an emerging network of neoprogressive Latin American evangelicals who discovered that others were seeking the same contextual answers to sociopolitical issues. Thus, at CLADE, Padilla, Escobar, the Peruvian-born British missionary Peter Savage, and others discussed the persistent paternalism of the missionary establishment and the scarcity of contextual Protestant evangelical theology in Latin America. This ad hoc group would later found the Fraternidad Teológica Latinoamericana (Latin American Theological Fraternity), which became the most influential Latin American Evangelical Protestant theological think tank. Surprisingly, the foundation of the FTL was probably not the most significant result of CLADE. Instead, CLADE taught a hard-learned lesson that would later reshape global evangelical organizational structure. The bold paternalism of CLADE played a significant role in the emerging diversity of Lausanne 1974's planning committee. Perhaps most important, this widely overlooked gathering of CLADE provides crucial background for the composition of the Lausanne Congress.

Trajectories of Inclusion and Exclusion

A significant and crucial question remains unanswered within not only our narrative but also current scholarship at large: why was the emerging Latin American Evangelical Left included in the proceedings of the Lausanne Congress of 1974? Put another way, if Costas, Padilla, and Escobar had pinged the radar of conservative evangelicals as theologically adrift, why were they given the most prominent platform for global evangelicals in the second half of the twentieth century? In part, when Billy Graham and colleagues searched for Lausanne's leadership, they looked through a lens that had been modified by CLADE.

René Padilla and Samuel Escobar's presence on the platform of the Lausanne Congress of 1974 represented the convergence of two key realities: a global evangelical student movement network that encouraged freedom from paternalistic influence and a growing awareness of the need for local leadership and control. These networks reached beyond Latin America, particularly in the case of Charles Troutman of the Latin America Mission (previously of the InterVarsity Christian Fellowship). Troutman attended CLADE I and explicitly referenced the lack of national leadership and contextual thinking there. Lausanne convener Jack Dain, who at the time was assistant bishop in the Sydney Anglican diocese, sent out letters requesting recommendations. In response, Charles Troutman urged Dain not to repeat the mistakes of CLADE I. If Escobar and Padilla were given plenary speeches at Lausanne, Troutman thought they might avoid a repeat of the CLADE debacle.

In his private recommendation letter, Troutman wrote, "I would strongly recommend that this steering committee consider . . . that the environment of the third world, and that the element of revolution is the natural habitat for the proclamation of the Gospel. I think a serious criticism that has been made against the speakers (with one exception) at the Bogotá Congress was that they all spoke from the standpoint of a stable industrial society, whereas the majority of ordinary delegates were living in the midst of Guerilla [sic] warfare and revolutionary governments." For evangelicals like Troutman, the core issue was sharing the true gospel: "This is a subtle thing for those of us from the Anglo-Saxon world to understand, but unless the Gospel is proclaimed in this context, I am afraid we are not saying what we think we are."[55] Troutman's experience at CLADE I also impacted his understanding of the contextual theology of mission. In sum, when Billy Graham and Jack Dain sought speakers for the Lausanne Congress, Troutman looked through a lens given by CLADE I. His focus on progressive Latin Americans like Costas, Escobar, and Padilla was a direct result of proximity through the evangelical university student movement.

Troutman's realization, however, is simply one example in a wider conversation among northern evangelical leaders. Many were increasingly aware of the vast growth of Christianity in the Global South. By implication, they set a wider table that included voices from diverse locales, even with its correspondingly complex conversation. With Billy Graham's blessing, Padilla and Escobar were ultimately invited by Dain to speak at Lausanne—an invitation that had manifest implications for the future trajectory of global evangelical conciliar discourse and political activism. The power of evangelical parachurch networks and resources, then, surfaced at Lausanne and influenced the trajectory of its legacy.

Ultimately, Latin American platform presence was both pragmatic and prescient. John Stott and Billy Graham realized that an emerging, younger generation of evangelical leaders was more concerned with social Christianity than previous ones. Stott himself had attended the WCC Uppsala assembly, where mainline Protestant theology had shifted decisively away from traditional understandings of mission.[56] Thus, he was by no means naive regarding the implications of widening the table for social Christianity. They also recognized the necessity of harnessing the energy of the younger generation, who were disproportionally represented by students and missionaries based on college campuses. For evangelicals like Graham, the advancement of evangelical evangelistic efforts was paramount. Thus, taking a risk with progressive Latin American evangelicals in particular was worth the potential backlash or unintended consequences.

CLADE, however, was a double-edged sword of inclusion and exclusion. While Orlando Costas's absence was the result of his own choices, his exclusion from the influential FTL was the result of a wider story that returns us to our opening theme of this chapter: dependency. In 1969, the same year as CLADE, Costas was pastoring in Milwaukee, Wisconsin, and actively involved in organizing Latinos for political activism. He had also recently joined the missionary staff of LAM and its seminary SBL. During his brief tenure with the SBL, Costas began a power struggle with rector Rubén Lores and the U.S.-based board of directors that were known colloquially as the "great white fathers."[57]

Orlando Costas and the War on Paternalism

Orlando Costas's arrival at the Costa Rican Seminario Bíblico Latinoamericano in the late 1960s placed him within accelerating conversations regarding missionary leadership, perceived paternalism, and local control in Latin America. His fierce protest of missionary oversight in particular represented his characteristic style—a "take-no-hostages" approach to American influence in the region. As an archetype of protesting paternalism, this story provides a fuller picture of Orlando Costas and his contested legacy within evangelicalism. The backstory of the SBL also reveals a widening scope of influence for the emerging Latin American Evangelical Left.

From its founding in 1924, the SBL was consistently led by LAM missionary faculty and its board of directors based in the United States. While conversations regarding nationalizing the seminary percolated for decades, they reached full boil in the 1960s. Once again, increasingly hostile conversations were not a Latin American monologue. Certainly, they were the result of pressure from Latin American faculty, perhaps principally Orlando Costas and rectors Plutarco Bonilla and Rubén Lores. No less important, however, was the early support of a significant segment of sympathetic American missionaries. The first indication of an openness toward the idea of nationalization appeared decades earlier in the annual report of rector and American missionary David Howard in 1956. Howard wrote, "Perhaps the greatest need at present in the Seminary is in terms of adequately trained and capable personnel to fill several vital positions. *A Latin rector is the first need*" (italics mine).[58] Though a Latin American rector may have been offered the job in 1956 and declined, American missionary Wilton Nelson was named the new SBL rector in 1957—continuing an unbroken line of American leadership until Plutarco Bonilla was elected in the academic year of 1969–1970.

Careful attention to oral history and archival documents from the San José archives of the SBL reveals that faculty, including many missionaries, were also beginning to test the boundaries of their evangelical institution in the early 1960s.[59] For example, in 1963, while SBL was still under North American missionary control, the American rector Wilton Nelson invited a Latin American Catholic priest to speak in the chapel. Nelson had issued the invitation without notifying what Berg called "the great white fathers" or the leadership of the LAM based in the United States. Recalling the episode in 2001, Berg said that he would "never forget the tongue lashing I had to sit through" from LAM founder Ken Strachan.[60] Strachan worried about the perception of Catholic cooperation among American evangelical donors and warned against future ecumenical endeavors. The operating fundamentalist and evangelical paradigm was, of course, that Catholics were to be the subjects of *conversion*, not *cooperation*. Yet, even while the board and founding president of LAM remained staunchly opposed to broad ecumenism (especially of the Catholic variety), this could not contain the influence of the Catholic Latin American context on SBL's conservative missionary faculty. Berg's recollection is revealing: "[The LAM missionary faculty] were all caught up in this post–Vatican II atmosphere, which was tremendous! Priests were coming into our bookstore and buying bibles. *Priests were!*"[61] The Second Vatican Council of the Catholic Church arguably affected Latin America more than any other region. It marked a turning point in Catholic-Protestant relations, not least categorizing Protestants as "separated Brethren," rather than sects or cults, and the possibility of salvation outside the Roman Catholic Church. More important for our purposes, Vatican II marked a turn toward local contexts and application, away from top-down paternalism. Within the SBL, Latin American faculty sought to capitalize on this accelerating momentum.

As these nationalizing conversations quickened in the late 1960s, Orlando Costas presented a paper to the annual assembly of the LAM titled, "On the Path Toward an Autochthonous Seminary."[62] While he pulled his punches in the first half of his paper, Costas came out swinging with his signature approach—fierce protest against paternalism: "Someone, certainly a missionary . . . has said that the [Seminario Bíblico Latinoamericano] is a child that has grown and now doesn't want to recognize her mommy. I would say [that we are] like a 48-year-old man whose mother, for reasons of cultural conditioning, has not been prepared to recognize her son's maturity with the promptness that it should, but that is gradually becoming conscious of his duties and possibilities."[63]

Costas thus presented what he viewed as an unambiguous crossroads for the U.S. LAM board: either release the seminary into Latin American hands or be caught colluding with a paternalistic status quo. Costas noted that the SBL had reached more than 50 percent of Latin American faculty, a significant milestone for the missionary-led seminary. He also highlighted the seminary's financial deficit that year. Though only $5,000, Costas seized on the deficit as a rejoinder to arguments in favor of missionary leadership as "financial stability."[64] He referenced this "frustrating" situation, asking how there could be such little money "to serve the Lord"—especially scholarships for Latin American students. The solution for Costas was undeniable: financial, organizational, and theological independence.

For Latin American SBL faculty members, gone were the days of dependency on North American theology, politics, and leadership. The seminary eventually won both its independence and soon a well-deserved reputation for radical theologies of liberation. Indeed, it quite quickly eschewed its evangelical ethos and embraced a diverse, ecumenical, and increasingly leftist political orientation. Costas's role in the SBL nationalization, alongside his participation in CELA III instead of CLADE, undoubtedly placed a question mark over his name—especially within conservative evangelical circles in the North.

While Costas played a major role in the nationalization and independence of the SBL, this agitation would undoubtedly sideline him from negotiation in later global evangelical conciliar discourse. Here, the words of LAM missionary Scott Nyborg represent the tension for many American evangelicals: "Orlando Costas is exactly like Rene [Padilla]. Great minds, brilliant, great theologians, founded in the word of God, love Jesus Christ, *but* always stirring controversy wherever they go—it's just the nature of them. And I think they're very very important to the Kingdom" (italics mine).[65] The embryonic Latin American Evangelical Left was simultaneously indispensable to the future of global evangelicalism and a bee in the American evangelical bonnet. As Peter Savage and Peter Wagner sought funds for the first gathering of the FTL, it became clear that the financial spigot would open only under certain conditions—namely, the exclusion of the entire Latin American segment of the SBL faculty, known colloquially as the "Costas Group."

Sustained attention to Latin American controversies brings the Lausanne Congress into wider focus. In this way, Lausanne 1974 was the dual product of American evangelical openness and resistance to materials from the Global South. The fierce rejection of the status quo by Latin Americans was the direct result of previous experience. Lausanne was not the first and would not be the last battle at the intersection of the United States and Latin America—especially over issues of paternalism and dependency. As a religious minority community in Latin America, the Protestant evangelical experience of *dependency* was multilayered. Evangelicals shared the Cold War sociopolitical context while remaining marginalized by a dominant Catholic majority. Simultaneously, evangelical churches were often dependent upon North American missionaries for funding and theologies. New forms of Latin American Christianity built upon layers of dependency with diverse materials from the fields of economics, education, and interdenominational religious communities.

Persistent dependency upon resources from the North provoked deep-seated frustration among progressive Latin Americans. This growing discontent then produced a context where emerging social Christianity and renewed calls for national leadership flourished. In this environment, the embryonic Latin American Evangelical Left played a key role in the development and diffusion of evangelical social Christianity. In particular, the struggle over evangelical boundaries uncovered these diverse factors and accelerated the fracture of evangelical theological consensus.

Ultimately, CLADE I would prove paramount for the acceleration of Latin American theological networks and social theology, owing almost exclusively to unintended consequences. Social Christianity had penetrated southern evangelical Christianity with lasting effect. Progressive evangelicals then turned inward toward their own context, negotiating in a similar way to CELAM in Medellín with Vatican II and the Catholic social theological tradition. For the Latin American Evangelical Left, deconstructing American managerial control was not enough; they also required a local construction site—the Latin American Theological Fraternity.

CHAPTER 4

Deporting American Evangelicalism

In 1971, Anabaptist ethicist John Howard Yoder, a leading voice in the emerging American Evangelical Left, wrote an article for *Certeza* magazine titled "Revolución y ética evangélica" (Revolution and Evangelical Ethics). Yoder challenged widespread evangelical beliefs regarding a private-public dichotomy of social ethics, arguing, "The Gospel has an undeniable political connotation since nothing of human life is beyond the reach of its transforming power."[1] He also spoke of the "revolution of Jesus," which includes sharing financial resources and applying Christian categories of sin and salvation to social conflicts.[2] The now controversial American ethicist drew upon longstanding emphases in his Anabaptist tradition to join an emerging Latin American conversation. This article did not follow the operating paradigm of global evangelical texts—importing the article from the North and rote translating its contents into Spanish. Instead, Yoder was living in Buenos Aires, collaborating with the leading minds of the emerging *Latin American* Evangelical Left—similar to visits by John Stott and Carl F. H. Henry during these crucial years leading up to the Lausanne Congress of 1974.

In Buenos Aires, Yoder taught at the ecumenical seminary ISEDET alongside key evangelical and liberation theologians while workshopping social theological ideas in Spanish journals and local think tanks. Yoder was also writing *The Politics of Jesus*, a book that would solidify his place in evangelical intellectual life and the leadership of the American Evangelical Left.[3] *Christianity Today* later named it the fifth most important Christian book of the twentieth century.[4] During this crucial epoch, Yoder undoubtedly benefited from conversation—and controversy—among an emerging Latin American Evangelical Left.[5] These hidden conversations represent the global reach and influence of Latin America.

This overlooked history requires a retelling of the global evangelical story—with a reset stage, revised script, and increasingly diverse cast of characters. We have already seen key relationships and controversies between conservative powerbrokers such as John Stott, Carl F. H. Henry, and the Billy Graham Evangelistic Association. Many in an emerging Evangelical Left also gathered in Latin America prior to the congress, including key players in the Radical Discipleship Group that pushed for the inclusion of social Christianity within the Lausanne Covenant. When John Howard Yoder, René Padilla, and Samuel Escobar convened the Radical Discipleship meeting in Lausanne, they drew upon earlier strategic synergies emanating from Latin America. While the gathering itself was spontaneous, the influential voices and networks drew from earlier conversations and controversies in the Global South. Latin Americans dragged their *local* battles onto the *global* stage. At Lausanne 1974, protests erupted from longstanding pressure beneath the United States. These conversations represented multidirectional flows—the rise of theological materials from the Global South *and* the surfacing of transnational networks formed in Latin America during crucial years leading up to the influential gathering.

For progressive evangelicals in Latin America, independent conversation on social Christianity and leftist politics was a victory in itself—the creation of space to discuss politics and social justice beyond the gaze of northern evangelical oversight. Deporting American theologies and methodologies was a decades-long process. Deconstructing American evangelical architecture, however, was both necessary *and* insufficient for the Latin American Evangelical Left. We have already uncovered postcolonial tools that chipped away at American evangelical ideologies. The construction site itself would be equally important for building a new evangelical brand of social Christianity. These crucial conversations took place primarily within the context of the most influential Latin American evangelical think tank, known as the Latin American Theological Fraternity (FTL). At times, they pursued collaboration with select North American and British evangelicals but within the context of their own national leadership and perceived independence.

In order to deport American evangelical paternalism, they required the intellectual and organizational space represented by the FTL. While this story has entered the scholarly stage, our view has been obstructed. The meager scholarship on these events has largely followed the oral historical

Figure 4. Pedro Arana, Washington Padilla, Samuel Escobar, and René Padilla
at the Second FTL Consultation in Lima, Peru, in December 1972.
Photo courtesy of René Padilla.

accounts of the main players—accounts the present researcher also heard
during his Spanish interviews. In a sense, one triumphalistic narrative has
given way to another: a North American story of soul saving has been replaced by a postcolonial story of the emergence of a truly independent
Latin American contextual theology. But careful attention to early planning, participation, and sources of funding for the first Latin American
Theological Fraternity gathering reveals a much more nuanced and complex
picture. This should not be seen as the beginning of a wholesale "shift southward" in global evangelical mission and discourse. Instead, strategic leaders
from the United States, Canada, and Britain joined an emerging, multidirectional conversation in Latin America. Members of the embryonic Latin
American Evangelical Left had been protesting American managerial control
for years. In that sense, Lausanne 1974 was simply their most prominent nego-

tiation. As Latin Americans pushed for local theological construction, they pulled global evangelicalism toward social themes.

Pulling Financial Strings

Despite the narrative of theological independence by the founding FTL membership, donors in the United States provided 100 percent of the funds for the first gathering in 1970. With financial dependence came strings attached. While it is true that the FTL set the trajectory for a new postcolonial and contextual brand of evangelical theologies, its emergence was contested and negotiated well into the 1970s. Thus, we must return to sources of funding, personal letters, and archival materials to clarify the origins and trajectory set there. In particular, how did early funding carve political and theological fault lines?

The early search for contextual theology in the FTL was marked by paternalistic growing pains. The first FTL consultation in Cochabamba was funded exclusively through American money—almost entirely through the Evangelical Foreign Missions Association (EFMA) and its executive secretary, Clyde Taylor.[6] Peter Savage took the lead in raising funds and providing organizational leadership, while Peter Wagner worked behind the scenes as the treasurer. American donors covered room, board, and travel expenses for the congress attendees.[7] For the majority, these expenses were not extravagant—board only cost U.S.$2.50 per person per day.[8] With money, however, came strings attached. As a result, René Padilla was initially excluded, along with José Míguez Bonino, Orlando Costas, Plutarco Bonilla, and the entire faculty of the SBL.[9] This blunted the influence of holistic emphases—but only temporarily.

Clyde Taylor responded to Peter Savage's request for funds on February 18, 1970, making clear that his support was contingent upon carving theological boundaries. He wrote, "Frankly, I am not interested in helping raise funds to get a group of theologians together who are going to condone [theological liberalism]."[10] The stated fear was not the Social Gospel but the theology of German Karl Barth in particular. Taylor further specified the dangers he saw therein: "As you know, there is considerable inclination toward Barthianism or neo-orthodoxy among some of our evangelicals in Latin America. I really don't know where Rene Padilla and Bonilla stand on this. We do know where Samuel Escobar stands. Míguez Bonino is neo-orthodox." Taylor made clear that the conservative evangelical establishment felt comfortable with Escobar but wary of Padilla. Thus, Taylor wanted Savage to participate fully: "I think this is why we felt quite safe in having you and Pete Wagner involved in this movement to be sure we did not allow those who would compromise the authority of Scripture in their whole theological concept."[11] Clyde Taylor openly wondered if Padilla was neo-orthodox and made clear his desire to exclude Míguez Bonino. As historian Gary Dorrien explained, for many North American evangelicals, "theological neoorthodoxy produced merely a more biblical-sounding version of the same compromised culture-faith" as theological liberalism.[12] Dorrien summed up this point of view well: "[Neo-orthodoxy] embraced the liberal dichotomy between faith and science, denied the propositional nature of revelation, and forfeited the objective truth character of the gospel."[13]

As time went on, Taylor continued to place pressure on Savage regarding the need to exclude those who, in his opinion, leaned toward neo-orthodoxy. In response, Savage attempted to place distance between the FTL and the ATE. He noted that the latter was led by Padilla and required "only" that members sign the IVF statement of faith—which Míguez Bonino happily signed.[14] Savage commented that the ATE's theological requirements had been outlined "naively" and that Padilla, Escobar, and Arana were now under a false impression about Míguez Bonino being truly evangelical.[15] Savage offered to circulate some of Míguez Bonino's work "to make members realise where this man stands."[16] Yet, Míguez Bonino was not the only theologian who was suspect.

When Western FTL donors and organizers initially sought to exclude René Padilla from the FTL, this plan was divulged to Samuel Escobar, who disapproved. Savage wrote in a confidential memo, "[Escobar] felt sore that René Padilla would be excluded and in a way feels that we are starting off on the wrong footing without him." Yet, Savage concluded his memo with, "In spite of this, [Escobar] seemed willing to attend without René."[17] Padilla was eventually included, certainly partially due to Escobar's concerns; it is doubtful whether Escobar would have proceeded without him.[18] Some, however, maintained their concerns about Padilla. For his part, Wagner hoped that IFES staff member Alec Clifford would attend FTL I, as he "exerts a moderating influence on René."[19]

The leadership of British missionaries was essential for the fledgling FTL and planning its first gathering—especially Peter "Pedro" Savage. As a Briton born to missionary parents in Peru, Savage was both bilingual and bicultural. He was thus a natural bridge and negotiator during these sensitive times. Indeed, "amidst this internal strife, the foundation of the Fraternity would have been almost impossible without the sensitive negotiations carried out by Pedro Savage."[20] Padilla and Escobar viewed Savage himself as a positive influence in national leadership here. In particular, Savage and Padilla were trusted friends; Savage eventually moved to Buenos Aires to help Padilla found his Kairos Community. They also copastored in Buenos Aires in the mid-1970s.[21] Once again, the persistent oversight of certain North Americans, however, pushed these friendships to a breaking point.

Battle for the Bible

For evangelical Protestants in North America in the 1970s, biblical inerrancy was the foremost theological boundary marker.[22] The Evangelical Theological Society (ETS, founded 1949), for example, made assent to the authority of scripture and particularly biblical inerrancy, its only theological requirement. This doctrine asserted that the Bible is "wholly and verbally God-given . . . without error or fault in all its teaching, no less in what it states about God's acts in creation, about the events of world history, and about its own literary origins under God, than in its witness to God's saving grace in individual lives."[23] The first FTL gathering, then, is much more than an abstract theological debate but rather a window into the battle over evangelical identity in the postwar period.

The fledgling FTL met from December 12 to 18, 1970, in the bucolic town of Carachipampa, just outside Cochabamba (although in later press releases, Cochabamba was cited for clarity). At the first FTL gathering, twenty-five leaders participated in the first meeting of the FTL, including speakers Pedro Arana, Andrew Kirk, Peter Wagner, Samuel Escobar, and René Padilla, among others—Orlando Costas and the SBL faculty were excluded.[24] Costas blamed "forces outside of Latin America" who had acted to "prevent the presence of those who, according to them, represented an anti-establishment line within the evangelical movement."[25] Costas also noted that Padilla and Escobar lodged protest against their exclusion.

Sensitivity to paternalism and imported influence was observable even in the published description of speakers. The edited volume listed every speaker's nationality except for Briton Andrew Kirk, who was the only non–Latin American speaker included in the volume. Similarly, while Peter Wagner presented a paper titled "Church Growth in Latin America," it was excluded from the published volume. This conference occurred less than a year after CLADE and the offense surrounding Wagner's book. Given the chronology and connection, it is easy to see why his paper was excluded here (though his was not the only paper excluded).[26] Once again, the embryonic Latin American Evangelical Left was not averse to outside influence of all kinds but rather influence that came with paternalistic (often American) baggage.

The influence of British ISEDET professor Andrew Kirk provides one such example. The chosen topic for discussion, hermeneutics, was most likely suggested by Kirk. The interpretation of the Bible, of course, became increasingly contested due to the radical approaches by ISAL and liberation theologians. But in a 2013 interview, Kirk denied that liberation theology was the impetus for FTL I's topic. Instead, he noted the Latin American evangelical relationship with fundamentalism, particularly its dispensational eschatology, which they perceived as a gateway to social quietism.[27] Similarly, Gutiérrez's book had not been released yet—the publication that catalyzed these discussions perhaps more than any other. Thus, FTL I represents the shared but unique path of Latin American evangelical discourse at this time.

Overall, the papers were representative of a Latin American push to negotiate new theological boundaries—as Escobar noted above, "That we as Latin Americans decide who is *evangélico* in America Latina and what it means to be *evangélico*."[28] At the FTL gathering, Escobar presented two papers, though only one made the later published volume. His unpublished paper, titled "The Bible and Social Revolution in Latin America," struck a notably promissionary tone: "I would like to underline the social dynamic introduced by the pure gospel preached and lived out." Then, in a surprising, pseudo-prosperity gospel argument, Escobar wrote, "This dynamic is evident in the rapid upward social mobility of the sectors of the population that have accepted the gospel." Escobar highlighted "Anglo-Saxon" missionary work with indigenous jungle tribes, alongside their subsequent literacy and economic savvy. Thus, he concluded, "Who can negate the transforming impact of the gospel?"

For Escobar, the picture of Christianity in Latin America was not all rosy, however: "In front of the eyes of the youth and all those who are conscious of the necessity for change, the gospel has become converted into the opium of the people." Escobar sharpened his critique toward conservative religion: "How is it that evangelicals have become a conservative force afraid to call into question the status quo and raise a prophetic voice? They jealously guard a sterile message which attempts at all costs to prove that the message is not dangerous, that it is not subversive and that it will not cause changes. Have we not diluted the Bible?" On the contrary, for Escobar, the gospel called into question longstanding political and theological loyalties in the region.

In his published paper titled "An Evangelical Theology for Iberoamerica," Samuel Escobar began the FTL gathering with a focus on "Biblical content and Anglo-Saxon clothing in Latin American theology." In particular, Escobar posited what he perceived as the fundamental problem of Protestantism in Latin America: the racial and cultural discordance between "Anglo-Saxon" Protestantism and Iberoamerica that is primarily Mestizo.[29] Ultimately, Escobar called for evangelicals to "leave the ghetto" to engage contemporary Latin American challenges—especially stripping the unnecessary clothing of the past.[30]

Fellow Peruvian Pedro Arana, who by then had joined the staff of IFES, presented a plainly Reformed-evangelical paper titled "The Revelation of God," drawing from Dutch Reformed statesman Abraham Kuyper and Swiss theologian Emil Brunner, as well as German theologian Karl Barth. In arguing from a Reformed perspective, Arana criticized four approaches to scripture that were present in Latin American Protestantism: what he called "liberal rationalism," "fundamentalist subjectivism," "existentialism," and "revolutionism." In response, Arana argued that the doctrine of revelation and inspiration should be informed not primarily by sociology or history but by the canon of scripture: "True originality in the Christian sense consists in returning to the *origin* of our faith: God and His revelation."[31] For Arana, this careful attention to Scripture then provides a wider picture of both historical situatedness and future hope. Arana concluded with a call to return to the Bible: "We believe that we are at a moment of crisis in the Evangelical Church in Latin America. Understanding crisis as *krino*, the moment is decisive and dangerous, that is: a moment of opportunity as well."[32]

At FTL I, one paper in particular threatened not only the theological bona fides of the emerging Latin American Evangelical Left but also key sources of funding for it. Indeed, the storm of controversy swirled around one paper in particular: René Padilla's "Autoridad de la Biblia" (Authority of the Bible). Padilla began his plenary speech at Cochabamba with a sweeping statement: "The authority of the Bible constitutes, without a doubt, the most complex problem of all the problems that bibliology poses."[33] Padilla's paper had two main sections: the basis of biblical authority and the recognition of that authority.[34] Padilla wrote, "This presentation concentrates its attention on the problem of the basis, but this limitation that we have placed should not lead us to lose sight of the fact that in the final analysis the principle of authority from the Christian perspective is not *the Bible*, but *the Holy Spirit who speaks in the Bible*—the Word and the Spirit."[35]

Padilla's argument was based on Bernard Ramm's 1968 work *The Pattern of Religious Authority*, part of a series of books produced by Ramm in the late 1950s and early 1960s.[36] These books were heavily influenced by Ramm's experience studying under Karl Barth in the academic year of 1957–1958.[37] Though Ramm never fully embraced Barthianism, Ramm would later call Barth "the best" evangelical answer to the Enlightenment and asserted that Barth's theology "may serve as a paradigm for the future of evangelical methodology."[38] Thus, by openly aligning himself with Ramm, Padilla signaled what many saw as a maverick approach at the outset of the FTL. Padilla wielded Ramm's understanding of scripture in order to reject inerrancy, though Ramm himself defended the doctrine in his 1970 work.

In his paper, Padilla posited not only positive affirmations but also refutations of popular Protestant evangelical understandings of scripture. Most prominently, Padilla placed the current North American Protestant evangelical formulation of the inerrancy of scripture in his sights. Padilla also made clear his thoughts on those who held to this understanding of scripture. According to Padilla, the inerrantist "rationalizes the faith, ignores its existential dimensions, minimizes the internal witness of the Holy Spirit. As a result he requires as the basis for the knowledge of God something that no one can provide him since it does not exist—a Bible without error."[39]

Ultimately, Padilla spoke of the irrelevance of the hypothesis of inerrant original manuscripts—for, according to him, the extant copies *do* contain errors: "In the final analysis, the only Bible that *we have today*, whether we like it or not, is a Bible about which the least that must be admitted is that it contains errors of transmission and (in the case of any version) or translation." Thus, the required response is simple: "Therefore, either we thankfully receive it from God as it is and accept it as authoritative, in spite of minor errors and with the faith that none of them affects the substance of the Gospel, or we insist on the necessity of an absolutely inerrant Bible and find ourselves without an authoritative Bible. There is no other alternative!" These "minor errors" for Padilla include ones of transmission and could include errors in "minimal detail of geography, history, natural sciences."[40] Padilla quickly attempted to ward off criticism, however, saying that he did not mean to pass judgment on inerrancy.[41] He wrote that his purpose was not to reject inerrancy but to speak of the Bible in reference to the history of salvation, the revelation of Jesus, and the witness of the Holy Spirit. Significantly, this last idea appeared in the Cochabamba Declaration.[42] Thus, Padilla's paper made a broad argument on the basis of biblical authority, within which his discussion of inerrancy occupied only a portion. A description of Padilla's paper in the FTL journal *Boletín Teológico* highlighted Padilla's desire to take Latin American evangelical understanding of the authority of scripture beyond "a sad doctrinal superficiality" and posited a "theological comprehension" rooted in "healthy doctrine and Christian maturity."[43]

Ultimately, the FTL papers signaled a refusal on the part of Latin Americans to submit to the theology of both British and North American conservative missionaries, organizations, and mission agencies—in particular, many of whom utilized biblical inerrancy as a litmus test of orthodoxy.[44] The public battles of members of the FTL—and their eventual survival from them—would signal to other evangelical leaders in the Global South that challenging conservative evangelical loyalties was possible. Due to the influence of the embryonic Latin American Evangelical Left, the Cochabamba Declaration that FTL produced did not include an explicit statement on the inerrancy of scripture. As Escobar later recalled, "We thought that to include the word 'inerrancy' was to bring an agenda from the United States to a situation where nobody ever doubted the authority of the Word of God!"[45]

After intense negotiation, progressive delegates within the FTL successfully rejected the rote translation of an English-language congress declaration for use as the Cochabamba Declaration. Peter Wagner had brought along the Frankfurt Declaration, written by Peter Beyerhaus and others in Germany, and pushed for this to be used as the congress declaration of the FTL.[46] Escobar reflected, "The custom was that the only thing we had to do was translate things and [it was] 'ready.' And clearly, we

wanted to discuss and make our own."[47] Escobar's recollection fits with
Wagner's own discussion of his missionary work in Bolivia: "I proceeded
to translate the Fuller curriculum into Spanish—and wondered why we
had so little success in training effective pastors."[48] Though the emerging
Latin American Evangelical Left certainly intended to challenge the evangelical theological establishment and its practice of rote translation, they
could not have foreseen the forthcoming controversy regarding the authority of the Bible.

The Business of Evangelical Boundaries

The Latin American evangelical struggle to define their own boundaries
spilled over onto the pages of American periodicals. In particular, the account
written in *Christianity Today* set off a firestorm of controversy that threatened to bleed funding from the global IFES. On January 5, 1971, Peter Wagner was commissioned by *Christianity Today* to write a firsthand summary
of the FTL gathering at Cochabamba. In his article "High Theology in the
Andes," he expounded a generally positive account—much like the accounts
of other North American evangelical publications. Wagner singled out Padilla's paper, which Escobar speculated was due to Wagner's own failure to
receive FTL support for explicit statements on inerrancy.[49] His initial description of Padilla's paper was straightforward and accurate: "In his position
paper on authority, Padilla argued that insistence on an inerrant Bible means
asking for something unavailable—since no present edition or version is free
from difficulties of transmission and/or translation." Thus, "The result, said
Padilla, is the danger of ending up with no Bible and no authority. Exagger-
ated insistence on inerrancy, he added, in effect saws off the limb that sup-
ports evangelical theology."[50]

   While Wagner's description may have been benign, his organizational
identification set off a firestorm of criticism. Wagner identified Padilla's paper with "what some called the 'Inter-Varsity bloc.'" Wagner also tipped his
hand by contrasting Padilla's position with that of Andrew Kirk. Wagner
wrote, "Not all were convinced by Padilla and his backers. Holding uncom-
promisingly to an inerrant Bible and verbal inspiration Andrew Kirk of Union
Seminary in Buenos Aires declared in his closely reasoned paper on hermeneutics, 'What the text of the Bible says, God says without reservation and
without reduction.'"[51]

Wagner's contrast was misleading—beyond belying his personal views on inerrancy. Padilla did hold to verbal inspiration and later protested vehemently against a supposed division between him and Kirk.[52] Wagner, however, accurately described fault lines that arose between those who wanted to include inerrancy in the final Cochabamba declaration—Emilio Nuñez, Andrew Kirk, and Peter Wagner—and others who wanted it left out—Arana, Escobar, and Padilla.[53] In the end, the response to Padilla's paper, as summarized by Wagner, from *Christianity Today*'s primarily North American readership was swift and overwhelmingly negative.

Soon after Wagner's article appeared, Padilla wrote to Savage that IFES had received *"una lluvia de cartas"* (a rainfall of letters), many asking that Padilla be formally disciplined for his view on the Bible.[54] One letter from a reader in Utah explicitly referred to the Padilla controversy and received a personal response from IFES General Secretary C. Stacey Woods himself. Woods assured her that all staff had signed the IFES statement of faith "ex animo," and Woods rejected Wagner's account of the event: "Personally, I do not believe that this man Wagner really reported correctly the situation. If you were to obtain a copy of the Cochabamba Declaration for which René Padilla was largely responsible, I believe you would be reassured and thankful." Woods then provided an abstract of Padilla's paper (no doubt provided by Padilla himself). Woods concluded with his personal endorsement of Padilla: "I personally am persuaded that René Padilla holds to a strictly biblical position."[55] That same day (March 4, 1971), Woods wrote to Padilla to express support and reassurance: "My dear René, First, may I assure you that as I believe I understand your position concerning the doctrine of Scripture, I do not believe that you differ very much from me and I am not upset."

In the process of defending Padilla, Woods lambasted Wagner: "However, the fact remains that wretched Wagner and his abominable article, willfully misleading in 'Christianity Today' is resulting in letters coming in to us regarding the position of the IFES, yourself, Samuel and Pedro."[56] Fearing even further backlash, Woods requested fifty copies of the Cochabamba Declaration in English. Woods also wrote to Arana, Escobar, and Padilla, requesting further documentation of their views on scripture. In it, he also continued to excoriate Wagner:

I really believe the wretched Wagner is malicious. If this sort of thing continues to spread, it could have a bad affect upon the work and its support. I want to do what I can, public relations wise, honestly and sincerely, to bury the ghost. I am writing letters to the effect that you subscribed to the statement of faith of the IFES without any reservation. I enclose this statement. I presume this is so without question. Have you any other suggestion as to how we could deal with these heresy hunters and troglodytes?[57]

Woods both expressed support and asked Padilla for further proof of his commitment to accepted Protestant evangelical understandings of biblical infallibility and authority—he requested statements concerning "a) divine inspiration b) historicity c) verbal inspiration d) propositional revelation e) infallibility f) authority."[58]

Woods continued to receive negative letters from around the world and responded by implementing a strategy of damage control. For his own part, Padilla also sought to minimize the damage. Padilla was defiant in the face of criticism: "I make no apologies for what I said in Cochabamba. The position expressed there was carefully thought through beforehand and when I stated it I very well knew that I was sticking out my neck and opening myself to all sorts of accusations and misunderstandings." The issue, for Padilla, was one of honesty: "Yet I felt that I would not be honest if I did not express my deep convictions that the big fuss that most evangelicals raise over inerrancy reflects a serious misunderstanding of the nature of Biblical revelation, tied up with a reductionist concept of truth." In fact, inerrancy was only one part of a larger picture: "My concern was not to deny inerrancy, but to show that the question of biblical authority is an infinitely bigger issue than that of textual perfection."[59]

Padilla's statement acknowledged that he understood that he would cause controversy in his rejection of inerrancy, yet Padilla valued intellectual freedom above organizational unanimity. Wagner, for his part, attempted reconciliation with Padilla, writing an open letter through the FTL in June 1971, defending church growth theory in the process.[60] Wagner resigned from his FTL responsibilities that year and left Latin America to return to the United States, where he was recruited by Donald McGavran himself at Fuller Theological Seminary (FTS) in Southern California.[61]

Careful attention to linguistic dynamics here also reveals a more nuanced picture than scholarship and Padilla himself have presented. Padilla defended himself publicly through a scathing letter to the editor in *Christianity Today* titled "Highly Misleading" on February 9, 1971—perhaps a play on Wagner's title "High Theology."[62] Padilla also defended himself behind the scenes to

Stacey Woods. He wrote, "Let me quote the paragraph on this question in my position paper."[63] Padilla then translated the entire paragraph from Spanish while redacting various controversial aspects. For example, Padilla's "translation" for Woods implied that his point was one of textual criticism, extant manuscripts, and accessibility. Padilla's "translation" read, "The one that demands absolute textual perfection as an indispensable requisite for accepting Biblical authority makes this demand because he assumes that from an epistemological point of view the only controlling principle in the relation of man with God is reason, and the only reality in revelation is its informative aspect."[64] The metaphrasal translation of what Padilla actually wrote and said at Cochabamba, however, was something quite different—especially for inerrantists themselves: "The one that demands an absolute precision in minimal details of geography, history, natural sciences, etc., as an *indispensable* requisite for acceptance of biblical authority, makes this demand."[65]

In the Spanish version of his FTL plenary paper, it appears Padilla was, at the very least, implying that the Bible's accuracy in science and history was open for debate. The distinction for inerrantists (particularly North Americans) is profound: errors of *transmission* are simply textual and would not affect the "original manuscripts." But errors of *content*, such as historicity and science, affect the accuracy of the original documents and thus God's words. This fluidity in translation can be seen in less controversial paragraphs, as well. Thus, the sentence above, "The [biblical writers] write more from the point of view of faith, as people committed to their message," was translated by Padilla as "[the biblical writers] write from the perspective of men who are completely committed to their message."[66] The juxtaposition between objective history and the subjective, faith perspective of the biblical writers was redacted.

It appears, then, that though Padilla wrote that he was "ready to maintain [his] position and face up to the consequences," he may have attempted to soften his stance after the fact.[67] In the same letter to Woods, Padilla placed the blame squarely on Wagner's shoulders: "I am sorry, very sorry for the extra work that Peter Wagner's article is causing you. I must say that it is hard for me to believe that his intention in writing it was not a vicious one."[68] This provides a more nuanced picture of Woods's subsequent defense of Padilla and of Padilla and Escobar's public denunciation of Wagner. Escobar defended Padilla, saying that Wagner "presented a tendentious and disfigured painting of our first consultation."[69] In Escobar's opinion, Wagner had a malicious intent from the start—his article was intended to place pressure on them within the organization of InterVarsity-USA regarding their stance on scripture.[70] Elsewhere, Escobar could not bring himself to name Wagner, simply saying he had "lamented the effort of a certain missionary for dividing us, polarizing us, and disfiguring our reality in writing a chronicle of this meeting."[71] In light of the above linguistic dynamics, the current scholarship should also be corrected regarding this event.[72]

Global evangelical networks connected Latin American evangelicals through mission agencies and, in the case of the embryonic Evangelical Left, the global evangelical student movement. Though major theological issues were at stake, this prolonged FTL inerrancy controversy must be seen in light of one primary factor: fundraising. IFES staff member Alec Clifford wrote a handwritten note to Wagner on June 19, 1971, decrying the financial impact of the inerrancy controversy. "The repercussions of your CT report have been most unfortunate and far reaching. The whole program of IFES and IVF (USA) seems to have suffered through a loss of financial support and confidence thanks to the article . . . I don't know what can be done to undo the harm at this stage."[73] The financial situation certainly motivated Stacey Woods to implement damage control measures. That year, 1971, IVCF-USA contributed 67 percent of IFES overall income and budget.[74] Any drop in funds from donors in the United States would reverberate around the world. Though IFES had movements in over ninety countries, financial generosity from the United States shared the overwhelming burden of funding its operations.

In hindsight, Clifford's fear of a decrease in American donations was only partially founded. Donations from the United States to IFES fell by 17 percentage points from 1971 to 1974, from 67 percent in 1971 to just over half in 1974. The overall income of IFES, however, rose from U.S.$243,279 to U.S.$347,440 in 1974. Minutes from the Executive Committee also make clear that IFES had been planning to wean itself off American financial dependency for some time. Thus, it is unclear whether this drop should be credited primarily to the inerrancy controversy or to active fundraising outside the United States. Regardless, this competition did not remain at the intersection of Latin America and the United States. Instead, evangelicals from across the Global South identified with these struggles and amplified their negotiation for local control and contextual theologies—especially social ones.

This theological controversy also reveals a few key points of historical significance. The first is that the FTL received the attention and concern of Western evangelical leaders such as Carl F. H. Henry, Peter Wagner (who was initially involved), and evangelical financial supporters across the United States. While Wagner was concerned with the social Christian turn that the FTL would take, Henry expressed optimism that the FTL would address a theological vacuum in a revolutionary situation.[75] (Wagner eventually embraced his own charismatic version of social Christianity in later years.) The second is that Padilla had become persona non grata among American conservative evangelicals well before the 1974 Lausanne Congress because he had become identified with the "wrong side" in the inerrancy arguments of the 1970s.[76] Similarly, this emerging progressive coalition had already made clear they would no longer defer to northern evangelicals for theological direction.

The Cochabamba Declaration was a small step away from prepackaged, translated theology and toward national Latin American evangelical leadership. In their own Cochabamba Declaration, they wrote of the need to "obey the clear demands of the Word of God . . . within the complex social, political and economic scene in Latin America, to become a community which expresses the spirit of justice, kindness, and service which the Gospel implies."[77] Thus, social action appeared in the declaration, though positioned within *implication* language with regard to the gospel.

Soon after the declaration, Samuel Escobar exclaimed, "The very fact that we gathered here in Cochabamba to make theology is exceedingly significant for the Latin American church. . . . We can expect to move ahead together, recognizing our present differences, toward the formulation of a truly evangelical and vitally relevant theology-in-formation for our continent."[78] The embryonic Latin American Evangelical Left was emboldened and catalyzed by Cochabamba (by both its negative and its positive experiences) and looked to develop their own organizational structure to encourage the maturation of this nascent theology. The next meetings of the FTL would diversify the network, cement their independence, and encourage new avenues for Latin American social theology. When seen in light of the purpose of the fledgling FTL, their theological negotiation fits a wider narrative of carving new avenues of organizational leadership and theological freedom. Indeed, similar scenarios occurred across Latin America during this period, including Carl Henry's controversy over liberation theology in Costa Rica (described in Chapter 3).[79]

The First Evangelical Consultation on Social Ethics

In October 1971, Samuel Escobar wrote to IFES General Secretary Stacey Woods outlining his plan to leave Latin America to lead the IVCF in Canada. Interestingly, two years prior to Escobar's letter to Woods (one which took Woods by surprise), Woods had warned Escobar of the danger of North America stealing him from the "need in Latin America," telling him that "it is far more important to concentrate in Latin America than to go to North America." Woods expanded, "North America is like a great octapus [*sic*], with its money sucking people from all over the world to be speakers, regardless of the prior needs of the work in their own milieu. Hence, we have constantly got to be on guard against this sort of thing."[80] Woods's response to Escobar's decision was one of obvious disappointment that he had not been included in Escobar's decision-making process.[81] Escobar's decision, one that was also opposed by Padilla, set in motion a series of events that would have both direct and indirect consequences for the development and diffusion of *misión integral*.[82]

In anticipation of Escobar's absence, Padilla was named director of Ediciones Certeza (IFES literature project for Latin America) and *Certeza* magazine.[83] One of Padilla's first actions as director of Ediciones Certeza was to organize the "First Evangelical Consultation on Social Ethics" from July 5 to 8, 1972, in Lima. Padilla invited Pedro Arana, Orlando E. Costas, North American sociologist Charles F. Denton, prominent Pentecostal Assemblies of God pastor Juan Carlos Ortiz, Samuel Escobar, José Míguez Bonino, Emilio Antonio Nuñez, and Cuban American Methodist historian Justo L. González as participants and writers (many of whom had notably been excluded from CLADE I and the first FTL gathering).[84] Nuñez was professor of systematic theology and dean at Instituto Bíblico Centroamericano (later Central American Theological Seminary or SETECA). These connections would prove crucial for the influence of the FTL the following years. Overall, the diverse group of thinkers was particularly noteworthy—conservative evangelicals such as Emilio Nuñez and Samuel Escobar, as well as an influential Pentecostal pastor in Ortiz, alongside ecumenically minded leaders such as Orlando Costas, José Míguez Bonino, and Justo Gonzalez. Escobar opined years later, "No other 'evangelical' entity would have invited them."[85]

Ironically, the funding for the consultation once again came from North American sources, in this case the National Liberty Foundation (now renamed the Arthur S. DeMoss Foundation), an arm of the Liberty Life Insurance Company, in Liberty, Pennsylvania.[86] The company was headed by Arthur and Robert DeMoss, Christian philanthropists concerned with the development of Majority World theology from a conservative perspective.[87] Arthur Demoss was also an early board member of Campus Crusade for Christ. According to Peter Savage, the NLF funded the majority of CLADE I but through Clyde Taylor and the EFMA. Now, in 1972, Savage gained direct access to the funds from the DeMoss brothers, who were less concerned with the actual theological content than social location.[88]

The proximity between ecumenical and conservative minds provided an important context for dialogue—particularly around the topic of ISAL. Padilla wrote that the consultation was "organized for the purpose of producing a book that would encourage the reader to 'a life commitment to Jesus Christ, a commitment embodied in the Latin American reality.'"[89] Padilla's own contribution to this purpose came in the form of a paper titled "Iglesia y sociedad en América Latina" (Church and Society in Latin America), referring to the WCC series of consultations described earlier.[90] Míguez Bonino was, of course, one of the key players in ISAL; Escobar recalled that this juxtaposition between Míguez Bonino and Padilla "made sure the discussion was valuable and lively."[91] Ultimately, the first event planned by the FTL proved to be particularly salient for the future trajectory of the fraternity. The inclusion of diverse thinkers enriched each side. José Míguez Bonino was asked to present a paper titled "El nuevo Catolicismo" (The New Catholicism), due to his recent attendance at the Second Vatican Council as the only Latin American Protestant observer. In a recent interview, Escobar recalled the FTL recognizing Míguez Bonino's "authority" on the topic of Roman Catholicism.[92] This reality also illuminates the extent and limits of FTL ecumenicity: Míguez Bonino's presence signaled a broad evangelical tent that extended beyond most ecclesiastical and organizational boundaries of the time.

In the same way, however, a Protestant was still the representative "authority" on Roman Catholicism, demonstrating that Latin American evangelical ecumenicity stopped short of including Roman Catholics themselves—a reality that largely continues to this day. Here, Escobar's recollection of the specific results of the Consultation on Social Ethics provides clarity on the wider commitments of the FTL: "From there onward, the FTL proved that in its task of reflection, it would not be conditioned by the missionaries and conservative mission agencies who wanted to impose a fundamentalist agenda. Gonzalez, Míguez and Costas brought a vision of ecumenical scope that enriched us all."[93]

John Howard Yoder and the Evangelical Left at FTL

From December 11 to 18, 1972, twenty-seven Latin American evangelical leaders gathered at the Seminario Bíblico in Lima, Peru, for the Second Consultation of the FTL under the theme of "The Kingdom of God and Latin America."[94] This meeting—its theme, location, and global representation—provides a crucial backstory for both the rise of the Latin American Evangelical Left and their later influence at Lausanne 1974. The leaders of the FTL undoubtedly chose SBL for what it represented: the ability to deport American evangelical influence. That year, 1972, the flagship fundamentalist seminary gained its independence from American missionary control under Orlando Costas's leadership. According to the Briton Andrew Kirk, a founding member of the FTL, this consultation was also influenced quite significantly by the presence of American Anabaptist ethicist John Howard Yoder. The combination of his famously Anabaptist pacifist ethics and the pull of violent revolution in Latin America made a potent mixture. Exporting the credit to John Howard Yoder, however, provides only a partial picture.

While influence here in Lima was multidirectional, Padilla would later wield his role as editor of the volume to blunt Yoder's influence. Five papers were presented at the gathering by Emilio Nuñez, René Padilla, José Míguez Bonino, Samuel Escobar, and American Mennonite John Howard ("Juan") Yoder. (Padilla recalled Yoder as the only American member of the FTL—though in reality Peter Wagner was the first.[95]) The plenary speakers were all increasingly prominent thinkers of the emerging Evangelical Left (with Nuñez as a notable dissenter) and demonstrated its emerging global networks emanating from Latin America. In Escobar's view, this consultation "continued with the same agenda" of the Padilla-planned Consultation on Social Ethics.[96] Indeed, he recalled, "René had convinced us of the importance of eschatology and of the kingdom of God for understanding the message of Jesus."[97] Padilla himself wrote that the consultation met with a "sense of expectation" after the first consultation in Cochabamba had "set a precedent for meetings of the Fraternity."[98] Thus, this FTL Lima gathering focused on the question of identifying the kingdom of God and

Figure 5. Delegates of the Second FTL Consultation, Lima, Peru,
December, 1972. Photo courtesy of René Padilla.

participating within it. This theme gains our attention in the following chapter, as the FTL influenced the construction of liberation theology in surprising ways.

Dispensationalism, according to the editorial introduction, "[had] exercised an incalculable influence on the message and life itself of the church in [Latin America]."[99] Thus, FTL organizers asked Salvadoran Emilio Antonio Nuñez to present on the kingdom of God from a dispensational perspective. Nuñez had completed his master's degree (ThM, 1964) and doctorate (ThD, 1969) at Dallas Theological Seminary, which is known as a center of an academically rigorous brand of dispensational theology.[100] At the time, Nuñez was a professor and dean of the influential Seminario Teológico Centroamericano de Guatemala, known today as SETECA. SETECA maintains close connections with conservative evangelicalism in the United States and trains Latin American evangelical pastors throughout the region. Nuñez's consistent participation in the FTL provides crucial nuance here. In particular, the FTL and the Evangelical Left cannot be fully conflated. Forums like this one represented a sincere effort to represent a broad swath of evangelicalism in the region and not simply those with progressive loyalties.

At this forum, Escobar associated Nuñez's position on the kingdom of God and dispensationalism with the Scofield Reference Bible, whose notes Nuñez translated for its Spanish publication.[101] These realities, coupled with Nuñez's status as "a very respected theologian" throughout Central America, provided an "excellent" debate among participants.[102] Nuñez placed his accent mark on a "future kingdom," explicitly rejecting not only a "Social Gospel" but also Barthian theology. He argued that the kingdom is yet to come, and he provided nuance that it is "imminent and transcendent."[103] His paper also provided a natural segue to the later intervention of René Padilla. Nuñez reflected, "We have not experimented properly with the tension between the kingdom that is coming and the kingdom that is already here with us."[104] Padilla's paper centered on this "already and not yet"—a central feature of his later plenary speech at the Lausanne Congress of 1974.

The second consultation of the FTL provided the space and encouragement to expand a Latin American evangelical understanding of the kingdom of God. Of particular importance, due to its later prominence on the Lausanne 1974 platform, was René Padilla's paper here. Indeed, Padilla's reliance on his PhD research is clear throughout—especially as eschatology serves as the framework for the paper, the "'already' and 'not yet'" character of the kingdom.[105] This paper also formed the basis of a significant portion of "The Mission of the Church in Light of the Kingdom of God"—the final chapter of his most famous work, *Misión integral*, and its English translation, *Mission Between the Times*. Padilla's paper sought a middle way between two opposing sides: the dispensational, future-oriented eschatology of the kingdom (represented by Emilio Nuñez's paper) and the "realized eschatology" of many liberation theologians and participants in ISAL. Under the title "The Church as the Messianic Community," Padilla presented the mission of the church with both an eschatological and a Christological framework. For the first time, Padilla expounded his view that the mission of the church finds its nexus in the kingdom of God.[106] For Padilla, the church carries out the mission of God in eschatological tension, reflecting the kingdom of God and carrying a wider gospel message.

While Padilla urged a recognition of realized eschatology, he tempered expectations on the ability of Christians to change society. He wrote, "The Church's hope rests not in the structures created by those powers, but in the new heaven and new earth 'in which righteousness dwells.' It looks at itself as a sign of God's new creation, that new creation in the light of which it is seen that every human effort to build a perfect society holds within itself the seeds of destruction."[107] Padilla rejected utopian goals of building the kingdom of God and finding hope in regime change. Yet, in the same paragraph, Padilla channeled Marxist language to excoriate evangelical social apathy. Ultimately, for Padilla, "It must, finally, place the mission of the church within the framework of God's plan to create a new humanity."[108]

At FTL II, participants certainly benefited from theological exchange and negotiation with José Míguez Bonino's paper, "The Kingdom of God and History: Reflections for a Discussion of the Topic"—a reality that gains focus in Chapter 6.[109] John Howard Yoder's paper, "Messianic Expectations of the Kingdom and Its Central Character for an Adequate Contemporary Hermeneutic," focused especially on expanded on layers of interpretation for the kingdom of God. This certainly had political implications, for he argued, "Whoever says Kingdom says Politics."[110] If one were to follow Yoder's "first guidelines of a different approach," then his conclusions would follow: "We would revise traditional doctrinal formulas (such as justification, reconciliation, regeneration) so that they more accurately reflect the reality and power of the kingdom. Because the promise and the summons to surrender are not reserved for tomorrow."[111]

Ultimately, the gathering at Lima provided the opportunity to dialogue with diverse theologians and to share resources with more overtly ecumenical streams of Protestant evangelical thought.

The official goals of the Fraternity were also defined at Lima as follows:

1. To promote reflection around the gospel and its significance for man and society in Latin America.
2. To set up a platform for dialogue between thinkers who confess Jesus Christ as Lord and God and that are prepared (*están dispuestos a*) to reflect in light of the Bible in order to build a bridge between the gospel and Latin American culture.
3. To contribute to the life and mission of the church of Christ in Latin America, without pretending to speak in the name of the church or assuming the position of theological spokesman for the evangelical people in the Latin American continent.[112]

These goals were a "triple commitment—with the Word, with the church and with Latin America." Indeed, the emphases at FTL II also became a central theme for the FTL in later years: "[The kingdom of God] became an axis for FTL theology and ministry in the following years."[113] This diverse gathering was only a foreshadowing of things to come for the FTL. The same key theologians—Arana, Padilla, Escobar, Míguez Bonino, and Costas—would continue in public dialogue throughout the 1970s.[114]

After this influential gathering, the subtext bled onto the pages of the edited volume. In particular, René Padilla penned searing critiques of John Howard Yoder. As a result, the influence of Yoder's paper was clearly stunted. The editorial introduction recalled that the "informality" of Yoder's presentation "disconcerted many in Lima and even prevented several to fully appreciate the intense exegetical work in it."[115] Padilla criticized Yoder for his last-minute preparation: "More than half the paper was written 'on the fly' in the days preceding its public presentation." Padilla also went out of his way to highlight the influence of Latin Americans on the published version of Yoder's paper: "It was only after the meeting that Yoder's presentation was more definitive. As a result, of all the papers, perhaps this one best reflects the questions that were planted during the consultation."[116] For an editorial introduction, this description was surprisingly critical. What was Padilla trying to communicate?

Given the growing prominence of progressive evangelical John Howard Yoder, especially with popularity of *The Politics of Jesus*, one could easily expect the spotlight to linger on Yoder's contribution here. Yet, similar to the personal letter to Carl Henry in our Introduction, René Padilla was unwilling to export credit from the embryonic Latin American Evangelical Left. The oral history and written recollections of main characters are also telling. Padilla later recalled this event as "important" due to "the rediscovery of the centrality of the kingdom of God in the life and ministry of Jesus Christ."[117] Elsewhere, he wrote, "It marked for evangelicalism the rediscovery of the kingdom of God as the basis for the mission of the church."[118] If the FTL had rediscovered a central tool for reshaping global evangelical mission, then they also refused to export credit for it.

This widely overlooked history requires nothing less than a retelling of the global evangelical story—with a reset stage, script, and cast of characters. Heated protest from a Cold War context reached full boil at Lausanne 1974. Many key members of an emerging Evangelical Left felt its heat prior to the Lausanne Congress as they gathered near its southern source. When John Howard Yoder, René Padilla, and Samuel Escobar convened the Radical Discipleship Gathering in Lausanne, they also drew upon earlier strategic synergies emanating from Latin America. These conversations represented multidirectional flows—the rise of theological materials from the Global South *and* the surfacing of transnational networks formed in Latin America during crucial years leading up to the influential gathering. In sum, the proximity of the evangelical right and left produced influential theologies and challenged longstanding political loyalties.

From its inception in 1970, the Latin American Theological Fraternity was surrounded by controversy and conflict as it sought to redefine evangelical boundaries in the aftermath of CLADE (1969). This early negotiation inspired networks of Latin American thinkers across denominational and theological boundaries, as well as accelerating the process of developing *misión integral* itself. Indeed, since the ATE and CLADE I gatherings in 1969, diverse theological sharing had pushed key thinkers in the embryonic Evangelical Left to publish their own writings. Transnational spaces, such as the ATE and FTL, also reinvigorated regional nationalism and identity that were contested by paternalism from the North. One event—the battle over scriptural inerrancy—also raised to the surface these diverse factors and accelerated the fracture of evangelical theological consensus.

Rather than treating the FTL as a monolith, we have also clarified the early contribution of key thinkers within it. The early FTL was not a Latin American monologue, as the presence of sympathetic British and American thinkers made clear. Andrew Kirk was a critical bridge for more conservative thinkers and the ecumenical ISEDET seminary in Buenos Aires. Similarly, the now controversial American Mennonite ethicist John Howard Yoder channeled longstanding Anabaptist emphases on the social dimensions of the gospel and incoherence of violence with the Christian message. René Padilla, in particular, shaped the FTL in his own image, as shown through its early focus on "the kingdom of God" in 1972. Similarly, Padilla's role, in contrast to that of colleagues Samuel Escobar and Orlando Costas, has also been clarified by placing the themes of early FTL gatherings in conversation with Padilla's own theological development. It has become increasingly clear that Padilla was the primary mind behind these progressive evangelical themes—that his colleagues took his lead and borrowed his main theological motif—the kingdom of God. In the same way, Samuel Escobar appropriated theological ideas that originated from Padilla's theological journey, developed in organizations formed primarily by him. Escobar would later wield them in more irenic ways in global forums and on the East Coast of the United States.

Ultimately, the FTL served as one of the most influential avenues for developing and disseminating *misión integral* to the rest of the world. The proximity of such a diverse network of thinkers sharpened their thought and spurred them on to productive writing. This legacy was particularly significant as many influential members of the emerging Latin American Evangelical Left were not professors with funded research leave. Orlando Costas, who himself was an academic, became frustrated with his colleagues for not publishing more freely and often.[119] Funding to participate in the FTL provided critical time and motivation to publish their own theological writings. The FTL consultations not only sharpened the thinking of the embryonic Evangelical Left in Latin America but also forced each thinker to publish his or her own work. As a result, they redefined evangelical political and theological loyalties in the region *and* among an emerging generation of global evangelicals.

CHAPTER 5

Marketing Social Christianity

"I cannot think of any believers spitting at an American missionary, or throwing rocks at him, yet I have seen mature Christians *tremble with indignation* at things done and said by some missionaries who have come from the United States to civilize and Christianize us." This statement appeared in a scathing anonymous article in the InterVarsity Christian Fellowship magazine *HIS* in 1959, entitled "Why Latin Americans Dislike Some American Missionaries."[1] The article described a series of cultural faux pas and offensive scenarios, concluding, "Only very godly men could stand some of these American missionaries."[2] The author identified the United States as the source of a shallow Christianity and pondered the racial-superiority complex of some American missionaries: "The attitude of the type of missionary I am thinking about is that of a man from a master race who is carrying the white man's burden in his missionary work among inferior races."[3]

The anonymous author described herself or himself by saying, "I am a native of one of the South American republics. We have had gospel work here for nearly a century." At first glance, this biting article appears to shed light on the often uneasy power balance, sporadic racial discord, and missionary work between Latin America and the United States. While on the surface this holds a degree of explanatory power, further attention to the anonymous author sheds light elsewhere: the growing progressive discontent with the conservative evangelical status quo. In fact, the diary of Paul Little, a staff member with InterVarsity Christian Fellowship–USA, identified the author as Alec Clifford, the son of British Brethren missionaries in Argentina and an International Fellowship of Evangelical Students (IFES) staff member.[4] While Clifford was born in Argentina, the wording of his article was, at best, misleading.

While initially anonymous and often subtle, a growing chorus of voices would increasingly challenge the U.S. exportation of Christian goods around

Figure 6. American missionaries Doug and Marilyn Stewart (IFES), Samuel Escobar, British missionary Felicity Bentley-Taylor (neé Houghton), Catharine Feser Padilla, and René Padilla. Photo courtesy of the IFES, Oxford, England.

the world—seen most clearly in the full-throated rebuke by some at Lausanne 1974. Perhaps surprisingly, some of the most salient protests, however, came from missionaries themselves. Many contended that protesting missionary *paternalism*, for example, was fully consonant with evangelicalism's missionary nature. There is no debate that Lausanne challenged widely held political and theological loyalties. But the story of Lausanne's negotiation also resists regional and vocational binaries. In other words, this was not a simple story of local Christians versus foreign missionaries. On the contrary, three northern missionary sources influenced our story in untold ways—especially the branding of evangelical social Christianity for mass consumption.

Christian Brethrenism is an evangelical Protestant movement that began in Dublin and southwest England within the period 1827–1831.[5] In Latin America, Brethren missionaries cultivated a legacy of releasing leadership to local agents, in large part due to a Brethren congregational polity that lacked paid clergy and hierarchy. Alec Clifford and IFES General Secretary Stacey Woods—both Brethren leaders—drew from a long history of denominational distinctives when they expressed frustration with American paternalism in the region. The Brethren tradition of pioneering publishing projects also created channels through which Latin Americans wrote their own theologies and developed a new brand of evangelical social Christianity.[6] Local leadership roles and publishing structures provided avenues for the promotion and diffusion of Latin American social Christian ideas. The global influence of many Latin American evangelicals directly resulted from Brethren leadership streams and their sustained emphasis on local leadership. These publishing platforms and leadership roles raised their profile prior to the Lausanne Congress of 1974 and, in doing so, fueled the evangelical renaissance of social Christianity.

The fledgling Latin American Evangelical Left sought to decolonize Jesus, identifying local images of Jesus as foreign imports from Spain and the United States. At the same time, they fiercely rejected exporting credit for their construction of local images of Christ. All the more surprising, then, is the consistent praise and credit given to the Scottish Presbyterian missionary named John A. Mackay (1889–1983). Mackay, who later became the president of Princeton Theological Seminary, was perhaps the most influential theologian in Latin America in the first half of the twentieth century. In particular, his monumental work *The Other Spanish Christ* (1932) decried the importation of a foreign Jesus and called for a decolonized, Latin Christ—one whose life and work were grounded in that local context. As a young college student in Peru, Samuel Escobar was especially impacted by the Scottish theologian in print and in person. This encounter catalyzed Escobar's search for social Christianity and confirmed, in his mind, its compatibility with evangelicalism. If the Brethren publishing legacy provided marketing means, Mackay partly inspired the brand itself—a truly "Latin Christ" far from the foreign importation of northern forms. Ultimately, Mackay's Latin American reception challenges categories of missionary and local leaders while parsing the individuality of the main Latin American players. In a similar way, Catharine Feser Padilla invites exploration of how our story has been obscured by a gendered context.

American missionary Catharine Feser Padilla's (1932–2009) impact on the emergence of Latin American evangelical social Christianity was as varied as it was complex. Her influence mirrored that of many American women missionaries before her: personal engagement in social projects, privately pushing her spouse to widen theology to include social Christianity, and actively concealing her own influence. Perhaps her primary influence was that of translator of *misión integral* through the work of her husband René Padilla. In turn, Feser Padilla became the primary linguistic bridge for early influential publications on social Christianity from Latin America.

When René Padilla entered Wheaton College as a freshman, he barely spoke a word of English. While he certainly improved his English significantly in the next decade, the move from language proficiency to native language precision is a significant leap. Accounts from Padilla's closest colleagues and family members confirm that Feser Padilla, a well-educated American missionary, edited nearly everything Padilla wrote. Indeed, their daughter Ruth Padilla DeBorst (an emerging evangelical leader in her own right) remembered her mother "proof-reading and commenting on the papers [René] presented in world forums."[7]

Editing, however, is never a neutral enterprise. It is always seasoned by the background and emphases of the editor herself. If the primary contribution of the emerging Latin American Evangelical Left was one of theological language and intellectual framing, then this translation process requires careful attention. Feser Padilla's consistent avoidance of the spotlight also invites a critical analysis of gender roles and restrictions in both Latin American and U.S. evangelical circles. Finally, as an American citizen, Feser Padilla also provided René with further license to critique American foreign policy. In doing so, she pushed him leftward theologically *and* politically. Much of his legacy depended on his ability to straddle the Spanish- and English-speaking worlds. While scholars have begun to highlight Padilla and Escobar's importance in the rise of social theology in Latin America and indeed global evangelicalism, nothing has been written (except by Padilla family members) on Padilla's closest colleague for nearly fifty years, Catharine Feser Padilla. Attention to her, in turn, provides a window into the lives and influence of Protestant evangelical women in late modern evangelical Protestant Christianity. The ability of the emerging Latin American Evangelical Left to communicate itself *evangelically* and *theologically* was thus tied to transnational sources as diverse as the movement of global evangelicalism itself. This raises crucial questions of the development and translation of social Christianity during this time and the role of Catharine Feser Padilla in developing *misión integral*.

Decolonizing Jesus

In 1953, a young Samuel Escobar journeyed home to his native Peru, after attending the World Baptist Youth Congress in Rio de Janeiro, Brazil. During a stop in Buenos Aires, he received word that the well-known Scottish theologian John Mackay was scheduled to deliver the Carnahan Lectures at the ecumenical seminary ISEDET in Buenos Aires.[8] At the time, Mackay was president of Princeton Theological Seminary and Escobar was a nineteen-year-old college student in Peru. To Escobar's surprise, after requesting an interview, Mackay provided over an hour of his time. Escobar also expressed surprise at Mackay's fluency in Spanish and range of conversation on Latin American philosophy and literature. The generous meeting was a "defining experience" for the young Peruvian.[9]

What is perhaps most surprising about Escobar's relationship with Mackay is what Escobar later recalled regarding the Scotsman's legacy. Escobar recounted, "Mackay helped me dialogue more [fully] with Latin American writers" and credited the social dimension of the gospel as "an inheritance from Mackay."[10] The surprising reception of Mackay's life and teaching deserves fuller attention that begins across the Atlantic in the nation of Scotland. In turn, this story offers critical nuance to individual contributions within the emerging Latin American Evangelical Left.

The decades of the 1930s and 1940s represented an intellectual low-water mark for evangelicalism in many parts of the world.[11] Though there were many individual exceptions, the nation of Scotland largely stood alone in terms of a robust theological development due to "the combined influence of a dominant Reformed tradition and an unrivalled system of public education."[12] This intellectual tradition, combined with a vigorous missionary-sending culture, produced influence around the world that was disproportionate to its size.[13] Most important for purposes here, Scotland provided the foremost Protestant evangelical theologian in Latin America in the first half of the twentieth century: John A. Mackay. Mackay influenced an entire generation of Latin American theologians across a wide denominational spectrum. The embryonic Latin American Evangelical Left found in him a rare contextual resource and a stark contrast to the operating paradigm of rote translation and importation from North America and Britain.

Mackay grew up in the Free Presbyterian Church in Inverness, later becoming a missionary of the Free Church of Scotland to Latin America from 1916 to 1932—though he often visited after his missionary tenure.[14] At a time when many global evangelical mission organizations were fixated on Africa and East Asia, Mackay chose Latin America. Crucial to this decision was his involvement with the Student Volunteer Movement at the Princeton Theological Seminary (PTS) in New Jersey, where he graduated in 1915.[15] That year, Mackay won a theological fellowship to study in Europe. Due to World War I, Mackay ruled out Germany and Britain. Mackay's PTS professor, the celebrated American Reformed theologian B. B. Warfield, suggested that Mackay study the Hispanic religious tradition in Spain in preparation for Mackay's missionary work in Latin America. This advice from Warfield would bear fruit for Mackay's entire career.

On Warfield's recommendation, Mackay later recalled, "I was taking up the incarnational approach. I wanted to become mostly related to, identified with, Latin America cultural reality, on an instrumental basis so that I would . . . win the right to be heard."[16] Mackay spent the year in Madrid drinking deeply from the well of Spanish and Hispanic intellectual tradition. Not only did he master the Spanish language, but he also developed a profound respect for the traditions of Latin America through his acquaintance with Professor Miguel de Unamuno, who later became a world-renowned philosopher. After a productive missionary career in Latin America, Mackay was eventually recruited to lead his alma mater Princeton Theological Seminary as president. He was formally installed on February 2, 1937.

Mackay's encounter with Latin American culture and literature convinced him that Christianity in the region was anything but indigenous. The Christian message had a foreign accent, and this hindered the acceptance of the gospel. Thus, Mackay wrote his most influential book, *The Other Spanish Christ*, in 1932 as an attempt to diagnose the problems of Latin American Christianity and provide a way forward to an authentically "Latin Christ." As an evangelically minded ecumenist, Mackay longed for Latin America to encounter a vibrant, living faith—the Christ of the scriptures. In Mackay's words, he sought to "introduce the evangelical into the cultural."[17]

In *The Other Spanish Christ*, Mackay decried the importation of a foreign Jesus to Latin America and declared the pressing need for replacing imported theology with contextual theology and national leadership.[18] Mackay also saw theological education as a mission field, arguing that theology must be contextualized for Latin Americans to truly grasp the gospel.[19] For the emerging Latin American Evangelical Left, Mackay's contribution in terms of the social element in the gospel is foremost here. In *The Other Spanish Christ*, Mackay expounded the message that the kingdom of God had social as well as personal elements. Mackay wrote, "Jesus' concept of the kingdom of God had a social as well as a personal aspect. It was a state of society as well as a state of the soul."[20] Because of Mackay's unique cultural sensitivity, his writing gained broad acceptance.

Mackay's life and work spoke into a context where contextual Latin American theology was lacking. In the midst of political and social ferment, Latin

American Protestants often searched in vain for religious literature that addressed their context. This was clearly seen in the previous chapter, in which Escobar asked for material to address a Marxist challenge. In return, he was given "a poorly translated Spanish version of the book *Christian Evidences* by E. Y. Mullins," the notable Southern Baptist theologian and educator.[21] Indeed, the vast majority of Latin American Protestant publications were rote translated and imported from North America, with little reference to political tumult or revolutionary movements. Thus, Mackay's life and work influenced an entire generation of Latin American Protestant evangelical thinkers. In Mackay, this generation found a rare bridge between faithfulness to the Latin American context and to their understanding of evangelical orthodoxy. It is no surprise Mackay wrote *The Other Spanish Christ* from Mexico City, Mexico.

One of the key Latin American contributions to evangelical discourse was the widening of the gospel to include social dimensions. In a 2013 interview, the present researcher asked Samuel Escobar about this progression, understanding social action as not only an *implication* of the gospel message but also *inherent* within it. Escobar was unequivocal: "I believe this is part of the heritage of Mackay."[22] Escobar expanded, "This had a strong influence, I believe, *possibly in René [Padilla] too*, in my understanding that the idea of loving neighbor and serving as an essential (*constitutiva*) part of the message of the Gospel—it wasn't added. So, the polemic was always for North American missionaries, and for many pastors, it wasn't part of the Gospel. So, in this sense, I believe that we received an inheritance from Mackay."[23]

Elsewhere, Escobar was explicit with regard to Mackay's influence on his colleagues: "The writings of Latin American ecumenical theologians like Emilio Castro and José Míguez Bonino, or evangelicals like René Padilla and Pedro Arana, show Mackay's pervasive influence."[24] Escobar was not alone in giving Mackay credit for catalyzing social theology. In a 2014 interview, Pedro Arana, successor to Padilla as general secretary for Latin America with IFES, also gave (unprompted) credit to Mackay for providing the category of an expanded gospel message.[25] Similarly, in a 2014 interview, Ruth Padilla DeBorst, who is an emerging evangelical leader and daughter of René Padilla, also spoke of Mackay's influence on the earlier generation: "He gave them a good model, inspiration, in different ways and different places they all cite him as just a helpful—model personally, but also his read of Latin American religiosity . . . I think that he was very influential on that whole generation."[26]

Padilla DeBorst also spoke of the influence of Mackay's *The Other Spanish Christ* in a 2007 article in *Christianity Today.*[27]

While Escobar, Arana, Padilla-Deborst, and others readily gave credit to outside influences for the development of their theological thinking, René Padilla was much more reluctant to do so. For example, when asked the same question as Escobar above on *implication* to *content*, Padilla was insistent that he simply read the Latin American context. Careful attention to his writings, however, does reveal a similar influence by Mackay. In a 2009 article, Padilla simply noted that reading Mackay reminded him of Latin America's theological poverty.[28] Yet, this later recollection is perhaps at odds with his comments in the 1960s. Indeed, in a 1966 article, Padilla wrote, "Over thirty years ago Dr. John A. Mackay wrote of the need in Latin America for a new type of evangelism—the 'lecture without cult,' in which the speaker takes the message to people in their own situation and presents it as something valuable in itself rather than as a part of a church service."[29] Here, Padilla was clear regarding the benefit of Mackay's work: "The relevance of this approach to the present-day university situation cannot be overemphasized." Padilla's footnote made clear he was referring to Mackay's most famous work, *The Other Spanish Christ*.

Elsewhere, Padilla described Mackay's book as "an outstanding example of the sort of apologetics that evangelical theologians felt compelled to articulate in the face of Roman Catholic hegemonic power in Latin America."[30] Padilla expanded, "This book became a classic and is still regarded as one of the best explanations of the *raison d'entrée* [sic] of Protestant Christianity in a Roman Catholic continent." Early in his own career, Padilla also noted that Mackay influenced his understanding of the need for a Latin American theological education led by Latin Americans themselves—an emphasis that became one of Padilla's enduring legacies.[31] René Padilla first discovered the importance of the kingdom of God during his PhD studies through the influence of neo-evangelicals such as George Eldon Ladd, but he *applied* the kingdom in social terms through the influence of thinkers like Mackay.

This brief discussion of the life and legacy of Scottish theologian John A. Mackay reveals a few preliminary conclusions. The first clarifies the educational trajectory of Costas, Padilla, and Escobar. Rather than moving northward, Escobar completed his formal education entirely in Latin America and Spain. Escobar's first impression of Padilla when they met in 1958 before the IFES Latin American congress was that Padilla was more "Anglo-Saxon" in his thinking, in contrast to Escobar's "Latin American philosophical training."[32] While certainly an overstatement, this quote reveals Escobar's perception and holds a degree of explanatory power. Padilla certainly took the lead on evangelical theological method, primarily due to his evangelical education, while Escobar at times was more sensitive to maintaining a truly Latin American character.

Second, Escobar's acknowledgment of an "inheritance from Mackay" with regard to social Christianity is also revealing. Escobar's openness to crediting sources in the North stems from his more irenic approach to global cooperation—particularly with Western theologians. This resulted in Escobar's inclusion in forums and gatherings from which Padilla would be excluded. Not only was Escobar seen as more theologically "safe" to a wide spectrum of evangelicals, but his cooperative approach also aided the spread of their Latin American brand of social Christianity among northern leaders.

Marketing *Misión Integral*

To this day, Latin American theologians struggle to access publishing arenas in their native languages. Seen in this light, the traditions of the Anabaptist Brethren movement were crucial to our story. The Brethren movement is known for publishing a variety of journals—many of which have roots in the nineteenth century. For example, in 1895, James Clifford began missionary work in Bolivia and subsequently pioneered a variety of publishing projects, many of which continue to this day.[33] (The Cliffords' legacy later intersects our story through their son Alec Clifford.) In its brief history, the two values of publishing and national leadership both complemented and clashed with one another. For the Brethren, publishing was not simply a luxury; it was a necessity. Because they lacked a denominational structure, hierarchy, and paid clergy, journals often served the purpose of mediating controversies.[34] Thus, it is no surprise to find many early examples of publishing within Brethren missionaries in Latin America from the 1890s forward.[35] Simply considered by itself, the Brethren emphasis on publishing is perhaps only an intriguing denominational characteristic or a minor contribution to our understanding of Protestant Christianity. Yet, this emphasis on publishing increasingly fused with a Brethren brand of internationalism. This pushed Brethren ideas outside of small pockets into global organizations and debates. Historian David Bebbington even went as far as to argue for Brethren preeminence in evangelical participation: "Their part in interdenominational activities that were distinctively evangelical were second to none."[36]

Whatever their ranking, the Christian Brethren were well positioned to not only participate in global evangelical gatherings but also influence their outcomes. Because of their lack of hierarchy and robust interchurch negotiation in journals, they had meted out their own convictions prior to global debates. Thus, "because it adhered to its own standards so fiercely, Brethrenism was well placed to act as a ginger group in the evangelical world."[37]

Brethren expertise on publishing—including channels of printing and distribution—played an instrumental role in the later dissemination of new, contextualized Latin American Protestant thought. One important bridge between a British missionary tradition and a new generation of Latin American leaders was Alec Clifford, the son of the British Brethren missionaries in Argentina described above. Alec Clifford spent the majority of his career as a staff member of the International Fellowship of Evangelical Students and became the editor of *Campo Missionero*, which his father James founded in the early twentieth century. It is no surprise that internal memoranda of the Executive Committee of the International Fellowship of Evangelical Students record Alec Clifford's push to establish a publishing work in Latin America centered at universities.

In 1957, the Publication Committee of the IFES met at Burg Schnellenberg Attendorn, Sauerland, Germany, between Saturday evening, August 31, and Monday evening, September 2, 1957. The minutes recorded, "There was considerable discussion of a project to issue a Quarterly Magazine in Spanish for South America." Similarly, it concluded, "It was finally—AGREED to recommend to the Executive Committee that it accept the proposals worked out in South America for the publication of a First Class Quarterly in Spanish for educated people (with students primarily in mind)." Two years later, the project finally received financial backing from the Executive Committee, which was chaired by Brethren Australian leader Stacey Woods. The minutes of the literature committee from August 25 to 28, 1959, also recorded that Alec Clifford had been appointed "Chairman of the Latin American Literature Committee."[38]

In 1962, the Spanish student magazine *Certeza* was founded in Buenos Aires, soon expanding from three issues to five in 1963. Each had an average printing of 10,000 copies. While *Certeza* was printed in Buenos Aires, it was also distributed in Brazil, Chile, Mexico, Peru, Venezuela, Argentina, Bolivia, Colombia, Ecuador, and "the countries of Central America and the

Caribbean."[39] Its highest circulation was in Argentina, perhaps principally due to Brethren networks across the country, though Argentina was a publishing hub for Protestant literature.[40] By 1974, IFES claimed that *Certeza* had become "the interdenominational magazine with the widest circulation in Latin America."[41] Ediciones Certeza, the publishing arm of IFES in Latin America, had also undertaken a massive publishing project, which, in 1969, was just beginning to expand. That year, Ediciones Certeza sold 5,498 books, but by 1973, it had sold 16,569. Nearly 50 percent of the sales were to university students.[42]

In 1965, the Executive Committee of the IFES met with the topic of enquiry, "How can we help indigenous writing?"[43] IFES at that time was under the leadership of another Brethren leader, Australian General Secretary C. Stacey Woods. As with Woods, Clifford was not content—like many of his colleagues from the United States—to create a dependent ministry based upon his expertise. Clifford mentored younger Latin Americans in publishing work—namely, Escobar and Padilla and, through them, Pedro Arana.[44]

Samuel Escobar moved to Argentina from Peru in 1960 and became friends with Clifford that year. There, Escobar recalled his own "horizon continued to grow" with regard to social Christianity. Given overwhelmingly negative narratives surrounding missionary work in Latin America, it is surprising to hear glowing endorsements of a British missionary. Escobar wrote in 1984, "By means of my adoptive father Alejandro Clifford, I not only received a significant school of the best evangelical journalism, but also a lasting professor of Church History in Latin America, and of ecclesiology that today we would call 'radical.'"[45] Escobar gave credit to Clifford not only for publishing know-how but also for mentoring him in a radical new approach to Christianity, which included antisectarianism and anti-institutionalism. This he attributed to Clifford's Brethren heritage: "My contact with the group of Brethren . . . demonstrated to me what could truly be called a lay, autonomous, and rich theological movement." Though Escobar was Baptist, Clifford's mentorship, combined with the wider Brethren movement, "was a laboratory of learning theologically, journalistically, and educationally."[46] In the 1950s, Clifford had also organized a robust journal-sharing program with all Protestant journals in Latin America. This was part of why, in a 2013 interview in Valencia, Escobar referred to Clifford as a mentor and teacher of both himself and René Padilla.[47] In 1966, Padilla described the magazine *Certeza* (at that time under Clifford's editorship) as "the most important contribution in this field made to student witness."[48] In Escobar's recollection, he and Padilla sought to position themselves against wider fundamentalist trends by reading widely and encouraged their students to do so as well.[49]

The ability to market *misión integral* was drawn in part from a Brethren heritage and legacy, especially through the influence of Stacey Woods and Alec Clifford. While missionaries founded key Spanish journals, Brethren denominational distinctives led them to release leadership to local Latin Americans—including to members of the later Latin American Evangelical Left. As a result, Padilla, Escobar, and Arana in particular received established channels for disseminating their emerging progressive ideas. While the publishing know-how was part of this legacy, this only partially explains their global influence. The ability to *market* these ideas in English to a particularly American audience was tied to the editorial influence of Catharine Feser Padilla and a holistic tradition of American women missionaries. In a way, both were strategic bridges for moving progressive evangelical ideas from pockets of Latin America to the broader evangelical world.

The Holistic Legacy of American Women Missionaries

The influence of Protestant women on the rise of Latin American social theology is a neglected area that has been obscured by multiple religious and cultural layers. These include the widespread influence of American fundamentalist missions and conservative cultural understandings of gender in the region.[50] Lingering American fundamentalist missionary influence presented a stark juxtaposition to Protestant evangelical women such as Catharine Feser Padilla: conservative gender roles in churches alongside an uncommonly progressive organizational structure of parachurch ministries. These parachurch organizations often allowed women near-equal access to preaching, teaching, and organizational leadership. The context of many female parachurch staff workers in postwar Latin America, then, was socially progressive initiatives within a conservative sociocultural and religious context. Within this multilayered setting, Feser Padilla condescended to her gendered context and exercised significant influence on the emergence of *misión integral*. In doing so, she carved out avenues for the global dissemination of integral mission themes through her bilingual editing and bicultural connections. If Feser Padilla's influence has been widely overlooked, how might uncovering her contribution shed light on the multidirectional, multilingual story of an emerging Latin American Evangelical Left? As the gulf between fundamentalism and neo-evangelicalism widened from the late 1950s onward, so did the diversity of roles for women in ministry—perhaps nowhere more acutely than within parachurch organizations. Parachurch organizations then exerted increasing pressure on traditional gendered structures and, in turn, wider influence on American evangelicalism.[51] Catharine Padilla followed in the tradition of early twentieth-century women in Protestant fundamentalist circles who turned to Bible teaching as the primary mode of carrying out a Christian calling.[52]

From Pennsylvania to Patagonia

Catharine Feser was born on November 5, 1932, in the city of Philadelphia. She grew up in a "very conservative Christian," well-educated family.[53] Her parents were both ordained ministers, earning graduate degrees from Eastern Baptist Theological Seminary (EBTS, now Palmer Theological Seminary [PTS]).[54] EBTS was founded on March 25, 1925. The seminary founders, according to PTS in 2014, "maintained that the agendas of conservative institutions were too narrow, particularly with regard to the prohibition of women in ministry and the absence of concern for social justice."[55] The theological training of her parents, then, grounded Feser Padilla in a progressive tradition of American fundamentalism. Her father, Walter, earned a master of theology degree (ThM) on May 17, 1933, and joined the pastorate soon after.[56] Catharine's mother passed away when she was just six years old—a loss that undoubtedly propelled the young Philadelphian toward independence. As a result, Catharine's father left the pastorate to care for his daughters.[57] Catharine later attended Wheaton College, earning a bachelor of arts (BA) in Bible with highest honor on June 14, 1954, and a master of arts (MA) in New Testament on January 29, 1960.[58] Her formal education at Wheaton, a bastion of the fledgling conservative evangelical movement, seemed destined to clash with her progressive upbringing, especially in terms of gender roles. Yet, at the peak of the civil rights movement in the United States in the late 1950s and early 1960s, other progressive issues were more pertinent on Wheaton's campus, such as economic inequality.[59]

At Wheaton, Feser Padilla began volunteering with Foreign Mission Fellowship (now International Mission Fellowship) and its mission work in a local Latino church.[60] As a Wheaton senior, Catharine began providing car rides to Padilla, who at the time was a freshman (René had entered university at twenty years old, two years later than was common among his North American classmates).[61] After graduating from Wheaton, Catharine returned to her hometown of Philadelphia to be near her widowed father and to teach in a "reform school for delinquent girls."[62] Catharine then joined the staff of InterVarsity Fellowship–USA for two years in Nebraska and South Dakota.

Joining an evangelical parachurch organization opened avenues for Catharine to exercise diverse gifts and roles that were widely restricted to men in Protestant evangelical churches. As historian Margaret Bendroth demonstrated, "The highest female career, that of Bible teacher, reflected the fundamentalist emphasis on public speaking as a sign of leadership and seemed, at least initially, not to contradict rules against women teachers."[63] Feser Padilla's work in these parachurch organizations demonstrates the ways in which women within conservative evangelical circles could take leadership roles in traditionally male-restricted fields.[64]

Catharine's work as a professor, editor, and parachurch staff worker extended her influence far beyond the context of her familial relationships. In a 1964 *Delaware County Times* newspaper article, her local pastor considered her "called out from his ministry" as a missionary. No mention was made of René.[65] A later fundraising letter also described her prioritization of both family and mission work: "Catharine devotes time to their home, women's work and Bible teaching. She teaches at the Christian and Missionary Alliance Bible Institute in Buenos Aires and often is invited to speak at conferences."[66] Catharine later became a Greek professor at Seminario Evangélico Interdenominacional in San Fernando and the Instituto Bíblico Buenos Aires (known in English as the Christian and Missionary Alliance Bible Institute).[67] She also published a variety of books, including a Bible commentary on 1–2 Thessalonians, a practical manual for the study of the Bible, and articles on women in ministry.[68] Much of her time was spent working behind the scenes, especially among the poor and as editor for her husband, René Padilla.

Multilingual Conduit

Because of what Padilla called his "language problems," he postponed the start of his undergraduate studies, instead working in the cafeteria for the first semester.[69] His linguistic challenges were also reflected in his Wheaton College transcript—his grades steadily improved as time went on.[70] Padilla also admitted that his ministry at a local Spanish-speaking church (where he met Catharine) curtailed his apprehension of the English language.[71] Much of Padilla's later influence, however, depended on his ability to straddle the English- and Spanish-speaking worlds. While René later became proficient in English, how might his marriage to a native English speaker have extended the reach of his ideas, especially in the early years of the 1960s and 1970s? After graduating from Wheaton College with his BA in philosophy in 1957, René rejected overtures from IFES General Secretary and later mentor C. Stacey Woods to join the staff of IFES.[72] Padilla completed his MA in theology in 1960, graduating in absentia from Latin America. From Latin America, Padilla proposed marriage to his long-time American friend, Catharine Feser.

Ruth Padilla DeBorst's above recollection of her mother editing Padilla's work was not limited to large public presentations either. "Nothing escaped her eagle eye when she edited countless manuscripts in Spanish and English for Ediciones Kairos," Padilla DeBorst expanded.[73] In a 2013 interview, René himself said, "[Catharine] edited nearly everything I wrote."[74] Padilla's colleague and successor as IFES general secretary for Latin America, Pedro Arana, also called Catharine René's "English editor" in a 2013 interview.[75] Catharine's extensive editing undoubtedly filled a gap between language proficiency and native language precision—expanding the reach of integral mission ideas.

"I Married Latin America—I Don't Want to Divorce"

On January 24, 1972, Samuel Escobar sent a "confidential" letter to IFES General Secretary C. Stacey Woods. In it, he informed the Australian of his impending move out of Latin America to Canada, accepting the role of general secretary for Canada's InterVarsity Fellowship. Escobar wrote, "There have been varied reactions from the members of the IFES staff and national leaders that I have been able to consult and meet. Most of them have encouraged me to go to Canada. Rene has been an important exception. He does not seem to share my plans for setting up a training ground for prospective staff."[76] Escobar's desire was to provide theological training for global IFES staff via various theological institutions in Canada (i.e., Regent College in Vancouver and the Institute for Christian Studies in Toronto). While Escobar shared a passion for theological education within Latin America, he saw Canada as a strategic opportunity that was too good to pass up. In contrast, Escobar penned, "Rene thinks, however, that it's not the point where my absence could be more critical." Padilla's foremost concern was with their fledgling development of social Christianity, particularly their IFES literature project in Latin America, *Certeza*, which was both a magazine and a publishing house.

By the early 1970s, René Padilla had seen many of his closest colleagues in Latin America leave for North America or Britain. Escobar eventually moved to the United States in the early 1980s and later succeeded Puerto Rican evangelical Orlando Costas at Eastern Baptist Theological Seminary from 1985 to 2005. Costas himself had already made clear his "real mission . . . was to be in North America," carrying out the majority of his career in the North.[77] In 1979, Professor Andrew Kirk, founding member of the Latin American Theological Fraternity, had also returned to his native Britain. Many American missionaries had also returned. In 1981, René Padilla pondered whether it was finally time for his family to leave Latin America.

That year, his request to remain director of the literature project of the IFES in Latin America (Ediciones Certeza and *Certeza* magazine) had been denied by IFES General Secretary Chua Wee Hian.[78] Observing his colleagues' well-worn path leading out of Latin America, in a 2014 interview, Padilla recalled looking northward to other opportunities in the United States. That year, Padilla also received a letter from Gerald Anderson, then director of the Overseas Ministries Study Center (OMSC) in New Haven, Connecticut, which sits adjacent to Yale Divinity School. Anderson, according to Padilla, offered him the role of associate director of the OMSC and to "take charge" of their journal.[79] Naturally, Padilla shared the letter with his wife, Catharine Feser Padilla, along with his belief that their prayers may have been answered. Faced with the opportunity to return to her homeland of the East Coast of the United States, along with greater financial stability and a larger platform for spreading social Christian ideas, Catharine responded firmly, "I married Latin America—I don't want to divorce."[80]

Catharine's response to the job offer revealed that *her* mission remained in Latin America. René thus wrote to Anderson declining the opportunity— René and Catharine would remain in Buenos Aires, Argentina, until Catharine's death in 2009.[81] Catharine's decision had manifest implications for the legacy of social Christianity in Latin America and the trajectory of global evangelicalism. The next year, they founded *Misión* magazine, which Padilla later described as his primary means of disseminating *misión integral*.[82] His social location in Latin America also cemented his legacy as publisher of young Latin Americans and a figurehead for the movement itself.

Catharine's refusal to "divorce" Latin America hearkened to René Padilla's twofold marriage proposal decades earlier—to marry him and to marry Latin America. Because of this, Catharine initially denied his proposal.[83] She had never even visited Latin America and felt apprehensive leaving her widowed father.[84] René insisted she reconsider. Catharine suspended her rejection and reconsidered for two full years—finally accepting his proposal in 1960. Catharine's prolonged decision finds continuity with nineteenth- and twentieth-century missionary wives' biographies, such as Adoniram Judson's proposal to Ann Hasseltine.[85] Like Hasseltine, Feser Padilla had to decide first if she would marry an unknown mission field, with a foreign culture and language. On the other hand, the mission field often offered American fundamentalist (and later evangelical) women greater freedom in ministry—due to the lack of male missionaries and the nature of missionary work as parachurch, as well.

Far from bystanders on the mission of their husbands, American women missionaries often leveraged marriage decisions in order to prioritize their own missionary calling. Dana Robert, in her groundbreaking research on American women missionaries, sheds light on the decision many American women missionaries had faced: "If one takes the evidence available from biographies of missionary wives at face value, it seems that only a minority of women chose the husband and then had to be persuaded to undertake the mission. Most of the time, the commitment to mission preceded commitment to the husband."[86] Thus, Catharine and René's daughter Ruth Padilla DeBorst could describe her parents' marriage and family as "grounded on a missiological covenant."[87] After Catharine and René's wedding in January 1961, Catharine bought a one-way plane ticket to Bogotá. Her commitment to the priority of mission in Latin America, within its cultural, linguistic, and sociopolitical context, had profound implications for not only the Padilla family but also the emergence of *misión integral* itself.

As a traveling secretary with IFES, René was constantly traveling throughout Latin America, often away from home for months at a time.[88] On January 14, 1960, Padilla wrote to Samuel Escobar, recounting a five-week trip he took to Venezuela in Mérida, Caracas, Maracay, Barquisimeto, and Maracaibo. This constant traveling continued into the 1970s. Indeed, Samuel Escobar wrote in 1977, "René Padilla does not appear to have a permanent home, since in his first months of work he was moved constantly through different university centers."[89] In his 1977 travel diary, John Stott wrote of René's inner turmoil after another five-week trip around Latin America and the joy of the Padilla children at seeing their father again.[90] Three years later, Stott accompanied the Padilla family on a camping trip in the Patagonia mountains of Argentina. Stott wrote in his travel diary, "They are a really delightful family. I think the world of René as a Christian leader, scholar and friend; Cathie is a marvelously unflappable, loving and capable wife and mother."[91] In continuity with many nineteenth- and early twentieth-century missionary wives, Feser Padilla's "unflappable" commitment to mission within her familial relationships allowed both René and her to prioritize mission.[92]

Escobar connected Padilla's ability to travel away from home to his later inclusion of social concern in ministry. In 1977, Escobar reflected, "These long travels . . . gave the workers a first-hand knowledge of the national reality in these countries, which added to the rising demand of students for guidance, eventually leading toward making social concern an ingredient of his ministry."[93] This same freedom allowed Padilla to travel on multiple occasions with John Stott, including a "birding" holiday in the Galapagos Islands—Stott's favorite pastime.[94] This relationship carved paths for the dissemination of social Christianity in global evangelicalism.

It is plausible to suggest that missionary longevity on the mission field in the nineteenth and twentieth centuries was often intricately tied to the ability of both spouses to adapt to the newfound context. Feser Padilla's thorough adoption of Latin America is perhaps most clearly shown through her eventual rejection of her own country, the United States.[95] Feser Padilla adopted Latin America as her own, alongside an intense solidarity with widespread rejection of American foreign policy in Latin America. In a 2013 interview, René Padilla recalled Catharine's frustration with the American invasion of Iraq (2003) and with American evangelical approval on Wheaton College's campus. In the academic year 2003–2004, René was a guest professor at Wheaton College in Illinois. On Wheaton's campus, Catharine attempted to engage Wheaton students and faculty with a critique of the war and American foreign policy. In René's recollection, "She was completely rebuffed." As a result, Catharine cut ties with her native country: "I am ashamed to be American," René recalled her saying. This posture persisted. Upon returning to Argentina from Wheaton, René was increasingly invited to speak and teach in the United States, but René recalled Catharine's consistent response: "I don't want to go to America. I am ashamed to be American."[96] She never returned.

Choosing the Background: Catharine Feser Padilla as Missionary Wife

Ultimately, like many missionary wives of the nineteenth and twentieth centuries, Catharine Feser Padilla worked tirelessly behind the scenes, actively eschewing the spotlight. Her daughter Elisa Padilla, now president of the Kairos Foundation and director of its literature project, Ediciones Kairos, described her mother as "always serving in silence."[97] This description of Catharine appears to be true of her educational work, as well. One of her former students, Gladys Amador, said about her teaching, "She did not speak a lot, but she said a lot with her actions."[98] As René gained increasing attention and demand as a speaker, Catharine did not waver in her rejection of personal attention. Careful literary analysis also reveals that René often received authorial credit, even when Catharine contributed significantly to the content.

For example, in 2003, they cowrote *Mujer y hombre en la misión de Dios* (*Man and Woman in the Mission of God*). The book was adapted from a 1991 conference where both Catharine and René gave plenary speeches. The first half of the book is taken from René's presentation but is designated as written by both Catharine and René. Indeed, in the first half, Catharine's name is added to René's republished presentation, yet for the second half—taken from Catharine's presentation—René's name is not added.[99] In a separate edited volume, Padilla also published his own section from the conference only under his name, leaving out Catharine's.[100] It is possible that René was simply sharing credit with Catharine here. Given her extensive editing shown above, however, it is equally as likely that she cowrote the original piece, only to give credit to René in the public presentation. Catharine's hidden influence is further confirmed by a 2013 account regarding her own book project, *La Palabra de Dios para el pueblo de Dios* (*The Word of God for the People of God*).[101]

In a 2013 interview, René recalled Catharine approaching him visibly distressed: "I don't want my name to appear on the book." René exclaimed, "How not? Why not?" Catharine retorted, "Well, why would I? I prefer that it not appear—I only want 'Ediciones Kairos' to appear." René recalled his response as, "No, it can't be." The debate was far from over. When the book was "practically ready for the printer," Catharine returned to René insistently, "I don't want my name to appear." René described his response: "So I said, listen to (me as) the editor of Ediciones Kairos, not (as) your spouse—I cannot publish this book without your name—your name is going to appear." René said she responded, "Well, you're the boss."[102] This brief anecdote sheds light on Catharine's consistent desire to eschew public recognition. Because of this, studies on her influence must, by necessity, discuss her choice to work within her familial relationships. In the same way, quantifying Feser Padilla's influence on René's extensive influence and publication is significantly problematized. Indeed, her influence appears to be inseparably linked to René's.

As we have seen earlier, Padilla lacked social theological categories in the early 1960s as he wrote his doctoral thesis in England. If in 1965 Padilla lacked social theological categories, from where did he obtain them? In Chapter 2, I argued that the same revolutionary university environment gave rise to both Latin American liberation theology and *misión integral*. Yet, context is never sufficient to explain the development of theological ideas.

In continuity with many nineteenth- and twentieth-century women missionaries, the themes of Catharine's teaching and ministry were holistic.[103] Dana Robert clarified, "Even in proclamation-oriented evangelical mission agencies, women were the ones to undertake ministries of compassion. Women's mission theory emphasized education, in the nineteenth century as the functional equivalent to preaching, and in the twentieth century for social liberation."[104] Prior to René Padilla's apprehension of social theological categories, Catharine was working among the poor, widowed, and substance abuse addicts (of course, in partnership with Padilla).[105] These holistic themes also appear in her later writing. At the 2008 Global Connections "Thinking Mission" Forum (the year prior to her death), her Bible study materials were distributed to participants. In them, she wrote,

> Is the problem that there is something missing in the Gospel message to which these people have responded? Is the message that has been preached to them only the offer of a place in heaven after death? Have

people received a truncated gospel that has prepared them for heaven but has not prepared them to live on this earth? . . . Has the Bible been left closed up in our churches instead of touching the every-day life in the home, in the workplace, or in society in general—as well as in the church?[106]

For Catharine, expanding the content of the gospel message was essential for impacting society.[107] It is plausible to suggest that Feser Padilla's consistent holistic ministry impacted Padilla's own view of Christian mission.

Equality of gender roles within the home and the church eventually became a staple of *misión integral* for both Catharine and René. Ruth Padilla DeBorst remembered her mother "wrangling with him [René] over the translation of Greek biblical terms."[108] Catharine's ministry and writing often focused on expanding opportunities for women in the church and the home. Indeed, Ruth Padilla DeBorst wrote, "Her articles, book chapters and published lectures . . . focus mainly on the role of women and men as equal bearers of God's image in the kingdom of God, the church and the world—something she so confidently modeled and inspired in her own children and in generations of Latin American women and men."[109] A literary analysis of René Padilla's own writing on women and *misión integral* (which space unfortunately does not fully allow) reveals a progression of thought toward equality for women in the home, as well as in the church—for example, from his first article in 1975 "La mujer: Un ser humano" (Woman: A Human Being) to his 1997 article "Hombre y mujer, coherederos del reino" (Man and Woman, Coheirs of the Kingdom).[110] Padilla also hired former political activist Marta Márquez as female copastor in his Buenos Aires Baptist church—a move that both split his church and led to significant numerical decline.[111] Catharine also preached on occasion.

When asked about the influence of Catharine on René with regard to women's equality, among other progressive issues, Pedro Arana answered incredulously, "[René and Cati] shared entirely the study of the Scriptures. Cati as a professor in Biblical Studies in . . . two seminaries. *How could they not* share the themes of women, social justice, among others?"[112] Catharine Feser Padilla's significance should be included in any discussion of René Padilla's influence, especially given René's own repudiation of the social dimensions of the gospel in his 1965 PhD thesis, the confirmation of oral historical accounts, and in the light of the holistic legacy of female American missionaries in the nineteenth and twentieth centuries.

An increasingly prominent, vocal, and diverse evangelical coalition challenged U.S. exported Christian goods around the world—seen most clearly at the epochal Lausanne Congress of 1974. Many of the most significant protests came from missionaries themselves who observed firsthand the failures and successes of mission from the Global North. Many contended that rejecting conservative politics, cultural passivity, and missionary *paternalism* was fully consonant with evangelicalism. Thus, our story does not fit into prepackaged stereotypes of local Christians against foreign missionaries. On the contrary, three northern missionary sources influenced the early development process of *misión integral* in untold ways. In a way, all three influences peaked at the Lausanne Congress of 1974.

The branding, marketing, and translation of *misión integral* was a shared project across denominations, nationalities, and genders. Within a wider context of persistent paternalism, British Brethren missionaries progressively released leadership to local Latin Americans, in large part due to their congregational polity that lacked paid clergy and hierarchy. The Brethren tradition of pioneering publishing projects created channels through which Latin Americans wrote their own theologies and developed a new brand of social Christianity. This allowed Latin American Protestant evangelicals to diffuse social Christian ideas to a wider constituency. Thus, while Christian Brethrenism is implicated in providing a theological structure for rejecting social reform in fundamentalism and dispensationalism, it should also be credited with providing an escape hatch from it.

John A. Mackay, Scottish missionary to Latin America and later president of Princeton Theological Seminary, influenced an entire generation of Latin American Protestant evangelical thinkers through his life and work. Samuel Escobar was particularly impacted by Mackay's sensitivity and use of Latin American philosophy to thoroughly contextualize the message of Jesus in Latin America. The emerging Latin American Evangelical Left found in Mackay a rare bridge between answering questions raised by the Latin American context and remaining faithful to their understanding of evangelical orthodoxy. Mackay's understanding of social Christianity and the contextualization of the gospel message provided both encouragement and targeted inspiration in their search for a new brand of evangelical social Christianity. As they sought to market these ideas to the English-speaking world, Feser Padilla provided a strategic and necessary bridge.

The story of Catharine Feser Padilla's influence is necessarily gendered, ultimately imbedded within her context of human relationships.[113] Within the Latin American contextual reality of male leadership and the pervasive influence of a machismo culture where women have historically been excluded and oppressed, Feser Padilla empowered a generation of evangelical women and men through theological education. Similarly, her multilingual editing carved out grooves for the spread of integral mission themes—expanding the influence of both integral mission and her husband, René Padilla. Her influence, one focused on a progressive understanding of gender and the kingdom of God, was infused into the origins, development, and spread of *misión integral*. Ultimately, this well-educated, bilingual American professor condescended to her gendered context in order to prioritize mission.

The extent of Feser Padilla's influence on the origins, development, and dissemination of integral mission, however, may never fully be known. As Pedro Arana eloquently stated in a 2014 interview, "I think that René's achievements are shared in a percentage that we'll never be able to specify with his partner, spouse, mother of their children, English editor and loving critic."[114] Catharine Feser Padilla, drawing from a tradition of holistic service within American women missions, exercised an incalculable influence on the development of an evangelical social Christianity.

This attention to foreign evangelical missionaries in Latin America provides further nuance to the intellectual history of the emerging Latin American Evangelical Left. This progressive coalition fiercely defended national autonomy but was not averse to foreign aid—provided it eschewed a paternalistic paradigm. The ability of Woods, Clifford, Mackay, and Feser Padilla to adopt local language, customs, and praxis built a bridge for their ideas to gain wider acceptance. Once again, the story of *misión integral* has emerged as transnational, multilingual, and increasingly diverse. The complex relationship between local Latin Americans and northern missionaries included positive and negative legacies—a dynamic interplay that should be reflected in the narrative.

CHAPTER 6

Crossing Boundaries

In June 1977, Orlando Costas, René Padilla, John Stott, and José Míguez Bonino descended a winding road tucked into the side of Irazú volcano, an active volcano in Cordillera Central, Costa Rica, just outside the city of Cartago. One topic dominated the conversation: the efficacy of Marxism versus capitalism and each one's compatibility with the Christian faith. As they navigated this narrow road, the four theologians stopped to watch "two teams of peasants ploughing a hillside field, and sowing it with potatoes." John Stott recorded in his travel diary soon after, "Two oxen were yoked to a simple wooden plough, while barefoot men walked up the furrows rhythmically scattering fertiliser and potatoes."[1] This living parable offered a vivid backdrop to discussing the relationship between Christianity and politics, theology and economics, along with power, corruption, and the future of Latin America.

Their conversation also provides us with a window into the new religious landscape of the postwar period—an increasingly diverse and increasingly global evangelicalism, represented by an Argentine Methodist liberation theologian in Míguez Bonino, a Puerto Rican evangelical in Costas, a British evangelical Anglican clergyman in Stott, and an Ecuadorian evangelical in Padilla. Few could deny its existence or importance after the events surrounding the Lausanne Congress. Yet, much of this story, one of ecumenism and theological exchange, however, remains hidden by linguistic, political, and ideological boundaries.

Latin American leaders crossed not only the fiercely guarded religious boundaries of many American evangelicals and Catholic liberation theologians but also the boundaries constructed by current scholarly literature. In other words, the boundaries that religious leaders sought to police have actually been aided by the ways in which scholars have narrated their history. The Latin American Evangelical Left faced closely guarded boundaries on both sides of the political spectrum—the Catholic left and the American evangelical right. This was due in part to their intentional positioning, defining themselves primarily against two perceived ideological excesses: Marxist-inflected theologies of liberation and the conservative political loyalties of the Religious Right. In the scholarly literature, intellectual exchange with theologies of liberation has been viewed as unthinkable, as the vast majority of Latin American evangelical churches were perceived as parroting the anticommunist, socially isolated, and moralistic theologies of their American counterparts. But even the identification of a Latin American Evangelical Left challenges this scholarly oversight and popular stereotype. Scholarship has presented the story of Latin American social Christianity as if these boundaries held—that religious segregation was successful, negating intellectual exchange and cross-pollination within a hotly contested religious marketplace.

South of the Rio Grande, the story of Latin American Protestant Christianity, in particular, has often divided individuals into prepackaged, binary categories such as liberal and conservative. Indeed, it has often pitted ecumenical and evangelical Protestant strands of Christianity against one another. While this narrative is generally true at the organizational level, it is often problematic when applied interpersonally. If binary categories of liberal versus conservative have obscured key intellectual exchange, how might closer attention to archival documents and oral history shed light on ecumenical boundary crossing? Chapter 2 argued that *misión integral* was far from a *version* of liberation theology. Here, the argument cuts across the grain of received scholarship and posits surprising and untold influence of evangelicals *upon* theologies of liberation. While the wall between ecumenical and evangelical Protestantism in Latin America was viewed publicly as insurmountable in the late 1960s and early 1970s, many events and relationships problematize this narrative.

In particular, the relationship between José Míguez Bonino and the Latin American Evangelical Left is a case study of theological exchange between liberation theology, mainline Protestantism, and Protestant evangelicalism. Recent scholarship has either ignored the relationship or labeled it as a historical aberration—the most recent designating its inception to the 1990s.[2] In the case of Míguez Bonino, collaboration was particularly important, as he "preferred to test his own ideas and theological under-standings within the milieu of group work."[3] If this was the process by which Míguez Bonino formed his theology, and his relationship with the Latin American Evangelical Left has been both ignored and misrepresented, what might be gleaned regarding the relationship between Protestant theologies of liberation and *misión integral*? The prevailing narrative welcomes interrogation and a return to strategic gatherings of the Latin American Theological Fraternity—with a focused lens on hidden relationships and causality.

From Public Dialogue to Hidden Story

José Míguez Bonino was born in Rosario de Santa Fe, Argentina, in 1924. Like many liberation theologians, Bonino left Latin America to study in the West—first studying at the Evangelical School of Theology in Buenos Aires (where he later became a professor); then Candler School of Theology (Emory University) in Atlanta, Georgia; and Union Theological Seminary, New York, for his doctorate (ThD, 1960). His doctoral thesis was entitled "A Study of Some Recent Roman Catholic and Protestant Thought on the Relation of Scripture and Tradition." It is not surprising, then, that Míguez Bonino is perhaps best known as the only Latin American Protestant observer at the Second Vatican Council from 1962 to 1965.[4] He often participated in Roman Catholic gatherings, such as the decade-long Catholic Inter-American Cooperation Program (CICOP) from 1964 to 1973, alongside Gustavo Gutiérrez and Juan Luis Segundo. Míguez Bonino exerted impressive influence at CICOP, for example, as a plenary speaker in 1967 in Boston, Massachusetts, where over 3,000 participants attended.[5] That year, Míguez Bonino was visiting professor at Union Theological Seminary in New York—though the spring semester was interrupted by student strikes.[6]

Míguez Bonino later became regional president of the World Council of Churches (WCC) from 1975 to 1983, after being intimately involved in the WCC discussion forum entitled "Iglesia y Sociedad en América Latina" (ISAL).[7] ISAL, under Míguez Bonino's shared leadership, exercised an incalculable influence on the rise of liberation theology—as we have previously seen.[8] Yet, Míguez Bonino's contribution to liberation theology was complex, as he deepened its Christian character and widened its dialogue with Marxism.⁹ He has been rightly described as a "participant-critic" of the movement.¹⁰ Míguez Bonino's books *Doing Theology in a Revolutionary Situation* (1975) and *Toward a Christian Political Ethics* (1983) are widely considered core liberation theology texts. The former's discussion of the theological motif of the kingdom of God became a central contribution to the discourse of liberation theology.

In the revolutionary postwar Latin American context, debate surrounding the kingdom of God was more than an abstract intellectual exercise. As guerilla warfare and Marxist revolution were live options, theologians grappled with the ability to identify the kingdom of God and understand participation in it. This theological motif would also later define their utopian ideals and quest to reshape religion and politics in Latin America. But in the early 1970s, the concept of the kingdom of God had not yet gained the prime of place in either theologies of liberation or the emerging understanding of the Latin American Evangelical Left. During this decade, Míguez Bonino's closest conversation partners were other liberation theologians—including Gustavo Gutiérrez, Rubem Alves, and Juan Luis Segundo. At least in the case of the kingdom of God motif, however, his understanding finds its origins in a surprisingly *evangelical* place.

In 1972, René Padilla planned a consultation titled "The Kingdom of God and Latin America" under the auspices of the newly formed Latin American Theological Fraternity (FTL). This was the first gathering after the U.S. evangelical-approved participants gathered in 1970 for the first FTL. More important, this was after the English translation and publication in northern journals ended and the white evangelical gaze largely subsided (as we saw earlier with the Wagner *Christianity Today* controversy). As a result of this perceived independence, René Padilla invited none other than José Míguez Bonino to give a plenary address alongside him. This was both Padilla and Míguez Bonino's first public explanation of their theologies of the kingdom—which would later become central themes for both liberation theology and *misión integral.* Orlando Costas was also included after Padilla and Escobar had protested his exclusion from FTL I along with that of other SBL professors. According to Costas, Escobar and Padilla "insisted that the doors be opened so that we could enter into a new theological friendship."¹¹ Costas expanded, "From this moment, my theological reflection has been linked to the itinerary of the Fraternity."¹² While Costas up until this point had been marginal to the movement, he increasingly joined these conversations as an ecumenical voice.

While Padilla shared the revolutionary university context with liberation theologians, his intellectual currents from the North were radically divergent from those of his liberation theology colleagues. René Padilla, for his part, had begun exploring the kingdom of God as a theme in his PhD thesis but had yet to expound his own understanding of the concept. Similarly, though Míguez Bonino would later write extensively on the theme, he had also yet to address the topic exclusively in a public forum. Indeed, Míguez Bonino's first two titles on the kingdom of God appeared in Protestant evangelical settings: the first for the evangelical journal *Cuadernos Teológicos*, though Míguez Bonino had certainly referenced the theme prior to this gathering.[13]

While the conference itself was Padilla's brainchild, he wrote in the introduction to the conference volume, "The paper by Míguez Bonino was probably the most debated of all."[14] At FTL II, Padilla and Míguez Bonino agreed at many points but clashed at this point of participation in the kingdom—who can participate and who is part of it?[15] Míguez Bonino argued that Christians must *name* and *manifest* the kingdom of God. This takes the form of obedience in "doctrinal and ideological mediations."[16] For Míguez Bonino, these instruments principally included Marxism and social scientific analysis. There was no place for "neutrality" in regard to history— one must choose sides and take action.[17] This, of course, reflected the primary methodological lens of liberation theology—the priority of praxis in theological construction. "Instead of defining theology as the ordered pursuit of understanding the eternal being and salvific activity of God, theologies of liberation prioritized first committed action and then empirical reflection in response to the condition of impoverished human beings in their particular social and political contexts."[18]

Eschatology played a central role in both *misión integral* and liberation theology, as well. Míguez Bonino actually deferred to Padilla on eschatology and mentioned that he "fully" agreed with the eschatological position presented in Padilla's paper.[19] Padilla situated the kingdom of God within the framework of the "already" and the "not yet" that was also present in his PhD thesis and plenary speech at Lausanne 1974. Yet, Míguez Bonino also strongly objected to Padilla's formulation of the relationship between the church and the kingdom of God. He pitted Padilla against what he called "the Protestants of the sixteenth-century Reformation" and "the case in the Old Testament." He argued that God "manifests his sovereignty in the world even through people who do not profess his name; and he also carries out his work

through them."[20] Thus, this participation in the kingdom of God and building a utopian society was open to non-Christians as well as Christians, though
the former would not name their work as "Christian." Padilla, on the other
hand, argued that the church *mediated* the kingdom of God to the world, and
he reserved participation in the kingdom for believers alone.[21]

Even so, Míguez Bonino worried about removing the Christian character of praxis: "We may soon be talking about 'love' or 'new person' or 'liberation' in which reference to the history of special revelation, and particularly
to Jesus Christ, is secondary, merely exemplary, and even dispensable. In
Christian terms, if that happens, reference to God himself has lost its
content. Of what God are we speaking? And of what kingdom?"[22] Once
again, Míguez Bonino was guarding the *Christian* nature of action in the
kingdom and manifesting his "participant-critic" credentials. Evangelicals
in the FTL also pushed Míguez Bonino to guard the Christian character of
the kingdom of God, as he sought to widen participation in it.

The evangelical push to construct a theology of the kingdom provides a
crucial intervention in the popular understanding of liberation theology and
Latin American social Christianity. Míguez Bonino's paper at this 1972 FTL
gathering later formed the basis of a key chapter in *Doing Theology in a
Revolutionary Situation* and the 1975 work, *Frontiers of Theology in Latin
America*, which appeared alongside essays by Rubem Alves, Hugo Assmann,
Leonardo Boff, Gustavo Gutiérrez, Juan Luis Segundo, and other prominent
liberation theologians.[23] The dependence of Míguez Bonino's influential chapters on his FTL presentation is clear, and in fact, large sections are simply
translations of his paper from the earlier FTL evangelical gathering.[24] Unfortunately, very few outside of a small group of Latin American evangelicals
were ever aware of these encounters.

Tellingly, in that liberation theology republication, *Frontiers of Theology
in Latin America*, Míguez Bonino made no mention of the Protestant evangelical roots of the essay, though the editorial preface promised readers that
the essays were either original to the monograph or the original source would
be given.[25] His redaction of the text is perhaps the most interesting aspect of
his translation and adaptation. He also moved his interaction with Padilla
from the body of the text to the endnotes. The republication, however, does
contain a lengthy interaction with the German theologian Jürgen Moltmann.
Míguez Bonino also softened certain Christian emphases, as well, such as
his specific allusion to the Christian character of orthopraxis, removing

"particularly to Jesus Christ" for the wider publication. In *Doing Theology in a Revolutionary Situation*, an endnote referring to the edited conference volume is the only indication of its roots (though the conference itself is not mentioned). What explains this telling redaction?

The timing of the FTL and both monographs took place at a sensitive time in the construction of liberation theology and a broader ecumenical coalition. As ecumenical interactions surfaced, scrutiny of these relationships followed closely behind. In 1975, the year *Frontiers of Theology in Latin America* was published, Míguez Bonino was elected regional president of the WCC. In a 2013 interview, René Padilla recalled Míguez Bonino receiving more scrutiny for his interaction with evangelicals: "At this time, people knew he was ecumenical and part of the WCC. And when he became the president of the WCC.... He entered a very difficult situation because the word 'ecumenical' is a bad word—especially from the United States. So, there was a problem—but it wasn't just from the side of evangelicals (*evangélicos*) but also from the side of the ecumenicals."[26] The WCC and evangelical Protestants were sharply polarized on a wide variety of religious issues. Publicly associating, let alone sharing, theological materials would have certainly been controversial for Míguez Bonino's leadership tenure.

The previously hidden dialogue at FTL II reveals several key conclusions and also invites further analysis. Padilla by no means introduced the concept of the kingdom of God, nor should he be given credit for Míguez Bonino's writings. Yet, Padilla pushed Míguez Bonino on the eschatological character of the kingdom of God, along with the church's central role in mediating the kingdom. In doing so, he became a key conversation partner and the FTL a guardrail within which Míguez Bonino formulated his understanding. In turn, Míguez Bonino himself became a guardrail for liberation theology, pushing many to guard and deepen the Christian character of its praxis. In the end, the concept of the kingdom of God became perhaps the most important theological concept within theologies of liberation and indeed a key product of ecumenical theological exchange. The Latin American Theological Fraternity provided both the environment for this dialogue and an evangelical flavor that seasoned the concepts.[27]

Ultimately, Míguez Bonino was clearly concerned by the prospect of being publicly associated with evangelical Protestants, though privately he participated in robust theological discussions that sharpened both him and the embryonic Evangelical Left. Perhaps more important for understanding the development of *misión integral*, one is able to see that leaders on both sides of the theological divide, both conservative evangelicals and ecumenical Protestants, were wary of being publicly associated with René Padilla. Thus, the emerging Latin American Evangelical Left faced multifaceted exclusion. Seen in a different light, Míguez Bonino ultimately hid his participation with the FTL in order to deepen it. He avoided official membership in the FTL in order to continue participation in both Protestant ecumenical *and* evangelical circles. In fact, his name often appears on the Spanish rosters of participants at the FTL, though Míguez Bonino avoided placing his name on the published membership roll. While he did not want to publicly associate with evangelicals prior to the 1990s (when he became an official member of the FTL), he drew deeply from friendship, collaboration, and intellectual exchange. Costas, Padilla, and Escobar, on the other hand, publicly negotiated power in the public square within influential circles of North American Protestant evangelicalism, such as *Christianity Today* magazine. This hidden participation and collaboration, then, is also emboldening. How might we take this analysis further? Deeper interrogation of oral history and prevailing understandings of *organizational* boundaries sheds light on the multidirectional development of social Christianities.

Ecumenical Boundary Crossing and Hidden Participation

The history of polarization between Latin American ecumenical and evangelical Protestant organizations provides further insight here. For many Protestants, the Primera Conferencia Evangélica Latinoamericana (the First Latin American Evangelical Conference, CELA I) of 1949 was the first Latin American–led Christian conference without influence or impetus outside of Latin America.[28] (The use of the word *evangélica* here should be understood in its broader gloss of "Protestant" rather than evangelical in the theological sense.) The second CELA gathering in 1961 drew influential ecumenical Protestant leaders such as British theologian Lesslie Newbigin, Scottish ecumenist John Mackay, and Míguez Bonino. Yet, the background of CELA II was a gathering three weeks earlier in Huampaní, Peru, from which the WCC-sponsored ISAL arose (described in Chapter 2). This gathering gave momentum to an emerging radical strand of ecumenical theology and caught the attention of conservative evangelicals who shared much in common with more conservative members of CELA.

By 1969, when the third CELA gathering was being planned, many evangelical Protestants in North America were increasingly concerned with the direction of the movement. Thus, rather than an ecumenism that was often discussed, CELA represented one side of a growing organizational chasm between the more ecumenical and evangelical strands of Protestantism. Indeed, José Míguez Bonino wrote, "Existing Protestant organizations with wide participation . . . either broke up or had to take sides in this confrontation."[29] Samuel Escobar blamed the shallowness of evangelical Protestant thought for much of the division: "I believe that if the (evangélicos) sectors would have done battle long before in efforts toward unity and cooperation, if we had been more serious in relation to theology and the pastoral (aspect) and less dependent on simplistic formulas, if we had learned to dialogue instead of escaping, there would be another panorama of Latin American Protestantism today. But by 1969 it was already too late."[30] The "breach" between an ecumenical sector represented by WCC-affiliated agencies and a "conservative sector" represented by CLADE had already revealed that the "breach was almost insuperable" by the early 1970s.

While this division certainly was true in many historic organizations, it was not always true interpersonally or within the fledgling Latin American organizations that arose in the late 1960s and early 1970s. Historians have often taken the reality of organizational polarity and applied these data to individual leaders within the organizations.[31] Individual theologians are then presented in binary categories of liberal/conservative to reflect the organizations within which they moved. Scholarship on CLADE I and CELA III has often been forced into predetermined categories of liberal and conservative, as well. But this binary classification has obscured the reality of ecumenical friendships and interaction, as well as intellectual exchange.

Widespread evangelical dissatisfaction certainly did arise against CELA III, including a group who succeeded in postponing the congress itself.[32] As Raimundo Barreto explained, "Despite succeeding in postponing CELA III for four years, the evangelical massive 'invasion' of that conference did not take place. Those evangelicals who did not feel represented in the theology guiding CELA III opted for organizing their own evangelical congress."[33] This other congress was, of course, the controversial CLADE I, planned by BGEA out of North America. Despite the efforts of many Latin American pastors, alongside the BGEA and North American donors, Latin American Protestants crossed religious boundaries dividing liberal and conservative camps.

Samuel Escobar has been raised as an example of the conservative side of this binary division—especially due to his influential speech at CLADE I. Yet, Escobar himself was an official observer at CELA III, unbeknown to North American leaders and, indeed, current scholarship. René Padilla also attended (perhaps in a fuller capacity) at the invitation of Emilio Castro, later WCC general secretary.[34] In a 2013 interview, Padilla spoke of a robust friendship with Castro, recalling multiple personal meetings while Castro was president of the WCC (1985–1992).[35] He later accepted Castro's invitation in 1991 to the WCC Assembly in Canberra, Australia. Padilla even recalled Castro offering him the editorship of the *International Review of Mission*—in Padilla's words, "to take over" the ecumenical magazine. Padilla described the offer as "an important gesture."[36] Castro's inclusion of evangelical Protestants such as Padilla was consistent with Castro's contention elsewhere that "the ecumenical movement remains incomplete" without evangelicals.[37] René Padilla later suspected that Míguez Bonino had pushed for his inclusion at CELA III, the start of significant ecumenical and evangelical collaboration with him and others in the WCC.[38]

Orlando Costas's presence at CELA III, described earlier, was less surprising. Indeed, Míguez Bonino reflected on Costas's legacy in terms of boundary crossing: "Orlando was convinced that some of the lines of separation in theology and church life (conservatives/progressives, evangelicals/ecumenics, orthodox/liberals) are drawn wrongly."[39] He then expanded, "With profound knowledge ... Orlando made great—and many times successful—efforts to show the falsehood of such images ... the constant and dis-respectful way in which he crossed frontiers was a call to define ourselves without fear."[40] While Costas found his home in diverse locations, he preferred the self-designation "radical evangelical."[41] Part of Costas's most significant legacy was pushing his evangelical colleagues to expand their influence beyond the borders of evangelicalism. In doing so, his was often an outsider's voice. Perhaps most significant here was the friendship of René Padilla and José Míguez Bonino, due to their longtime residence in the city of Buenos Aires. Their friendship was especially marked by both longevity and depth: from 1967 onward, these two leaders, who represented diverse strands of Latin American Protestant Christianity, shared public theological dialogue, writing projects, phone calls, interviews, Argentine *parrillas* (traditional Argentine grills), books from their personal libraries, and extensive partnership through the Latin American Theological Fraternity and the Buenos Aires–based Kairos Community.

Figure 7. René Padilla at the Kairos Center for Christian Discipleship and Integral Mission, Buenos Aires, Argentina, September 2013. Photo by author.

Ecumenical and Evangelical

"For the moment Latin America says a 'GOODBYE.' With bereaved sadness we lose one of our illustrious sons and president of the Fraternity but at the same time with pride we offer him to Canada as the first missionary from the Third World to this far away land."[42] These words in Padilla's article in *Boletín Teológico* appeared alongside a farewell to Samuel Escobar, perhaps symbolic of Padilla's role in fulfilling his own call. After Samuel Escobar left Latin America to lead the Canadian IVCF in October 1971, one of René

Padilla's first actions as director of Ediciones Certeza was to convene the First Evangelical Consultation on Social Ethics from July 5 to 8, 1972, in Lima. Here in Lima, Padilla's plenary talk was a searing critique of "Iglesia y Sociedad en América Latina" (Church and Society in Latin America), the series of consultations that were connected to the World Council of Churches and operated under the leadership of Míguez Bonino.[43] These consultations had become increasingly radicalized in the late 1960s and into the early 1970s. Thus, while progressive evangelicals like Padilla cultivated friendships across religious boundaries, they sought to do so without compromising their convictions regarding Christian orthodoxy.

Padilla left no doubt regarding his view of the radical theology emanating from the World Council of Churches and ISAL: "The last few years have seen the emergence of a theology that *pretends* to provide an interpretation of the Christian faith pertinent to the Latin American situation: the theology of 'Iglesia y Sociedad en América Latina'" (italics mine).[44] In attacking ISAL, Padilla was not simply throwing stones from afar but was interacting with what he observed at CELA III and in friendship with Míguez Bonino. Padilla's paper expanded on a critique he wrote in July 1972 in the FTL journal *Boletín Teológico* and within the LAM journal *Pensamiento Cristiano* in September 1972. At the FTL gathering, Padilla honed in on ISAL's hermeneutic, saying, "The inevitable conclusion is that concentration on an ethical and political hermeneutic has resulted in a theology that does not do justice to the totality of the biblical witness."[45] Similarly, he rejected the use of *ideology* as its dominant hermeneutic: "In the end, ISAL's theological problem is finding a hermeneutic that justifies a line of political action which has been selected from an ideology in advance."[46] As an evangelical Protestant, Padilla wanted the Bible to provide both the theological framework and the marching orders for orthopraxis—letting interpretation be informed by the historical situation rather than vice versa. This contrasted heavily with liberation theology's priority of praxis, governed by Marxist social scientific analysis.

The robust dialogue here foreshadowed a public pattern of discussion between Padilla and Míguez Bonino that flourished in the 1970s. Míguez Bonino himself had already critiqued aspects of ISAL in 1969, saying, "Where is the church?" in the thought of ISAL.[47] He also defended the use of Marxism as a necessary tool to evaluate orthopraxis.[48] Míguez Bonino ultimately looked back with measured disapproval on what he called "utopian Protestantism."[49] Indeed, under the section heading "What to Do with This

Failure?" Míguez Bonino spoke candidly about the need for "reinterpret[ing] and re-liv[ing]" this legacy. What is clear, as well, is that Míguez Bonino listened to and took seriously the concerns of FTL leaders.

In his most famous work, *Doing Theology in a Revolutionary Situation*, published a few years after this FTL gathering, he quoted Pedro Arana's paper from the Padilla-led ATE. Arana had written, "In the ideology of ISAL, God is translated by revolution; the people of God by the revolutionary hosts, and the Word of God by the revolutionary writings. Nobody will fail to see that all of this is Marxist humanism."[50] While Míguez Bonino ultimately disagreed with Arana, he also wrote, "We shall see further on that the criticism is not without significance. In fact, it seems to me that our Latin American theology of liberation has not yet become sufficiently aware of the weight of this risk and consequently has not yet developed adequate safeguards against it."[51]

Padilla's own theological method also moved closer to theologies of liberation in order to critique them. For example, Padilla wrote, "The only theology that the Bible knows is a 'functional' theology, that is to say, theology in dialogue with concrete reality, theology in service to praxis."[52] Padilla was willing to utilize the language of liberation theologians even within his own critique of insider groups. Padilla also employed the language of "status quo" in order to critique both received theologies from the West, as well as Western critiques of liberation theology itself.[53] Indeed, in his article for *Christianity Today*—the magazine's first article to directly address liberation theology—Padilla warned American evangelicals to address their own ideological biases before critiquing liberation theology.[54] Padilla wrote in 1973,

> The need for a liberation of theology is then as real in our case as in the case of the theology of liberation. In fact, aside from the grace of God all our theological reflection is always apt to become a subtle façade for our own ideas and prejudices; theology is turned into a rationalization by means of which we avoid obedience to God in the historical situation. The theology of liberation should be a warning to us against the temptation to adapt the Gospel to our way of life instead of adapting our way of life to the Gospel.[55]

What was the answer, then? Though Padilla ultimately rejected ISAL and its method, he was sharpened by its stinging critique of a socially vacuous evangelical status quo. In his 1972 FTL article, after sidelining ISAL, Padilla concluded, "Then, where? Where is the theology that responds to the questions that the Latin American situation presents the Christian faith? Will we have to settle for repeating abstract doctrinal formulas, manufactured in other situations?" This hypothetical question was met with a call for interrogating the gospel message itself: "The work that this historic moment imposes upon us is to reflect ourselves, Christians in Latin America, and discover *the dimensions of the Gospel* in our own situation. Until we do this, the Gospel will not be something entirely ours nor exercise the critical function that it should exercise in relation to the totality of life" (underline original, italics mine).[56] Padilla demanded a "gospel for the poor" of Latin America, contextualized to their revolutionary situation.

The answer, then, was a gospel not just for the American middle class, imported into Latin America. Instead, wider dimensions were needed, a gospel for the poor, the oppressed, and those touched by the Latin American reality. Padilla, Escobar, and the FTL did not critique ISAL from an ivory tower or posit in its place a fully formed solution. Instead, they acknowledged the void from which ISAL arose and called evangelical Protestants to fill in what was lacking. Ultimately for the emerging Evangelical Left, this void existed in the gospel message itself.

In the course of their respective lives, Míguez Bonino increasingly identified himself as evangelical, while Padilla increasingly identified himself as ecumenical. During the 1970s, when Padilla was certainly influencing Míguez Bonino with regard to evangelical Protestant themes, Míguez Bonino was writing widely on ecumenism.[57] Padilla recalled Míguez Bonino becoming disillusioned with what eventually became of ISAL.[58] In the late 1990s and early 2000s, Míguez Bonino began to publicly praise his progressive evangelical colleagues at conferences and in print while increasingly identifying with them.

"I have been variously tagged a conservative, a revolutionary, a Barthian, a liberal, a catholic, a 'moderate,' and a liberationist. Probably there is truth in all of these. It is not for me to decide." In his 1993 Carnahan Lectures at the ecumenical seminary ISEDET, Míguez Bonino was candid in his self-reflection on labels and theological camps. This rumination led to a telling identification from the Argentine thinker: "When I do attempt to define myself in my innermost being, what 'comes from within' is that I am *evangélico*. It seems that it is in this soil that my religious life and ecclesiastical activity have been rooted throughout more than seventy years." Míguez Bonino reflected further, "From this origin have sprung the joys and the conflicts, the satisfactions and the frustrations which over time have been knit together. There my deepest friendships, and also the most painful separations, were engendered; there lie the memories of dead ones I loved and the hope of generations I have seen born and grow." Acknowledging the complexity of his own journey as a churchman and liberation theologian, he concluded, "Whether in truth I am *evangélico* is not for me to say. Nor am I concerned that others affirm or deny it. What I am truly belongs to the grace of God. At least an *evangélico* is what I have always wanted to be."[59]

Míguez Bonino located his "deepest friendships" within the *evangélico* community—a community engendered by complex negotiations of belonging. Given Míguez Bonino's diverse ecumenical participation, which community was he actually identifying with? He was clearly describing more than the WCC and ISAL communities, for his membership in those communities was uncontested. His chapter on the "evangelical face" of Latin American Protestantism clarifies his self-identification.

For Míguez Bonino, the solution to social quietism lay not within the liberal organizations within which he associated for over half a century but within what he identified as the "evangelical renewal." Thus, he concluded his chapter, "The Evangelical Face of Latin American Protestantism," by highlighting the Latin American Theological Fraternity: "The *evangelical renewal* . . . in Latin America, has been represented mainly by the Latin American Theological Fraternity, which we associate with the names of René Padilla, Peter Savage, Samuel Escobar, Pedro Arana, Emilio A. Nuñez, and many others, and *which has exerted an ever growing weight in the evangelical world since its origins in 1970*" (italics mine).[60] The FTL was "the way out" of social quietism and dispensational trends in Latin American evangelical history. This was a telling recognition from the "Dean of Latin American Protestants."

Míguez Bonino then turned to highlight what he called the "most significant features" of the FTL. These included a retrieval and recovery of "an evangelical tradition, linked especially to the Anabaptist movement . . . and to the evangelical awakening of the eighteenth century in England and the United States."[61] He then concluded, "The work of Escobar, Arana, and Padilla shows us that this is not a mere vindication of a tradition but rather a search for elements that can fertilize theological reflection and evangelical practice for today's Latin America."[62] The second aspect Míguez Bonino highlighted was its emphasis on "the *centrality of Scripture*," quoting the FTL Cochabamba Declaration at length. Míguez Bonino then turned to Padilla specifically, highlighting his Lausanne 1974 paper. Here, he noted Padilla's rejection of "'acculturation' to the cultural norms of the missionary sending nations" and the "American way of life."[63]

Progressive evangelicals like Samuel Escobar, in turn, gave credit to Orlando Costas and Míguez Bonino for pushing the boundaries of ecumenism within the Latin American Theological Fraternity.[64] Similarly, Costas himself gave the credit to Míguez Bonino for influencing him in this realm. Míguez Bonino's choice of the term "evangelical" as a self-descriptor may have also been influenced by Costas. Costas had critiqued an earlier article by Míguez Bonino, which sought to categorize Latin American religious subgroups.[65] Here, Míguez Bonino identified the "charismatic," "revolutionary," and "conservative" families. Costas wrote that Míguez Bonino had ignored the "Evangelistic or Kerygmatic family," which he associated with proclamation.[66] Costas also posited a fourth group, in which he placed the FTL—the *Didaché*, the Greek word meaning teaching.[67] Thus, in a similar way to Padilla's dialogue with Míguez Bonino on the kingdom of God, Costas pushed him to incorporate in his categorization a theological "family" that, in Costas's opinion, took the church and the Bible seriously. At every turn, the FTL encouraged Míguez Bonino in this direction—a label with which Míguez Bonino ultimately self-identified. This was even seen during crucial early years. For example, Míguez Bonino was invited by John Stott to give the London Lectures in Contemporary Christianity in 1974, presumably on Padilla's recommendation. He gave a provocative lecture titled "Christians and Marxists: The Mutual Challenge to Revolution."[68]

As Míguez Bonino increasingly identified with evangelical sectors of Latin America, Padilla (and ultimately the FTL with him) increasingly identified as ecumenical. From the mid-1980s, Padilla began to see ecumenicity as an essential component of *misión integral*.[69] In a recent interview, René Padilla seamlessly moved from discussing his friendship with Míguez Bonino to Padilla's own appropriation of the terminological pairing of "evangelical and ecumenical."[70] For Padilla, the two realities—a relationship and a self-identification—went hand-in-hand. Reflecting upon Míguez Bonino's influence in 2013, Padilla said, "For me, he helped me a great deal. I appreciated his position a lot in reference to the unity of the church. Because he was very convinced that unity had to remain in concrete situations. More than talking about unity was to know people of different churches and to do things together to work together."[71] Similarly, Padilla spoke of the necessary connection between integral mission and ecumenicity: "If we talk about integral mission, we have to talk about this theme—the mission of the church that isn't a separatist mission but a mission of reconciliation. Reconciliation with the other as a brother in Christ if he says he confesses Christ as Lord." With these words, Padilla revealed both the maturation of his own methodology and a long-held conviction regarding evangelical boundaries. His friendship with Míguez Bonino represented this contested journey and the wider FTL embrace of a spectrum of Latin American Protestantism.

Contested Friendship from Beginning to End

"The largest and most representative gathering of Latin American Protestants in our century has taken place." With these sweeping words, Samuel Escobar began his analysis of the third CLADE gathering in Quito, Ecuador, from August 24 to September 4, 1992. René Padilla became general secretary of the FTL from 1984 to 1992, culminating in the organization of the third CLADE conference in Quito. Padilla had generally avoided official administrative responsibility in the FTL due to his leadership of the IFES movement in Latin America for over a decade. Thus, his general secretary role in FTL was almost certainly due to his 1981 retirement from the IFES. Padilla's stint as general secretary concluded with CLADE III, which, he declared, "will undoubtedly mark a milestone in the history of the Church in Latin America."[72] Ecumenicity had become a central tenet of the Latin American Evangelical Left, but not everyone appreciated the growing ecumenism among a politically conscious, evangelically minded coalition. The fraught history of the WCC and global evangelicalism tinted the lens through which ecumenical leaders viewed these emerging ecumenical gestures. Thus, Escobar, Padilla, and Míguez Bonino would face increasing pressure to disassociate themselves from one another even into the 1990s.

CLADE III included 1,080 delegates. Its cohort included prominent theologians such as Padilla, Escobar, and Míguez Bonino, as well as younger leaders, including Mexican theologian Carmen Perez de Camargo, Nazarene theologian and economist Wilfredo Canales, and a handful of other young

Latin American thinkers—the fruit of intentional mentorship by FTL found-ers. The title of CLADE III was "The Whole Gospel for the Whole World from Latin America," signaling a maturation of social theology that had been gestating for at least the previous two decades. This emphasis on expanding the gospel itself was a fitting bookend to the first CLADE I. For Padilla, CLADE III was a dual homecoming: a physical homecoming to his home-town of Quito, as well as an intellectual return to the conference that birthed the Latin American Theological Fraternity. CLADE III also represented the rise of Majority World evangelical leadership, as both Anglican Bishop Da-vid Gitari from Kenya and Church of South India Canon Dr. Vinay Samuel attended. According to Escobar, they attended "representing African and Asian Evangelicals who have been partners of the Latin Americans in the re-discovery of the wholeness of the Gospel, the search for new missiological paradigms, and the effort to express the strong evangelistic dynamism of their churches in a way that will recover the transformational nature of the Gospel."[73]

As had been his characteristic practice throughout the previous two de-cades, René Padilla (as executive secretary of the FTL) invited Míguez Bonino to play a prominent role in the third CLADE conference of 1992. Míguez Bonino reflected on the gathering in his book *Faces of Latin American Prot-estantism*: "[CLADE III] went beyond the limits of the Latin American Theological Fraternity to become a truly 'Latin American Protestant Con-gress,' as much due to the breadth of its representation as to the wealth of materials and the freedom of debate. We were there present at a truly 'ecu-menical event' . . . of Latin American Protestantism."[74] The contrast be-tween BGEA-led CLADE I and the FTL-led CLADE III was striking. Padilla also asked Míguez Bonino to write a reflection on CLADE III for the FTL journal *Boletín Teológico*.[75] The result was an article titled "CLADE III as Ecumenical Meeting." After acknowledging Padilla's role in the article, Míguez Bonino declared, "CLADE III would probably be marked in the history of Latin American *evangélico* churches as the start of a new era."[76]

Perhaps most important, Míguez Bonino highlighted the inclusion of "the whole gospel"—though some disagreed with the concept during a robust debate at the congress. He wrote, "At the same time the experiences that are had at the local level will demonstrate that practice<<integrity (*integridad*) of the gospel>>—the whole gospel—that was so central in the work of CLADE III."[77] Escobar, in his report, also highlighted the "rediscovery of the wholeness of the Gospel."[78] In a 2013 interview, Padilla also recalled Míguez Bonino speaking at CLADE III of the faithfulness of FTL to the church and lamenting that the WCC's ISAL had been part of division.[79] In this way, the legacy of *misión integral* was clearly shown in CLADE III in terms of ecumenism and theological methodology. Much more could be said regarding surprising ecumenicity at the origins of Latin American social Christianity. For example, one could certainly expand on these partnerships, especially within the Buenos Aires–based Kairos Community. When Padilla invited missionaries to Buenos Aires, they often stayed in Míguez Bonino's home.[80]

Ultimately, Míguez Bonino continued to face pressure to dissociate himself from the FTL-sponsored CLADE. In a 2013 interview, Samuel Escobar recalled that Míguez Bonino faced criticism from the "ecumenical world" for being part of the FTL. Similarly, in 2013, Padilla retold a story that Míguez Bonino had narrated regarding his flight to the fourth CLADE gathering in Quito, Ecuador. Prior to boarding his flight to Quito, another Methodist leader saw Míguez Bonino in the airport and asked where he was flying. He replied that he was flying to Quito. "What are you going to?" the ecumenical leader asked. Míguez Bonino responded, "I'm going to attend CLADE, the congress on Latin American evangelization." To this the Methodist leader replied incredulously, "Why are you going *there*?" (The reader should note this is Padilla's recollection of a story told by Míguez Bonino.) Padilla commented, "José told me this because there was always prejudice like this." Padilla leaned back and said with a laugh, "We were more ecumenical than the ecumenicals."[81]

At the height of the global Cold War, conservative religious leaders—both Catholic and Protestant evangelical—were gripped by widespread fears regarding the Marxist penetration of Latin America and the spread of communist ideologies. In response, many conservative leaders heightened their theological boundary making, in an attempt to ward off "liberal theology" and reject compromised leaders from their organizations. But lines of liberal versus conservative blurred when applied to Latin America. They were often true organizationally, but when applied interpersonally and intellectually, they do not account for intellectual exchange and cross-pollination that took place within a hotly contested religious marketplace.

Latin American theologians crossed boundaries—not only the fiercely policed religious boundaries of American evangelical leaders but also the boundaries within which scholars have prepackaged Latin American social Christianities. In other words, the boundaries that conservative evangelicals and Catholic liberation theologians sought to police have been aided by the ways in which scholars have narrated their history. Theologians from the same generation shared political and intellectual resources—a reality that our narrative here should reflect. Perhaps more provocatively, in the case of José Míguez Bonino, the Evangelical Left shared raw materials with liberation theology, helping to carve the contours of one of their most prominent theological motifs—the kingdom of God.

The motif of the kingdom of God represented the diverse tapestry of postwar evangelicalism. Indeed, the apprehension of the kingdom of God as a theological category reveals the hybrid nature of the intellectual journey for Latin American evangelicals and was the primary means by which they challenged accepted evangelical norms. Contrary to widely held assumptions, the FTL did not borrow this emphasis from the ecumenical ISAL gatherings or Catholic liberation theologians. On the contrary, early FTL gatherings sharpened key liberation theologian José Míguez Bonino's understanding of this theological motif and the trajectory of his later influence. Equipped with the kingdom of God, progressive evangelicals in Latin America wielded this theological motif to widen the Christian gospel to include social elements and, in turn, challenge the political loyalties of evangelicals around the world.

This brief historical survey and interpersonal case study only begins to describe the extensive collaboration between key evangelical and ecumenical leaders. This chapter does not pretend to be exhaustive, but instead various preliminary conclusions may be further posited. First, as Methodist liberation theologian Míguez Bonino became increasingly disillusioned with ISAL and its radicalization, he turned publicly toward private relationships that had been maturing for nearly two decades. As a self-described *evangélico*, Míguez Bonino was committed to the local church *and* its vibrancy in service to the poor. Second, historians should avoid the interpretive jump from organizations to individual leaders, especially with regard to theological polarization. This proximity between Míguez Bonino and the emerging Latin American Evangelical Left makes sense when considering Costas's consistent boundary crossing and Padilla and Escobar's roots in the global evangelical student movement. Parachurch organizations such as the evangelical InterVarsity and IFES and ecumenical SCMs displayed the sometimes discordant proximity between progressive and conservative leaders. Within Latin America, this proximity was even closer.[82] Thus, once again, the evangelical and ecumenical student movements provided both mentorship and tools that aided the development of an evangelical brand of social Christianity.

Ultimately, narratives of polarization between evangelical and ecumenical Protestantism in the postwar period should be problematized. The relationship and collaboration between these leaders demonstrates robust theological exchange and negotiation, despite organizational polarization. The proximity of José Míguez Bonino in particular shaped the FTL's understanding of ecumenicity and its relationship to *misión integral*. It appears, then, that the Latin American Evangelical Left and Míguez Bonino—seen internationally as symbolic representatives of ecumenical and evangelical Protestant traditions—formed their ideas *en el camino*—a path they often shared.[83]

CHAPTER 7

The Reshaping of Global Evangelicalism

"Do something now!" Pastor Louie Giglio's voice echoed throughout the Georgia Dome in Atlanta in 2011. The lobby was dotted with interactive stations highlighting various causes—eye surgeries in Uganda, combatting sex slavery in the Philippines, and building water wells in India. The present researcher observed college students struggling to carry 40-pound water jugs around a replica mud hut designed to mirror the walk that many Indian women and children make daily.[1] Giglio challenged the students throughout the conference to "glorify God" not only by "reaching their campus for Christ" but by "doing something now" through social activism. At the Passion Conferences, the student response has been enormous. In 2013 alone, a year dedicated to anti–sex trafficking, organizers reported donations of over $3.1 million.[2] The year prior, U.S. President Barack Obama invited Giglio to give the invocation prayer at the 2012 presidential inauguration—public recognition of Giglio's influence among young evangelicals.[3] By 2014, the Passion Conference consisted of 60,000 evangelical college students from 56 countries and 2,300 universities.[4]

One might expect this brief case study from Social Gospelers, Catholic social theologians, or mainline Protestant activists—groups long known for various brands of social Christianity. Instead, the Passion Conference is a flagship gathering of conservative evangelicals led by speakers such as Baptist pastor John Piper and Christian writer and speaker Francis Chan. At this influential evangelical gathering, social action was not justified by its evangelistic fruit but rather as a "mission to answer God's call" to justice.[5] These themes of justice were often mediated to conservative evangelicals through mission and relief organizations such as Compassion International and World Vision. In the postwar period, these organizations became a constant presence in conservative evangelical churches, magazines, radio stations, music festivals, and the homes of everyday evangelicals through pictures of "sponsored children" stuck to refrigerator doors. They no longer justified their presence exclusively through the language of evangelism or saving souls. Indeed, they shifted decisively in terms of what they were saving the world *from*—souls *and* bodies saved from eternal damnation *and* temporal suffering. In one of the clearest examples, the president of World Vision, Richard Stearns, later titled his book *The Hole in the Gospel*, rejecting a private, individual salvation in favor of the gospel of the kingdom.[6] Elsewhere, Piper spoke of being "gripped" by the Lausanne Congress as "globally seismic in the transformation of mission."[7]

Today, "integral mission" is utilized as the official phrase and model by nearly 600 mission and relief agencies—including World Vision, Compassion International, Food for the Hungry, International Justice Mission, and World Relief. An integral mission—a synthesis of pursuing justice and offering salvation—is widely assumed within diverse communities of global evangelicalism. Even while many American evangelicals reject the political and structural solutions of our protagonists, the broader appropriation of integral mission themes represents a global reflex—the rise of Christian forms from the Global South. Seen in a different light, *misión integral* also became a victim of its own success.

The political edge often rounded as integral mission themes became increasingly appropriated in the Global North. According to influential Indian evangelical leader Vinay Samuel, this depoliticization was a purposeful project of Christian nongovernmental organizations (NGOs) and their fundraising campaigns in the United States.[8] In particular, anti-American politics did not *sell* to conservative American evangelical donors—the main fundraising bloc of these NGOs. Instead, they would rather pitch the concept of justice for an individual "sponsored" child—especially outside the borders of the United States. American evangelicals would rather donate to a world-saving project than a lecture on the "sins" of U.S. missionaries and foreign policy.

Global Christian mission and relief organizations followed developments in Latin American evangelical social Christianity with marked anticipation. In 1971, *World Vision* magazine, for example, highlighted the publishing prowess of "the liberal element of the Protestant church" and featured the inaugural FTL gathering and its "Cochabamba Declaration." The 1971 feature continued, "Though small, [the liberal element of the Protestant church] has made a powerful impact on theology and social ethics, outpublishing the evangelicals on these topics fifty pages to one." The *World Vision* editorial then concluded optimistically, "It is hoped that the Evangelical [Cochabamba]

Declaration and the publication of the position papers, will mark the beginning of a *new era* of theological discussion calling the church back to the Bible and the message of true evangelism" (italics mine).[9] This new era of global evangelicalism did, indeed, arrive—represented by a reshaping of leadership and Christian mission. As a result, it signaled a wider evangelical embrace of Christian relief organizations as members of the family rather than former foes of the Social Gospel. In this sense, Latin Americans widened the boundaries of evangelicalism.

The Lausanne Movement, driven by vitality from the emerging Latin American Evangelical Left, played one part in a broader reshaping of Protestant evangelical mission and relief. It also played a crucial role in widening the family of evangelicalism to include (or reintroduce) social Christianity. As prominent evangelical leaders embraced a new approach to social action, fear of the Social Gospel, modernism, and the shifting mission of the World Council of Churches gradually subsided. For Christian mission and relief organizations, such as World Vision and Compassion International, this meant they "could now appeal to the evangelical constituency as family, without the fear of either being rebuked for preaching the 'social gospel' or being charged of compromising on evangelism."[10] This family reunification took place through the mediation of global evangelical networks, organizations, and institutions that deserve fuller attention here.

The reshaping of global evangelicalism can be clearly seen especially in the trajectory of the Lausanne Movement itself—from 1974 to 2010. Indeed, the global evangelical table is set in a markedly different configuration today compared to the years prior to the Lausanne Congress of 1974. Leaders from the Global South are no longer "guests" welcomed in an American or British evangelical home. Instead, they often play the role of "host," setting the table and determining the proverbial menu. In turn, the presence of these increasingly diverse leaders challenged longstanding theological and political assumptions in evangelicalism within power centers in the United States and Britain.

The story of the diffusion of Latin American evangelical social Christianity is also one of irony. *Misión integral* spread primarily through relationships and networks that orbited the Global North. Latin Americans renegotiated the theological and political loyalties of global evangelicals, influencing key evangelical leaders and organizations in the process. Yet, appropriation by northern leaders also obscured Latin American influence and the contributions of the Latin American Evangelical Left. The exportation of Latin American intellectual goods was often accompanied by exporting credit to conservative evangelical powerbrokers such as the British Anglican statesman John Stott. Ultimately, the prevailing story of the Evangelical Left has largely focused on political and theological defeat at the hands of the American Religious Right. When seen through the lens of Latin Americans, however, a revised picture emerges. Here, the scope of our lens should match the size of their influence.

While the political edge rounded in evangelical NGOs, it sharpened among a significant minority of American evangelicals—the Evangelical Left. Key American leaders processed Latin American theological and political goods that were exported from Lausanne and the FTL. They found not only critical continuity with their own ideas but also a *theological* framework for their political engagement. By appropriating the language of Latin Americans, they continued to challenge broad evangelical political sympathies for conservativism and the Republican Party.

Converting Conservative Powerbrokers

John Stott's influence upon postwar global evangelicalism was probably unrivaled. "If evangelicals could elect a pope, [John] Stott is the person they would likely choose," one *New York Times* columnist argued in 2004.[11] Even Billy and Ruth Graham could share, "John Stott is the most respected evangelical clergyman in the world."[12] According to Stott's publisher, InterVarsity Press, Stott's books have sold millions of copies around the world and have been translated into dozens of languages. Stott's 2011 obituary in the *New York Times* called him "one of the world's most influential figures in the spread of evangelical Christianity over the past half-century."[13] This was perhaps primarily tied to his career-long connection and attention to college students on five continents.[14] As evangelicalism became increasingly diverse, Stott's global vision and friendships placed him at the center of evangelical negotiation over social Christianity, especially among an emerging younger generation. Stott was perhaps uniquely positioned to draw upon his personal repository of global friendships and theologies as he helped guide a worldwide coalition. His biographer put it succinctly: "Stott's *ambition* was global" (italics mine).[15] Stott's sensitivity to national leadership and local theological construction also changed his own thinking in untold ways—especially on social Christianity.

Figure 8. John Stott in his personal library in the early 2000s.
Photo courtesy of Langham Partnership–USA.

Stott's public conversion to social Christianity in the 1970s was a crucial moment of legitimacy for *misión integral*, as it signaled to a broad constituency—including large swaths of conservative evangelicalism—that social Christianity was not the boogeyman of the past. Stott's public reversal also raises crucial questions in this story. In the period of less than a decade, Stott widened his understanding of the mission of the church to include social dimensions. Careful attention to Stott's personal papers from Lambeth Palace in London, including his travel diaries, reveals the importance of his relationships with and attention to leaders from the Global South.

John Stott and René Padilla first met in July 1959 at Tyndale House in Cambridge.[16] Padilla, who was finishing his final year at Wheaton College, was in Europe to attend the Paris IFES general committee along with Escobar, Stacey Woods, and Wayne Bragg, who was an IFES staff worker in Puerto Rico.[17] Padilla met Stott again four years later in London, as Padilla began his PhD work at Manchester University. Padilla remembered fondly, "He called me by name. I was astounded. He was one of the best people with names."[18] This anecdote reflects on one of Stott's most enduring legacies: his interest in Majority World leaders. Indeed, Escobar shared a strikingly similar story of Stott recalling his name. His travel diary reveals that Stott kept detailed notes on individuals he met, including names of spouses and ages of children. Stott and Padilla remained close throughout the next three decades, including extensive travel and family vacations together. Their last meeting took place in 2008 at Stott's retirement home at St. Barnabas College in Lingfield, Surrey.[19] Padilla dedicated his own book, *Mission Between the Times*, to Stott in the front matter (along with Padilla's wife Catharine), and Stott's Langham Monographs republished the 2010 version. Stott's public conversion to *misión integral* began not in Latin America, however, but at the World Congress on Evangelism in Berlin 1966. There, he presented an unambiguous rejection of its core tenets.

"The commission of the Church, therefore, is not to reform society, but to preach the Gospel . . . the primary task of the members of Christ's Church is to be Gospel heralds, not social reformers."[20] John Stott concluded his address at the World Congress on Evangelism in Berlin 1966 with emphatic words on the primacy of evangelism in Christian mission.[21] As if to not be misunderstood, Stott repeated, "Again, the commission of the Church is not to heal the sick, but to preach the Gospel."[22] John Stott had set out to "re-examine our marching orders" but concluded the orders remained the same.[23] For evangelicals like Stott, the church's mission was unambiguous—evangelism was primary, and social reform, at best, was the work of converted individuals in response to this verbal message. At worst, it was a distraction from the primary task of evangelism.

In January 1974—six months prior to the Lausanne Congress—Stott and Padilla traveled together throughout Latin America, preaching and lecturing under the stated title "Towards Holistic Christianity." Alongside Padilla, Stott visited "hardline communist" political prisoners in southern Chile who had been "interrogated under torture" by the military regime.[24] During this trip, Stott scribbled in his diary, "[Padilla's] stature impresses me increasingly." A week after this entry, Stott preached on "the revolution of Jesus, changing persons as well as structures" in another southern Chilean prison. Afterward, "a mass of [imprisoned] students thronged" to speak with Stott and Padilla.[25] As a result of the experience, Stott increasingly pondered the implications of oppression and poverty for Christian mission. In Padilla's words, he "began to think that word and action are inseparable."[26]

In the aftermath of the Lausanne Congress, Stott announced a sharp reversal. In 1975, Stott published *Christian Mission in the Modern World*, publicly revealing his change of mind on the place of social action in Christian mission.[27] He admitted he would "express himself differently"—the Great Commission *did* include social responsibility.[28] "I now see more clearly that not only the consequences of the commission but the actual commission itself must be understood to include social as well as evangelistic responsibility, unless we are to be guilty of distorting the words of Jesus."[29] As the Protestant evangelical world gradually shifted toward more holistic emphases, Stott's name continued to emblazon the front pages—including the edited documents of the International Consultation on the Relationship Between Evangelism and Social Responsibility, held at Grand Rapids, Michigan, June 19–25, 1982.[30]

Because of his influence on editing the documents, Stott has been widely credited with communicating this through a famous metaphor—social action and evangelism working in tandem like two wings of a bird. This metaphor first appeared in English through the International Consultation on the Relationship Between Evangelism and Social Responsibility held in 1982 in Grand Rapids. This document declared, "[Social action and evangelism] are like the two blades of a pair of scissors or the two wings of a bird . . . kerygma (proclamation) and diakonia (service) went hand in hand [in Jesus' ministry]."[31] Careful attention to Spanish publications from this crucial decade, however, reveals that this groundbreaking declaration was influenced significantly by René Padilla. Indeed, the language and metaphors here exactly reflected his wording in his 1970 article, "Teología Latinoamericana: ¿Izquierdista o Evangélica?"[32] The Spanish article reveals Padilla not only used this metaphor in 1970 but also the Greek words *kerygma* and *diakonia* in his explanation, leaving little doubt of the origins of Stott's idea.

It is not surprising, then, that in a 2013 interview, Padilla recalled his own influence on Stott's shift toward holistic themes.[33] Samuel Escobar later expanded at the 2010 Lausanne Congress in Cape Town:

In 1974, in January, John Stott traveled all over Latin America. . . . In his presentations in several Latin American countries, organized by the Latin American Theological Fraternity, John Stott and Latin Americans discussed some of the issues that later on were going to come in the covenant. *John said that this trip to Latin America had helped him to change some of his views in light of the way in which the church was reading the Scripture in Latin America.* (italics mine)[34]

Rather than simply "Latin Americans," the influence from the South can be further specified. Escobar was living in Canada during Stott's lectures in the early 1970s and did not travel with Stott or attend any of Stott's lectures. Stott's itinerary also reveals that Padilla rarely left his side during their lectures throughout Latin America—from Mexico City, to Lima, to Santiago and southern Chile, and Buenos Aires.[35] Indeed, Padilla was Stott's translator for every lecture and often gave his own lectures alongside him during their month together. They mostly stayed in the same hotel room, with rare exceptions. At Lausanne, Escobar would undoubtedly push Stott behind-the-scenes during the drafting of the Lausanne Covenant. Escobar later recalled, "We spent long hours discussing diverse and sometimes conflicting positions."[36] Escobar also developed a deep personal friendship with Stott mostly after the key events of the Lausanne Congress.[37]

Stott's full embrace of holistic mission from 1974 to 1975 should be seen in light of movements within evangelical Anglicanism and the wider evangelical world at Lausanne. However, it is plausible to suggest that the primary influence was his friendship with leaders from the Third World. During the crucial years leading up to Stott's public "conversion," influence from Latin America was primarily from René Padilla himself rather than simply emanating from Latin America in general. To be sure, Stott's shift on Christian mission was influenced by events and ideas as diverse as his global networks— including the National Evangelical Anglican Congress at Keele in 1967, which he chaired.[38] Padilla would also benefit from Keele years later. The Christian relief organization TEAR Fund was founded in 1968 out of momentum from Keele, and Padilla would later become the international president of TEAR Fund UK and Ireland.[39]

As Stott shifted to holistic themes, then, he pulled many global evangelicals with him. Influence within these relationships was multidirectional— Stott on emerging evangelical leaders and the latter on Stott. If Stott was key in the distribution of evangelical social Christianity, Padilla, Escobar,

Costas, Arana, and the FTL were key in what language was used in spreading the message. We return to this key relationship as we explore the role of the Lausanne Movement in spreading Latin American social Christianity. Integral mission latched onto a wagon that was already moving in the United States—that of the American Evangelical Left. The legacies of Padilla and Escobar also diverge at that point, as well. While Padilla turned inward to Latin America, Escobar and Costas sought wider influence in Canada and the United States, eventually landing at key educational institutions of the Evangelical Left in the Global North.

Orlando Costas, Samuel Escobar, and the American Evangelical Left

On Thanksgiving weekend in 1973, an emerging coalition of progressive evangelicals gathered in the basement of the YMCA in downtown Chicago. The delegates of the "Thanksgiving Workshop of Evangelical Social Concern" included Anabaptist Ron Sider (who took a leading and organizing role), theologian Carl F. H. Henry, Sojourners president Jim Wallis, Fuller Theological Seminary professor Richard Mouw, and Samuel Escobar. Together, they produced the influential 1973 Chicago Declaration, which called for a resurgence of social justice among evangelicals. They also caught the eye of the *Washington Post*, which highlighted their primary goal: to "launch a religious movement that could shake the political and religious life in America."[40] Much of the narrative surrounding this emerging Evangelical Left has focused on political defeat at the hands of the Moral Majority and Religious Right. But a global lens refocuses this story, uncovering victories and defeat, negotiation and resistance for social Christianity in particular. The gathering deepened channels for the flow of social Christian ideas through its global friendships and networks. The Latin American Evangelical Left (and the FTL) was well positioned here: Samuel Escobar attended, as did John Howard Yoder, who had just returned from his sabbatical in Buenos Aires. Once again, prior to the Lausanne Congress, transnational and multidirectional conversation began to shift evangelicalism in untold ways.

The year of the Thanksgiving Workshop, Escobar was the general director of the InterVarsity Christian Fellowship in Canada (1972–1975). His move northward—opposed by Padilla—placed him squarely within these strategic conversations. The year prior, Escobar had met Ron Sider on the campus of

Eastern Baptist Theological Seminary—a meeting that undoubtedly aided his inclusion.[41] Escobar recalled, "This encounter [with Sider] marked the beginning of a long friendship in a common pilgrimage."[42] Escobar and Sider later became close faculty colleagues at EBTS, including a study tour to Peru together in 1999.[43] This location and friendship would have manifest implications for the widening of evangelical discourse on social Christianity. More specifically, Escobar's move placed Sider in conversation with the emerging Latin American Evangelical Left and Escobar in deeper conversation with the social Christianity of the Anabaptist-Mennonite community in particular.

In Chapter 5, we noted the tremendous influence of Anabaptist-Brethren missionaries in Latin America. In our story, American Mennonite Anabaptists played a crucial role in developing and spreading social Christianity in global evangelical circles.[44] Indeed, "the evangelical left [in the United States] in fact featured a disproportionate number of Anabaptists," pushing evangelicalism toward "prophetic social engagement."[45] This was a broad coalition of Anabaptist leaders, including Ron Sider, Art Gish (Church of the Brethren), Dale Brown (former moderator of the Church of the Brethren), Myron Augsburger (president of Eastern Mennonite College), and John Howard Yoder, who became increasingly prominent in the evangelical community in the 1960s and 1970s. Their tradition had long emphasized the ethical dimensions of Christian discipleship. Influential Mennonite presses such as Herald Press and Reformed presses such as Eerdmans gave these ideas increasing visibility.[46] Sider himself was also paying careful attention to Latin American Christianity, calling liberation theology in 1980 "probably the most significant theological development in recent years."[47]

Sider's article also showed surprising similarity to Padilla's double-sided critique of Latin American liberation theology and the ideological captivity of conservative evangelicals. Padilla and Sider both concluded with a call for an *evangelical* theology of liberation—though Padilla did so seven years prior.[48] Sider also rejected the dichotomy between social action and evangelism, in critical continuity with the Latin American Evangelical Left. In 1979, Sider wrote, "The time has come for all Christians to refuse to use the sentence: 'The primary task of the Church is. . . .' I do not care if you complete the sentence with evangelism or social action. Either way it is unbiblical and misleading. Evangelism, seeking social justice, fellowship, teaching, worship are all fundamental dimensions of the total task of the church. They must not be confused with each other although they are inextricably interrelated."[49] Sider was undoubtedly referencing the legacy of the Lausanne

Movement here. Similarly, Padilla, Escobar, and Costas are cited throughout Sider's *Good News and Good Works: A Theology for the Whole Gospel.*

While it is doubtful Sider borrowed from Padilla and Escobar here, given the long history of Anabaptist-Brethren social Christianity, it reveals critical continuity between a global Evangelical Left. The multidirectional influence of Sider and progressive Latin Americans produced a diverse theological exchange that became characteristic of postwar evangelicalism. In the United States, institutions with Anabaptist leadership also played a strategic role in this story. For example, Palmer Theological Seminary became a petri dish for the embryonic social Christianity of the Evangelical Left in the 1970s.

Palmer Theological Seminary and its Eastern University (which is now independent) consistently pulled progressive evangelicals into its institutional orbit. In doing so, it provided space, resources, and encouragement to widen the evangelical tent for social Christianity. Of course, in Chapter 4, we saw the influence of Palmer through Catharine Feser Padilla and René Padilla. Puerto Rican Orlando Costas was the first progressive Latin American evangelical to join the faculty of Palmer, being named Thornley B. Wood Professor of Missiology and director of Hispanic Studies and Ministries at Eastern Baptist Theological Seminary (later named Palmer) in 1980.[50] Costas's time at EBTS was short and largely symbolic. Four years later, Costas left Palmer for Andover Newton Theological Seminary, a move that represented his desire for dialogue *outside* of evangelicalism. This is perhaps where his primary legacy remains, cut short by his untimely death in 1987 from stomach cancer at the age of forty-five.

Costas's fierce protest against American influence gained critical continuity with sentiments in the Evangelical Left in the United States. For example, the Costas-led protest against the Panama Canal was printed in Sojourner's *Post-American*, IFES and InterVarsity's *His* magazine, and other influential magazines in the North.[51] The *Post-American* was founded in 1971 by Jim Wallis, then a seminary student at Trinity Evangelical Divinity School in Deerfield, Illinois. The magazine was fueled by student protests against American foreign policy in Vietnam. The open letter read, "Your precious 'American Way of Life' . . . feeds in no small proportion on the blood which gushes 'from the open veins of Latin America,'" referring to the Eduardo Galeano book of the same title.[52] Costas, though an American citizen, lambasted U.S. foreign policy in critical continuity with progressive evangelicals in the North.

Figure 9. Samuel Escobar speaking to college students in Peru, c. 1989. Photo courtesy of the International Fellowship of Evangelical Students, Oxford, England.

Eastern became a center of protest against American political and theological influence abroad. Tony Campolo, a sociologist at Eastern for many years, ran for the U.S. House of Representatives in 1976 as a Democrat and became one of the most prominent voices in the eclectic coalition of the Evangelical Left.[53] Campolo later spearheaded the "Red Letter Christians" coalition with New Monastic activist Shane Claiborne. Claiborne's first book, *Irresistible Revolution: Living as an Ordinary Radical* (2006), became a best seller.[54] The name Red Letter Christians referred to the words of Jesus that are often printed in red ink within Bibles. They indicted white evangelicals for ignoring Jesus' words on justice for the poor and oppressed.[55] Prior to running for political office, Campolo was influenced by his trips to Latin American countries where he perceived American exploitation.[56]

More than anything, Costas and Escobar's academic posts on the East Coast represented the institutionalization of integral mission within the structures of evangelical education and its diffusion across the United States. Samuel Escobar replaced Costas as the Thornley Chair at Palmer in 1984, cementing one of Escobar's key legacies—distributor of integral mission goods in the United States. Escobar and Costas's connection to an emerging American Evangelical Left in the United States was crucial to its spread. Escobar and Padilla's networks overlapped significantly, even as their influence was often unique. Just as Escobar's location in North America set a trajectory for his influence, so too did Padilla's choice to remain in Latin America. Padilla's passion, in particular, was to edit and publish *other* Latin American writers—indeed, he published more than 200 books. But he also maintained perfectionist tendencies that slowed his own publishing projects.[57] Though their lives and influence are often conflated, Samuel Escobar and René Padilla's careers diverged sharply in the 1970s. What Escobar called his "Canadian interlude" and later academic posts in the United States had manifest implications for his influence and the networks he developed. This, combined with his affable personality and cooperative approach, undoubtedly cemented his presence in key gatherings, such as the Lausanne Continuation Committee.

Church Growth and the Scourge of Segregation

René Padilla rejected racial and class segregation in his plenary speech at Lausanne 1974. His social location in Latin America and rejection of academic posts in the Global North did not mute or soften his critique of the United States. Perhaps his most searing critique was an indictment of American church growth and segregation within white suburban evangelicalism. Padilla especially critiqued its intellectual justification—the Homogeneous Unit Principle (HUP), first articulated by the influential Fuller Theological Seminary professor Donald McGavran. McGavran had argued that individuals tend to prefer converting to Christianity without crossing boundaries of race, tongue, or class.[58] Churches that only target one racial group were more "successful" because they grew numerically. Thus, church mission strategy should be carried out with a goal of *homogeneous* churches that have intercongregational interactions. The HUP was widely adopted by American evangelical leaders, even while some did not know its name. HUP provided an escape hatch from Martin Luther King Jr.'s famous indictment that Sunday morning was "the most segregated hour in America."[59] Segregation, then, could be seen as an unintended consequence of pursuing church growth.

At Lausanne, Padilla rejected HUP not only for promoting what he saw as racial segregation but also because of its implications for Third World leadership. If technology and numerical planning were the impetus for mission, then the center of decision making would be squarely in the "West."[60] To Padilla, "No amount of exegetical maneuvering" could allow this strategy in the light of biblical mandates on unity.[61] Padilla's plenary speech was not the first time he had excoriated the Homogeneous Unit Principle. In 1971, Padilla's response to Wagner's *Latin American Theology* had been strongly critical of McGavran and HUP.[62] McGavran wrote Padilla a private letter in response, hoping to sort out their differences in person.[63] Padilla later identified the letter as an attempt to silence him and appears to have ignored the gesture at the time.[64] Elsewhere, Stacey Woods supported Escobar's own critique of McGavran, saying, "I am very thankful that you are sensitive to the scurge [*sic*] of McGavran's Armenian [*sic*] thinking."[65] Instead of writing McGavran or meeting with him privately, Padilla took his grievances to the world stage of Lausanne 1974 and continued to publish on the issue up until and after the HUP consultation.[66] Padilla's clash with Fuller Seminary professors at Lausanne and later in Pasadena represented broader growing pains for the increasingly diverse global evangelical community. While Padilla could ignore MacGavran's appeal for dialogue, ignoring John Stott would prove more difficult.

John Stott invited René Padilla to participate in the Consultation on Homogeneous Units and Church Growth at Fuller Theological Seminary in Pasadena, California, from May 30 to June 2, 1977.[67] Padilla declined Stott's invitation, saying the topic did not interest him. Stott, however, was determined to include Padilla in worldwide consultations. Stott had previously agreed to visit Latin America in 1976–1977 under the auspices of the FTL. When Padilla declined Stott's invitation to the HUP consultation, however, Stott reneged on his commitment to visit Latin America. According to Padilla's 2013 recollection, Stott responded, "If you don't accept this invitation [to the HUP consultation], I'm not coming to Latin America." To this "threat," Padilla recalled responding, "This is extortion!" (Padilla recalled this response with a laugh.) In response, Padilla acquiesced and attended the meeting. When asked in 2013 about the consultation, he shook his head and recalled it as "terrible, terrible." He added, "It wasn't a dialogue. They didn't listen. At all, at all." Padilla continued, "They had made up their mind so they weren't ready to talk about any of it, at all—at all. No dialogue."[68] Stott's travel diary confirms Padilla's recollection. Stott wrote, "I was surprised how threatened the SWM team [Fuller's School of World Mission] obviously felt and, in consequence, how defensive they were in their presentations and contributions. I did not feel they were really 'open' and it saddened me that when René Padilla got up to speak, they (quite unconsciously, no doubt) put down their pads and pens, folded their arms, sat back and appeared to pull down the shutter of their minds."[69] Padilla's persistent criticism of the HUP produced mixed results.[70] Many Majority World thinkers have joined in this criticism, while the HUP continues to hold credence in many circles through its corollary "unreached people groups" designation. Ultimately, the mutual influence between John Stott, Padilla, and Escobar continued well after the Lausanne Congress of 1974. Stott not only channeled their influence at the Mexico City gathering with Billy Graham but also pushed Padilla to participate in consultations that were largely spurred by his plenary speech. The Lausanne Theology Working Group, created at Lausanne and led by Stott, organized four consultations that reflected themes raised in Padilla and Escobar's plenary speeches. These, in turn, largely set the trajectory for the later Lausanne Movement: (1) the social content of the gospel message; (2) a clarion call for Third World leadership; (3) the relationship between the gospel and culture, including the need for a simple lifestyle; and (4) a pointed critique of racial segregation within Christian mission, especially the Church Growth Theory and the Homogeneous Unit Principle.[71] These four reached their climax at a 1983 gathering in Wheaton, Illinois, entitled "Consultation on the Church in Response to Human Need." Thus, the themes raised by the embryonic Latin American Evangelical Left at Lausanne continued to surface throughout the 1970s and early 1980s. Stott negotiated on behalf of the Latin American Evangelical Left and welcomed their ideas into previously hostile conservative circles, as well.

"A Dialogue of the Deaf" and the Rise of New Global Missionary Structures

The emerging Latin American Evangelical Left grew increasingly frustrated with the conservative direction of the Lausanne Movement. Even as they gained control over local Latin American organizations, they grew discontent with the global evangelical status quo that they argued persistently favored conservatism and North American influence. As a result, they took three distinguishable paths: First, they turned inward to develop social Christianity in Latin America *within* their own organizations. Second, they developed their own global organizations to create space for likeminded Asian, African, and Latin American theologians. And third, they continued to press global organizations to widen their understanding of the gospel message.

This discontent was on full display at the third FTL gathering in 1977. From February 22 to March 5, 1977, fifty-five Latin American evangelical leaders from twelve countries gathered in Vila Kostka, Itaici, Brazil—nearly 100 kilometers northwest of São Paolo. This international consultation was the first FTL gathering outside of Spanish-speaking countries and its first consultation since the Lausanne Congress of 1974. It also marked a noticeably "pastoral" shift from more technical theological discussions.[72] In doing so, it provided a platform for the nascent Latin American Evangelical Left to increasingly criticize the conservative evangelical mission establishment. Yet, diplomatic members like Escobar continued to attempt a tightrope walk with the American public.

While in English Escobar spoke positively of the "dialogue" at Lausanne,[73] at FTL III (and later published within the FTL Spanish journal *Boletín Teologico*), Escobar decried the direction of Lausanne as a "dialogue of the deaf."[74] In doing so, Escobar utilized his bilingualism to his diplomatic advantage. He wrote,

> New voices, developers of a Biblical and theological ferment, to a certain extent unexpectedly, made their voices heard at Lausanne . . . in my very personal opinion, supported in part by my active participation in the organization of the Congress, leads me to affirm that the currents of opinion today in the evangelical world did not enter into real dialogue. There was rather a dialogue of the deaf. Those who expressed a renewal current from the Lausanne 74 platform, lost the battle in the organizational effort that came later.[75]

This "dialogue of the deaf" did not discourage Latin Americans from continuing their own politically diverse conversations within the FTL. While the global appropriation of integral mission themes continued to soften its political edge, the FTL remained a space for debate on the place of leftist politics in evangelicalism.

After Samuel Escobar's presidential address at the third Latin American Theological Fraternity (FTL) gathering, Orlando Costas pulled him aside with an incredulous tone: "Where was the class analysis?" Escobar and Costas sparred over the role of Marxist analysis in understanding urban life—a debate that extended beyond the session for over an hour.[76] In response, Escobar exclaimed, "But I'm not a Marxist!" raising his volume to match the "trumpeting voice" of his Puerto Rican colleague.[77] In Escobar's 2013 retelling, he accused Costas of naïveté, attributed to Costas's education in the United States and later life in Costa Rica—a "tranquil country without a military." In the Costa Rican context, "You can say radical things and there isn't a danger," an obvious reference to Escobar's life under repressive military regimes in Peru and Argentina. Escobar had *lived* the negative repercussions of Marxism firsthand in the universities, he argued.[78] After pausing for a moment, Escobar concluded, "I believe [Costas] was maturing . . . some of his ideas were changing because of the Fraternity—it was because we discussed these ideas!" At the third FTL gathering, the growing discontent of Latin Americans with the Lausanne Movement also surfaced. In response, they not only invested heavily in local spaces but also turned to likeminded African and Asian theologians to develop a global response.

The discourse of global evangelicalism increasingly reflected its demographic center in Africa, Asia, and Latin America. Majority World mission thinkers sought not only to reform traditional evangelical mission structures but also to build their own. As the decade of the 1970s wore on, progressive evangelical influence had been largely blunted within traditional missionary structures. Frustration reached a tipping point in June 1980 at the Second "Lausanne" Congress held in Pattaya, Thailand.

Early in the conference gathering, a group of Majority World delegates drafted a "Statement of Concern for the Future of the Lausanne Committee on World Evangelization" with a list of demands for the Lausanne organization leaders.[79] These included calling for new leadership, a "World Congress on Evangelical Social Responsibility and its implications for evangelism," and, perhaps most controversially, guidelines on how "evangelicals who support oppression and discrimination . . . can be reached by the Gospel and challenged to repent."[80] This statement indicted many conservative evangelicals not only as opponents of justice but also as non-Christians in need of conversion. According to Orlando Costas, nearly one-third of delegates signed the document within a few hours. Yet, he recalled the official committee response as "cool and disappointing" and "unsatisfactory."[81]

During the nine years between the Pattaya (1980) and Manila (1989) congresses, the conservative bloc rallied and continued to dominate global evangelical conciliar gatherings.

"Lausanne from its very beginning, for me, has just been somewhat schizophrenic." In a 2013 interview, Ruth Padilla DeBorst described two strands of the Lausanne Movement working in tandem up until that point: "One that is much more pragmatic, strategist, managerial mission. And another one that is in my estimation deeper theologically, and I would also say more humble and more holistic. And those two strands—they were evident in 74—and there's been this pendulum swing between those strands ever since."[82] Padilla DeBorst recalled that Manila had marginalized their progressive strand: "Manila was just the triumph of the managerial perspective—the unreached peoples, church growth, and all of that. And the other strand was hardly [evident]." Their fears were confirmed by the Pattaya Declaration of 1980, which clarified, "Nothing contained in the Lausanne Covenant is beyond our concern, *so long as it is clearly related to world evangelization*" (italics mine).[83] René Padilla later wrote, "Quite clearly, the Pattaya Consultation on World Evangelization failed to cope with the debatable issue of the relationship between evangelism and social responsibility. The tension already present in the Lausanne Covenant between . . . evangelism and sociopolitical involvement . . . and that 'in the church's mission of sacrificial service evangelism is primary' (paragraph 6) remained unresolved."[84] Thus, many southern evangelicals felt the movement was steadily drifting from the holistic gains made at Lausanne 1974. This, of course, mirrored conservative political gains in the United States, where the rise of the Evangelical Left seemed like a distant memory in the face of the Moral Majority.

This perceived conservative advance spurred Majority World leaders to form their own organization for the promotion of social Christianity. More important, it connected African, Asian, and Latin American evangelicals for a shared project of theological and political construction. In doing so, the global evangelical power structures increasingly reflected its demographic center in the Global South. In a 2014 interview, Indian evangelical leader Vinay Samuel described shared frustration of many Majority World Lausanne delegates with the Western mission establishment: "The space [at the time] was only available in the mission of the West. *They* controlled the spaces, *they* invited you, controlled publications—therefore if you wanted space internationally or globally and you wanted space to critique and innovate and to think through where God was leading you, you had to do it in the space of the people who were suspicious of you and you had to mind your-self." This was, according to Samuel, the impetus for forming a new organization in the 1980s. Thus, Samuel and other theologians from the Developing World sought to create breathing room for their own postcolonial thinking. Samuel saw their own perspective as something quite different: "We were the ones dealing with poverty on the front lines. We need to engage it and critique and find new ways of dealing with it. *At that point we needed to create our own space*" (italics mine).[85] That space for exploring mission theology out of the Majority World came to be known as the International Fellowship of Evangelical Mission Theologians or INFEMIT.

Twenty-five theologians gathered for the first INFEMIT consultation in March 1982, in Bangkok, Thailand.[86] The Kenyan Anglican bishop David Gitari reflected in the official conference volume, "This was a historic meeting. It was the first time that theologians of evangelical conviction from the Two Thirds World had met at their own initiative."[87] Padilla was elected chairman; David Gitari, vice chairman; Vinay Samuel, executive director; and David Bussau of Australia, treasurer.[88] The influential theologian Kwame Bediako of Ghana was intimately aware of the theological developments coming from Latin America. For example, Bediako and Padilla were delegates together at the Ninth General Committee of IFES held at Schloss Mittersill Castle in Austria from August 20 to September 1, 1975. The minutes record Bediako responding to Padilla's presentation on "indigenous" leadership and theology. It recorded, "Dr. Kwame Bediako (Ghana) stated that he was encouraged to note that the Latin Americans were developing indigenous forms of training and teaching."[89] This INFEMIT development represented joining forces between African, Asian, and Latin American evangelicals. Samuel described INFEMIT as the brainchild of three "fraternities": the Latin American Theological Fraternity, Partnership in Mission Asia (PIM-Asia), and the African Theological Fellowship (ATF). In reality, the ATF was founded at the second INFEMIT gathering in 1984 in Tlayacapan, Mexico. As these global evangelicals discovered each other, they plotted gains across the evangelical world.

INFEMIT, in turn, founded the Oxford Centre for Mission Studies (OCMS) in 1983, which enabled Third World leaders to complete postgraduate work from their own contexts.[90] OCMS aimed at the educational power structure of evangelicalism that largely remained in Great Britain and the United States. With Padilla at the helm as board chairman of both OCMS and INFEMIT, these two organizations also published the academic journal

Transformation (which transferred from the World Evangelical Fellowship [WEF] to INFEMIT/OCMS) from 1984 and a book publishing arm, Regnum Books, from 1987.[91] Vinay Samuel recalled, "René was key to Regnum [being set up] because he was very keen that we would publish our own things."[92] According to Samuel, the early gatherings of INFEMIT focused on the theme of integral mission. According to Samuel, the second motivation, behind frustration with Western missionary structures, was "the whole area of integral mission—not having to fight the battle of integral mission." Without the worry of white evangelical disapproval, they could focus on their own theological and political goals. The Latin American Evangelical Left fiercely fought for the *inclusion* of Majority World leadership but also, according to Samuel, the *exclusion* of anyone from the West: "It was a particular viewpoint of Latin Americans, both René and Orlando Costas and the Africans. They said we can't have white scholars from the establishment while we are thinking through these things. I was never fully for it, but I accepted it."[93] Once again, it was Latin Americans who set the direction and format for evangelical discourse. This time, they became the doorkeepers, largely excluding North Americans from their gathering.

The multidirectional discourse of global evangelicalism included a wide variety of interlocutors. As it diversified, the influence and example of Latin Americans remained. Padilla DeBorst recalled, "Latin America . . . the name, the experiences, and the intentionality was honed in Latin America but the spread also had to do with other faithful radical evangelicals in other contexts also grappling with the realities of their context." She then clarified, "INFEMIT gave them a space to find a common terminology. And to strengthen that vision for all of them. It also contributed to their appreciating each other, and encouraging to do theology within their own context not just regurgitating what was given to them from the North."[94] This "common terminology" was often that of *misión integral*, formed by the Latin American Evangelical Left.

From Foe to Family

The growing acceptance of *misión integral* provided strategic opportunities for Christian mission and relief organizations. Seen in this light, they walked through doors opened by Latin Americans. As a result, Christian NGOs pitched their organizations as key partners in Christian mission rather than a threat to evangelism. They utilized this language of the "social dimensions of the Gospel" and in particular the specific phrase "integral mission." There was a hole in the gospel and they could help fill it. The founding of the Micah Network in 1999 provides a clear example. As of 2014, the Micah Network comprised 578 member organizations in eighty-six countries. Notable member organizations in the United States include Compassion International, Christian Community Development Association (CCDA), Food for the Hungry, International Justice Mission, Latin American Mission, SIL International, Wheaton College Humanitarian Disaster Institute (HDI), the World Evangelical Alliance (WEA), and World Relief. Notable European member organizations include All Souls, Langham Place, International Aid Services, TearFund, Leprosy Mission International, and Wycliffe UK. The Micah Network was formed in 1999 under the stated, unifying principle of integral mission. This marked the most prominent usage of the English phrase "integral mission" to date. Compassion International alone had an operating budget of nearly $645 million in 2012–2013 and was the fifteenth largest U.S. charity in 2014.[95] While the broader movement of progressive evangelicalism found varying degrees of failure and success, the formation of the Micah Network reveals another piece of this global diffusion of evangelical social Christianity. The phrase is increasingly a catchall term for holistic mission in the evangelical Protestant community.

In a 2014 interview, David Westlake, director of integral mission at TearFund, spoke of the environment for Christian mission and relief organizations in the mid-1990s: "There was a sense among lots of Christians doing mission that we needed to 'up our game' theologically and in terms of identity."[96] According to Westlake, Steve Bradberry, then the head of TearAustralia, contacted René Padilla and began planning the formation of what would later become the Micah Network. The Micah Network held its first consultation in Oxford in September 2001. The consultation was divided into five days, each with its own theme. The first day's program simply read "INTEGRAL MISSION," underscored by a plenary address from René Padilla titled "Integral Mission—Past and Present."[97]

The Micah Network can be seen as the high point of evangelical conciliar discourse that accelerated in the early 1980s, albeit in small pockets. Four broader consultations led to a June 1983 WEF consultation in Wheaton titled "The Church in Response to Human Need." The Wheaton document clarified, "The mission of the church includes both the proclamation of the gospel and its demonstration. We must therefore evangelize, respond to immediate human needs, and press for social transformation."[98] Of this declaration, missiologist David Bosch wrote, "For the first time in an official statement emanating from an international evangelical symposium, the perennial dichotomy [of the two mandates between evangelism and social action] was overcome."[99] If this widening of Christian mission produced winners and losers, perhaps the most prominent winners were Christian mission and relief organizations—represented by the Micah Network. The reach of these ideas continued to expand, coming full circle in 2010 at the third Lausanne congress on world evangelization in Cape Town.

Integral mission was included for the first time in the official documents of the Lausanne Movement at Cape Town 2010. "The Cape Town Commitment" quoted the "Micah Declaration on Integral Mission":

> The Bible declares God's redemptive purpose for *creation* itself. Integral mission means discerning, proclaiming, and living out the biblical truth that the gospel is God's good news, through the cross and resurrection of Jesus Christ, for individual persons, *and* for society, *and* for creation. All three are broken and suffering because of sin; all three are included in the redeeming love and mission of God; all three must be part of the comprehensive mission of God's people. Christian unity is the creation of God, based on our reconciliation with God and with one another.[100]

Perhaps most important, the Cape Town Commitment's adoption of the language of integral mission gave a stamp of approval to Latin American evangelical social Christianity, albeit a somewhat depoliticized version.

At the 2010 Cape Town congress, two full days were dedicated to each section of the main theme: the Whole Church, the Whole Gospel, the Whole World. Padilla and Escobar were slotted for the third plenary session, where they shared their understanding of the history of the Lausanne Movement and their concerns with its future. Padilla's concerns at Cape Town were threefold. The first was unsurprising: the concern for discipleship rather than conversion—teaching believers to obey *everything* Jesus commanded, he said. The second, however, reflected later Padilla emphases, namely, globalization: "Globalization—globalization of what? Globalization of an unjust economic system that is destroying humankind. It's affecting people all over the world but especially the poor all over the world." Third, Padilla raised "the whole question of the destruction of the ecosystem."[101] In this sense, we can see the continued multidirectional influence of a global Evangelical Left. Many in the American Evangelical Left had been emphasizing "Creation Care" for years, including *Sojourners* and Red Letter Christians. *Misión integral* grew and changed as it was debated in progressive circles. This theological framework also found critical continuity with new ecclesiological movements among the Evangelical Left in the United States.

The Theological Framework of the Emerging Church Movement

In February 2005, *Time* magazine's cover story highlighted the "25 Most Influential Evangelicals in America," which included Billy Graham and John Stott.[102] Maryland pastor Brian McLaren was also named under the heading "Paradigm Shifter"—identifying him as the "elder statesman" of the Emerging Church Movement.[103] The Emerging Church Movement is largely defined by a decentralized, often postmodern approach to theology and church practice (as seen in the Emergent Village network). In the mid-1990s and early 2000s, McLaren traveled extensively in Latin America in order to learn about holistic mission from local churches. In a 2014 interview, McLaren said, "In almost every case, someone would say, 'We were influenced by the writing of René Padilla.'"[104]

McLaren met Padilla in 2005 through Elisa Padilla, who had been attending Cedar Ridge Community Church (CRCC) in Spencerville, Maryland. McLaren founded CRCC in 1982 and left in 2006 to pursue his writing and speaking career. At lunch after a 2005 church service, Padilla invited McLaren to travel with him for five weeks from August 10 to September 14, 2006. McLaren enthusiastically accepted. This 2006 trip included preaching, teaching, and ministering together throughout Latin America, including Mexico, Guatemala, Honduras, Chile, Costa Rica, and El Salvador—where they were joined by Ruth Padilla DeBorst. McLaren completed his influential 2006 book, *Everything Must Change*, while staying at Padilla's Kairos Center in Buenos Aires, Argentina—a sprawling campus and retreat center in the Pacheco region. In a 2014 interview, McLaren said, "That whole trip had a profound effect, especially on the final two chapters of the book." McLaren also introduced the 2005 Emergent Convention to the term "integral mission."[105]

McLaren had known of Latin American evangelical influence since the 1970s, when he cheered the inclusion of social emphases in the Lausanne

Covenant.[106] He recalled, "What I was exposed to in the 70s was the Lausanne Covenant and the section on social responsibility. I remember being so relieved and impressed and so happy that that was there." In a 2014 interview, McLaren spoke of integral mission operating under "a different theological ecosystem." By this, McLaren meant the emphasis on the gospel as the "Gospel of the Kingdom" and "the Gospel of justice" rather than an emphasis on "penal substitutionary atonement centered theology," which has long characterized evangelical theology.[107] For McLaren, "What seemed to be much more real in René [Padilla]'s work was that, no—this was actually a different system. A different theological ecosystem. And that really, really helped me." In a reflective moment on the influence of René Padilla, Elisa Padilla, and Ruth Padilla DeBorst, McLaren opined, "I would have to say, whatever small impact I've had in recent years, their flavor has seasoned everything I've done."[108] By appropriating aspects of *misión integral*, McLaren ultimately rejected a traditional Protestant evangelical understanding of both mission and salvation—rejecting many convictions Padilla and Escobar would continue to hold. Indeed, whether McLaren would accurately be described as "evangelical" today is unclear. Regardless, Latin American evangelical social Christianity provided a theological framework for McLaren and others in a new generation of the Evangelical Left.[109]

The prevailing story of the Evangelical Left has largely focused on political defeat at the hands of the American Religious Right. When seen through the lens of Latin Americans and the global diffusion of *misión integral*, the story is one of victory and defeat, resistance and appropriation on the global stage. The global diffusion of evangelical social Christianity from Latin America to the West is a crucial story in the history of evangelicalism. Latin Americans played a key role, widening evangelical Protestant discourse and influencing evangelical leaders and organizations in the process. This influence cut across political and theological divides.

The embryonic Latin American Evangelical Left highlighted progressive political and theological themes that were previously relegated to the margins of global evangelicalism in the 1960s and 1970s. While many of these ideas existed within the Brethren-Anabaptist tradition, progressive Latin Americans shined a spotlight on them. They consistently raised progressive themes at influential global gatherings, often in controversial, antiestablishment ways. In a similar way, Costas and Escobar increased the surface area for reactions and exposure to social Christianity by taking academic posts in the United States. In doing so, they provided theological justification for many white American evangelicals who were frustrated by their own communities. By widening the dimensions of the gospel itself, they demanded the reexamination of conservative theological and political loyalties. These Latin American voices joined growing protest within a restless and emerging American Evangelical Left.

The conversion of conservative powerbrokers such as the English clergyman John Stott was crucial to this project. Latin Americans and their "revolutionary ferment" pushed Stott toward a wider embrace of evangelical social Christianity. René Padilla's intimate relationship with Stott was especially influential at the Lausanne Congress of 1974 and the crucial years leading up to it. Oral historical accounts and Stott's personal diary from his travels with Padilla speak to the impact of the Latin American context on Stott's missiology. Stott's friendship with Padilla deepened during the critical chronological gap between Berlin 1966 (and Keele 1967) and the Lausanne Congress of 1974. When Stott wrote about his own understanding of these holistic themes, he borrowed from Padilla's language and thinking—speaking strongly to Padilla's significance here. This is not to say that Padilla was the primary influence on Stott's theology or even his missiology. Stott was sensitive to contextual issues and distinctively connected to a younger generation of evangelical leaders from the Global South, including in Africa and Asia. Padilla was simply one influence but a very significant one at a critical time in postwar global evangelical history and Stott's theological revision. Stott's public shift had manifest implications beyond an emerging Evangelical Left or those sympathetic to progressive themes. Stott was both respected and *safe* to a significant sector of conservative evangelicalism in the North. As Latin Americans negotiated the place of social Christianity, Stott channeled their influence to a wider constituency.

Padilla and Costas's controversial style opened up avenues for more diplomatic Majority World leaders to exert increasing influence upon the global evangelical community—particularly their colleague Samuel Escobar. Escobar's ability to criticize evangelical mission and practice, while maintaining friendships and collegial relationships with Americans and Britons, was partly due to Padilla and Costas's heightened rhetoric. We can see, for example, the contrasting styles of Padilla's blistering critiques in *Mission Between the Times* and Costas's *The Church and Its Mission: A Shattering Critique from the Third World* compared to Escobar's decidedly irenic *The*

New Global Mission.[110] Escobar's invitation to lead InterVarsity Christian Fellowship of Canada and his inclusion on the planning committee of Lausanne 1974 shed further light, as well.

Global mission and relief organizations watched these developments with hopeful anticipation. They welcomed a new era of global evangelicalism, one represented by a reshaping of leadership and mission emphases from the Third World. A wider evangelical embrace of Christian relief organizations signaled their acceptance as members of the family rather than former foes of the Social Gospel. Traditional Western missionary structures and relief organizations also widened their mission by appropriating the language of *misión integral*. Today, "integral mission" is utilized as the official phrase and model by nearly 600 mission and relief agencies—including Compassion International, Food for the Hungry, International Justice Mission, and World Relief. The Lausanne Movement in particular played a leading role in the widening of evangelical discourse—carving a path for future leaders to walk through. The reshaping of global evangelicalism can be clearly seen especially in the trajectory of the Lausanne Movement itself—from 1974 to 2010.

A Global Reach

"The Gospel has become too white, too privileged, too American, too male!" On October 11, 2011, Jim Wallis debated Al Mohler on the campus of Trinity Evangelical Divinity School (TEDS) in the suburbs of Chicago. These two prominent political activists—a progressive evangelical and a conservative seminary president—represent progressive and conservative evangelicalism perhaps more than anyone else. The proposed debate question cut to the core identity of this often polarized family: "Is Social Justice an Essential Part of the Mission of the Church?" In his rebuttal to Mohler's negative response, Wallis declared, "I have more in common with the global body of Christ than I do with my fellow American citizens . . . the [global] evangelical movement is talking about the *integral* gospel." Leaving little doubt where he had retrieved this holistic language, Wallis continued, "The Lausanne Covenant, a whole evangelical movement, pilgrimage, has made it clear that the proclamation of the Gospel includes how *justice* is integral to the Gospel, integral to the gospel!"[1]

For Wallis and the American Evangelical Left, authentic Christianity required an *integral* gospel—a gospel for the poor, the oppressed, and the marginalized. The gospel of the Religious Right was "too white, too male, too privileged, and too American." Unfortunately, the same can be said of how some have told the story of the Evangelical Left. Simply focusing on the American Evangelical Left obscures not only the wider story of the renaissance of evangelical social Christianity but its origins, as well. The transnational networks of global evangelicalism flowed multidirectionally, often emanating from an eclectic and progressive coalition in Latin America.

The *political* inspiration of the American Evangelical Left was drawn from student protests that raged during the 1960s and early 1970s during the Vietnam War and civil rights era. As evangelical Christians, however,

Figure 10. Al Mohler, Chris Firestone (moderator), and Jim Wallis. Courtesy of the
Carl F. H. Henry Center at Trinity Evangelical Divinity School, Deerfield, Illinois.

the Evangelical Left required *theological* justification for their political
action—the *evangelical* in the Evangelical Left. When searching for words
to describe a gospel for the poor, key members of the Evangelical Left turned
to the Global South and theological language that was forged within the Cold
War. The raw ingredients of evangelical social Christianity arose not primarily from the United States but from the unlikely and overlooked context
of Latin America. In the words of Brian McLaren, the Latin American Evangelical Left provided a "different theological ecosystem."[2]

The reach of Latin American evangelical social Christianity extended far
beyond the geographical and institutional boundaries of its main characters.
In particular, the penetration of social Christianity into evangelical conciliar discourse was a decisive stamp of approval from a sizable portion of the
global evangelical community. Thus, when the Evangelical Left sought to
prove their evangelical bona fides, they found the language of integral mission particularly useful. Similar to McLaren and the Emerging Church Movement, Jim Wallis has continued to use the language of integral mission to
describe the social dimensions of the gospel. When asked in 2013 how integral mission impacted politics in the United States, he responded, "I didn't

have the words for it then, but I do now . . . there in Latin America, the integral gospel is a way of life. 'Atonement only' works for the affluent only."[3] Many in the Evangelical Left found critical continuity with the theological methodology of Latin Americans. The story of the global Evangelical Left is not simply one of American political decline during the Reagan years but rather one of transnational diffusion of evangelical social Christianity around the world. Focusing on the rise of the Latin American Evangelical Left has clarified the origins and extent of this influence and pushed the implications deeper and wider. For Americans, a diversifying global evangelicalism produced divergent results at home and abroad.

Many progressive American evangelicals leveraged momentum from global gatherings to push for political reformation at home. In his bestselling *Rich Christians in an Age of Hunger* (1978), Ron Sider, the Anabaptist evangelical colleague of Escobar and Costas, concluded, "We must demand a foreign policy that unequivocally sides with the poor. If we truly believe that 'all men are created equal,' then our foreign policy must be redesigned to promote the interests of all people and not just the wealthy elites in developing countries or our own multinational corporations."[4] The drive to reform American influence abroad was not confined to progressive pathways either. For example, *Rich Christians in an Age of Hunger* was promoted at Campus Crusade for Christ's (CCC's) winter conferences in the late 1970s. By 2011, CCC employed an estimated 25,000 staff members in 191 countries—by far the largest Christian student organization in the world. The pages of *Christianity Today*, the flagship evangelical magazine, also balanced the strategic tension between polarized politics and theologies. *Christianity Today* was both a table of negotiation for Latin American evangelical independence (such as the inerrancy controversies in Chapter 4) and a strategic venue for editor Carl Henry and founder Billy Graham to spread their ideas of saving the world. These multidirectional conversations encouraged robust intellectual exchange within the increasingly diverse and connected evangelical world.

The rise of this progressive coalition and the shifting trajectory of evangelical conciliar discourse overlapped with key developments north of the Rio Grande. As American evangelical influence was growing politically at *home*, much of the theological rationale for social action came from *abroad* in the postwar era. During these crucial years of 1966–1974, in particular, evangelicals increasingly perceived the exportation of development projects and international aid as central to their world-saving project.[5] The renaissance of evangelical social Christianity, then, speaks broadly to seemingly contradictory trajectories. The first is the softening—or at least reformation—of American evangelical influence abroad. The rise of the Latin American Evangelical Left certainly loosened American power in various locales. Yet, their ideas also may have helped solidify American influence on a global scale. This preliminary assertion comports with wider scholarship, both on the global connections of American evangelicals and their continued influence around the world.[6] Similarly, if global evangelical mission included the dissemination of material resources as integral mission required, then the United States (and Britain) would maintain an outsized role due to affluence and global soft power, as well.

It is thoroughly probable that the renaissance of evangelical social Christianity buttressed American foreign policy during these crucial years. While certainly preliminary, this suggestion joins a robust scholarly conversation on "evangelical internationalism." One historian aptly concluded, "As the planet itself was undergoing revolutionary changes, evangelicals had adopted a thoroughly global consciousness that wedded a belief in America's global manifest destiny with a faith in the redemptive power of world Christianity."[7] Thus, while the Evangelical Left certainly lost the battle for American evangelical hearts during culture wars, the legacy of progressive evangelical ideas became widely assumed in American foreign policy. The wider embrace of evangelical social Christianity had manifest political consequences in the United States.

Our story is not one of a growing chasm between evangelicals in the Global South and North. Rather, "as the world becomes increasingly interdependent, Christianity in the United States is becoming transcultural, responding to the realities of globalization by actively and intentionally engaging in activities that span borders."[8] This broader transnational influence, while at times directly tied to progressive Latin Americans, often was mediated through mission and relief organizations such as Compassion International and World Vision. These organizations aggressively marketed their mission in conservative evangelical churches, magazines, radio stations, music festivals, and the homes of everyday evangelicals through pictures of "sponsored children" stuck to refrigerator doors. Theologically, they no longer justified their presence exclusively through the language of evangelism or saving souls. Indeed, they shifted decisively in terms of what they were saving the world *from*—souls *and* bodies saved from eternal damnation *and* temporal suffering.

Why did many evangelicals in the North greet these ideas as *family* rather than *foe* in contrast to their reaction to the so-called Social Gospel of the late nineteenth and early twentieth centuries? They baptized their project as *integral mission*—dripping with the words and schema of the Latin American Evangelical Left. Evangelicals across the political spectrum have utilized language from Latin America to speak of this Christian mission—from progressive political activist Jim Wallis and Emerging Church leader Brian McLaren to British evangelical Anglican statesman John Stott and nearly 600 Christian mission and relief organizations, including Compassion International and World Vision. Long after the decline of the Evangelical Left as a political force in the United States, this new expression of social Christianity gained acceptance even among many evangelicals that rejected the political movement. Yet, the theological framework of many in a global Evangelical Left was built not within the American public square but within Cold War Latin America.

The global Cold War profoundly shaped this new style of evangelicalism from Latin America. Within the petri dish of Latin American university campuses, new cultures developed in economics, education, and religion, particularly from 1930 to 1969. At the same time, a disproportionate number of the key thinkers of the embryonic Evangelical Left had been nurtured in universities and theological colleges that were centers of radical protests.[9] While protests raged around the world, those in Latin America were particularly violent and widespread. As Latin American evangelical theologians awoke to dependency on the North, they turned inward to their social context—one marked by revolutionary ferment and a perceived religious vacuum. It was here they began to build the scaffolding of their evangelical social Christianity.

The origins and development of this revived evangelical social Christianity followed a trajectory that was both clear and complex. In the 1960s, a shift from theories of development to theories of dependency was the background for the emergence of Catholic theologies of liberation, perhaps best known in the career of Peruvian Dominican priest Gustavo Gutiérrez and his 1971 book, *Teología de la liberación*. This conversation was not simply a Catholic monologue, however, but crossed denominational boundaries, developing transnationally through conversations with European political theologians and North American Protestants in the World Council of Churches. Indeed, the embryonic Latin American Evangelical Left shifted from the conservative evangelical emphases of the day within a wider intellectual context that was increasingly being *conscientized* to its dependence on the North—politically, economically, and theologically. This maturation had manifest implications for how evangelicals related to the powerful interests in North America.

Rather than responding to the emergence of theologies of liberation, progressive Latin American evangelicals appear to have been primarily reacting to a shared set of social and political forces that were reshaping postwar Latin America: rural-urban migration flows, the resulting complications of urbanization, and the rapid expansion of the universities, where Marxist ideas of revolutionary change presented a growing appeal to students. One can hardly overstate the influence of the Cuban Revolution here. What made the Cuban Revolution so shocking to the U.S. political establishment was a clear juxtaposition: the dominance of American influence under the Batista regime and how thoroughly the Castro regime eschewed it. The Cuban Revolution also played a crucial role in rupturing American managerial control of global evangelicalism—no less shocking due to the pervasive influence of conservative evangelicalism in the North. More broadly, new approaches to Christian political activism and mission flourished within an intellectual context that increasingly embraced theories of dependency. The Latin American Evangelical Left led an insurrection of many nonwhite and non-Western evangelicals, rejecting widespread dominance of American influence within global evangelicalism.

The toolkit of the emerging Latin American Evangelical Left was drawn primarily from their negotiated and hybrid identities. Indeed, this generation of Latin American evangelicals came of age within a context of violence, oppression, and exclusion at the hands of a Catholic majority. They were also uniquely positioned between deeply personal relationships with American missionaries and the growing anti-American sentiment on Latin American university campuses. These biographies then fused with evangelical intellectual developments such as critical evangelical biblical scholarship that emerged in the 1960s. Evangelical intellectual trends were necessary but insufficient. Our emerging progressive coalition spoke of the theological poverty of Latin America and complained that local questions were being met with foreign answers.

As the story of *misión integral* has been told by the main players, however, one triumphalistic narrative has given way to another—a North American story of soul saving has been replaced by a postcolonial story of the emergence of a truly independent Latin American form of social Christianity.

By paying careful attention to archival documents and personal papers, as well as interrogating this oral history, a revised understanding has arisen—one that sheds light on the sources of funding, foreign theological boundary making, and continued intervention from northern evangelical leaders. Thus, while it is true that the emerging Latin American Evangelical Left set the trajectory for the new contextual brand of evangelical theologies, its emergence was contested and negotiated well into the 1970s. Latin American Protestant evangelicals shared a postwar intellectual context with liberation theologians yet negotiated a unique path that intersected persistent evangelical missionary paternalism.

The intersection of imported theological and political influence from the North and a growing awareness of dependence in the South shifted global evangelicalism to new theologies and political loyalties that were unashamedly local. Rather than a wholesale shift southward for global evangelicalism, then, this marked the beginning of a multidirectional conversation with a wide variety of interlocutors. In other words, Latin American evangelicalism was always connected to and in conversation with the wider world.

The critical interface between missionaries from the North and an emerging progressive coalition in the South created friction and fissures that threatened long-established loyalties. Indeed, the reemergence of evangelical social Christianity on the global stage in 1974 quite nearly ushered in a civil war. While "America's Pastor" Billy Graham called for world evangelization, a new generation of evangelicals, who were largely nonwhite and non-Western, refused to accept the northern-planned agenda for the rest of the world, where issues of social justice often remained marginal.[10] Careful attention to unstudied audiotapes and personal letters also reveals that the conservative evangelical establishment was largely unaware of an emerging Evangelical Left in Latin America. At Lausanne, the transnational nature of postwar evangelicalism connected northern leaders with a new style of evangelicalism from Latin America.

This book has attempted to understand to what extent the emerging Latin American Evangelical Left—individually and collectively—can be appealed to as a source of influence within this global evangelical conciliar thinking. One aspect of this significance can be seen by examining the clear contrast between Berlin 1966 and Cape Town 2010. Comparing the statements from Berlin 1966 with that of Cape Town 2010 reveals an enormous development and contrast. Berlin 1966 clearly defined mission as evangelism, relegating social action to a secondary, muted status. Cape Town 2010, as described in the previous chapter, included integral mission and social Christianity in its official statement. This reality left us with a crucial question: how does one explain the massive shift within evangelical mission that took place within a fifty-year period? The answer has emerged as both clear and complex.

The intellectual toolkit for the Latin American Evangelical Left was stocked by a wide variety of global suppliers. Thus, parsing individual contributions of the Latin American Evangelical Left has provided a fuller picture of origins, development, and diffusion of influence. The motif of the kingdom of God occupied a prominent place in this diverse tapestry of postwar evangelicalism. Indeed, the apprehension of the kingdom of God as a theological category reveals the hybrid nature of the intellectual journey for Latin American evangelicals and the primary means by which they challenged accepted evangelical norms. As fundamentalism and dispensationalism went out of vogue, conservative evangelical biblical scholars—especially in Britain and the United States—searched for alternative understandings of the "end times" that would address postwar social realities. In response to this perceived vacuum, many neo-evangelicals turned to the theology of the kingdom or abandoned the language of the "end times" altogether.[11]

Contrary to widely held assumptions, the FTL did not borrow this emphasis from the Mainline Protestant ISAL gatherings or Catholic liberation theologians. In fact, there are some examples of borrowing in the other direction. Thus, early FTL gatherings sharpened the Methodist liberation theologian José Míguez Bonino's understanding of this theological motif and the trajectory of his later influence. Equipped with the concept of the kingdom of God, progressive evangelicals in Latin America wielded this theological motif to widen the Christian gospel to include social elements and, in turn, challenge the political loyalties of global evangelicals. The energy and tools for blazing new evangelical trails, then, were drawn from unique and shared tools. While Latin America and the Cold War have been widely credited with inspiring Catholic social teaching, this same context has been widely overlooked in the story of the Evangelical Left. At issue was nothing less than the reshaping of global evangelicalism.

In 2009, Rick Warren, the American megachurch pastor and author of *The Purpose Driven Life*, reflected on the future of global evangelicalism: "If you want to know the future of evangelicalism, it is in [Africa, Asia, and Latin America] . . . it ain't here, ok?" While the vast majority of Christians lived in Europe and North America in 1910, today the vast majority live where Warren suggested—in the Global South.[12] The reshaping of global evangelicalism, then, reflects its growing demographic center among people of color, women, and minorities in diaspora.

Progressive Latin Americans became trailblazers, playing the role of controversial truthtellers and prophets, bringing to bear the reality of the Majority World into the consciousness of powerbrokers in the North. Ultimately, evangelicals in the North would ignore the voices of their brothers and sisters in the South at their own risk, for the tides of change were sweeping over global evangelicalism, reshaping for many what it meant to be a faithful Christian in contexts of injustice, oppression, and inequality. The role of progressive Latin Americans as a bridge between younger, emerging evangelical leadership in the Global South and the evangelical establishment was crucial to the task of challenging evangelical loyalties. In fact, it is fair to say that one cannot understand the contextual turn of global evangelicalism in the postwar period without understanding their role within it.

Progressive Latin American evangelical leaders insisted on the noninterference of Western missionary leaders and the relentless priority of theological independence for the Global South. As Latin American evangelical theologians shifted to new contextual and holistic themes, they pulled many global evangelicals with them. This is simply one example of many where Latin American evangelicals dictated the terms of negotiation. While certainly not a representative study, this argument provides nuance to the widespread assumption that theological conservatism always equals political conservatism. On the contrary, the *theologically* conservative Latin American Evangelical Left defined themselves and their theology in opposition to North American fundamentalism and conservative evangelical political ideology—in particular, the loyalty of many evangelicals in the United States to the Republican Party.

This gospel for the poor was not a gospel for the poor only. Instead, it attempted to strip the gospel message of its American cultural dress and widen its parameters to include social content. Thus, in this way, the story speaks to wider issues today. Their dynamic interplay speaks clearly to Christians in contexts of poverty, inequality, and injustice. Social questions will continue to challenge Christians everywhere as Christianity increasingly shifts southward. In this sense, the question is not *if* the gospel speaks to contexts of oppression and injustice but *how*.

NOTES

Introduction

1. Carl F. H. Henry Archives, Trinity Evangelical Divinity School, "Personal Letter from René Padilla, August 10, 1972," Box 5, Folder 26. See also C. René Padilla Papers, Buenos Aires, Argentina, "Breve apreciación sobre la obra estudiantil en América Latina," 1965. Here, Padilla associates focus on tobacco, alcohol, and dance with missionary influence.

2. C. René Padilla Papers, Buenos Aires, "Breve apreciación sobre la obra estudiantil en América Latina," 1965.

3. Carl F. H. Henry, *The Uneasy Conscience of Modern Fundamentalism* (Grand Rapids, MI: Eerdmans, 1947). For Henry's reflections on the trip, see Carl F. H. Henry Archives at TEDS, "Personal Reflections on the Latin American Trip," Box 5, Folder 26.

4. See Chapter 3.

5. Ibid. According to his personal diary, Henry respected Padilla's wishes and avoided the topic on his speaking tour.

6. The Carl F. H. Henry Archives at Trinity Evangelical Divinity School, "Personal Letter from René Padilla, August 10, 1972," Box 5, Folder 26.

7. *Evanglii Gaudium*, 1.198.6. Prior to Francis, this language was most well known in the work of Latin American liberation theology—especially the work of Peruvian Dominican Gustavo Gutiérrez—and the writings of the Latin American Episcopal Council (CELAM). See especially Chapter 3, pp. 56, 20–21, for a discussion of CELAM at Medellín, Colombia, in 1969 and Puebla, Mexico, in 1979.

8. Odd Arne Westad, *The Global Cold War: Third World Interventions and the Making of Our Times* (Cambridge: Cambridge University Press, 2007), 3–4.

9. Ibid.

10. C. René Padilla, "My Theological Pilgrimage," *Journal of Latin American Theology* 4, no. 2 (2009), 104; cf. C. René Padilla, "My Theological Pilgrimage," in *Shaping a Global Theological Mind*, ed. Darren C. Marks (Burlington, VA: Ashgate, 2008).

11. See especially David Swartz, *Moral Minority: The Evangelical Left in an Age of Conservatism* (Philadelphia: University of Pennsylvania Press, 2014); Brantley Gasaway, *Progressive Evangelicals and the Pursuit of Justice* (Chapel Hill: University of North Carolina Press, 2015); Randall Balmer, *Redeemer: The Life of Jimmy Carter* (New York: Basic Books), 2014.

12. Balmer, *Redeemer*.

13. Swartz, *Moral Minority*, 7.

14. Ondina E. González and Justo L. González, *Christianity in Latin America: A History* (Cambridge: Cambridge University Press, 2008), 184–206.

15. Ibid., 206–207.

16. Washington J. Padilla, *La iglesia y los dioses modernos: Historia del Protestantismo en el Ecuador* (Quito: Corporación Editora Nacional, 1989), 249–297.

17. Ibid., 164. Washington Padilla was an Ecuadorian professor, evangelical missionary, and René's older brother. He received a BA at Rockmont College in Denver, Colorado, in 1953 and a MDiv at Fuller Theological Seminary in 1956. He was chaplain and professor of philosophy, ethics, and Bible at Colegio Teodoro W. Anderson de Quito (1969–1975), as well as professor of English at La Universidad Central del Ecuador (1964–1965), and worked with a variety of evangelical ministries such as HCJB "The Voice of the Andes" radio ministry, the United Bible Society, and Biblical Society of Ecuador.

18. Alvin M. Goffin, *The Rise of Protestant Evangelism in Ecuador, 1895–1990* (Gainesville: University Press of Florida, 1994), xx.

19. Washington J. Padilla, *La iglesia y los dioses modernos*, 280.

20. For more on the Protestant community in Ecuador, see Jeffrey Swanson, *Echoes of the Call: Identity and Ideology Among American Missionaries in Ecuador* (New York: Oxford University Press, 1995).

21. Washington J. Padilla, *La iglesia y los dioses modernos*, 285–287.

22. Gabriel A. Almond and James Smoot Coleman, *The Politics of the Developing Areas* (Princeton, NJ: Princeton University Press, 1960), cited in *Latin American Radicalism: A Documentary Report on Left and Nationalist Movements*, ed. Josué De Castro, Irving Louis Horowitz, and John Gerassi (London: Random House, 1968), 148.

23. M. Epstein, ed., *Statesman's Yearbook, 1935* (London: Macmillan, 1935), 1117.

24. Ibid., 1087.

25. Todd Hartch, *The Rebirth of Latin American Christianity*, Oxford Studies in World Christianity (Oxford: Oxford University Press, 2014), 96, 99.

26. See, for example, Hartch, *Rebirth of Latin American Christianity*, 59–61.

27. Carlos Mondragón, *Like Leaven in the Dough: Protestant Social Thought in Latin America, 1920–1950* (Madison, WI: Fairleigh Dickinson University Press, 2010), 19. This reality has been recounted to the researcher by several evangelical Protestants within North America (Chicago, Mexico), the Caribbean (Dominican Republic), and South America (Argentina).

28. See, for example, the account of SCM staff worker and later general secretary Valdo Gallard, Yale Divinity School Archives, World Christian Student Federation Papers, Collection 46, Box 284, Folder 2500. For an early twentieth-century account, see Will Payne and Charles T. W. Wilson, *Missionary Pioneering in Bolivia, with Some Account of Work in Argentina* (London: H. A. Raymond, 1904).

29. Pew Research Center: Religion & Public Life, "Religion in Latin America," http://www.pewforum.org/files/2014/11/Religion-in-Latin-America-11-12-PM-full-PDF.pdf, 4.

30. Ibid. Countries with the largest Protestant communities are largely located in Central America (Honduras, El Salvador, Guatemala). Two countries now no longer have a Catholic majority—Honduras and Uruguay (46 percent and 42 percent, respectively).

31. David Brooks, "Who Is John Stott," *New York Times*, November 30, 2004.

32. Heath W. Carter, "Social Christianity in America," in *Oxford Research Encyclopedia of Religion*, May 24, 2017, http://religion.oxfordre.com/view/10.1093/acrefore/9780199340378 .001.0001/acrefore-9780199340378-e-424

33. Brian Stanley, "Evangelical Social and Political Ethics: An Historical Perspective," *Evangelical Quarterly* 62 (1990): 27.

34. B. F. Westcott, *Social Aspects of Christianity* (London: Cambridge University Press, 1887), 96. Cited in Stanley, "Evangelical Social and Political Ethics," 27. See also David Thompson, "John Clifford's Social Gospel," *Baptist Quarterly* 21, no. 5 (1986): 207.

35. Thompson, "John Clifford," 207.

36. See pp. 90–96, 123–127.

37. See, for example, David O. Moberg, *The Great Reversal: Evangelism Versus Social Concern* (Philadelphia: Lippincott, 1972). Most recently, Gasaway, *Progressive Evangelicals*, 7.

38. For a brief biography of Taylor, see Timothy George, James Earl Massey, and Robert Smith Jr., eds., *Our Sufficiency Is of God: Essays on Preaching in Honor of Gardner C. Taylor* (Macon, GA: Mercer University Press, 2010), x–xxi. For more on his life, see Gerald Lamont Thomas, *African American Preaching: The Contribution of Dr. Gardner C. Taylor*, vol. 5 of *Martin Luther King, Jr. Memorial Studies in Religion, Culture, and Social Development*, ed. Mozella G. Mitchell (New York: Peter Lang, 2004).

39. We return to this theme through the case study of Catharine Feser Padilla in Chapter 5. Dana Lee Robert, *American Women in Mission: A Social History of Their Thought and Practice* (Macon, GA: Mercer University Press, 1996).

40. David Bebbington, "Evangelicals and Reform: An Analysis of Social and Political Action," *Third Way* 6, no. 5 (1983): 10–13; David W. Bebbington, *The Nonconformist Conscience: Chapel and Politics, 1870–1914* (London: Allen & Unwin, 1982), 37–60.

41. David J. Bosch, *Transforming Mission: Paradigm Shifts in Theology of Mission* (Maryknoll, NY: Orbis Books, 1991), 403.

42. See, for example, Henry, *The Uneasy Conscience*.

43. See Grant Wacker, *America's Pastor: Billy Graham and the Shaping of a Nation* (Cambridge, MA: Harvard University Press, 2014), 199. For Graham's take, see Billy Graham, *Just as I Am: The Autobiography of Billy Graham* (San Francisco: HarperSanFrancisco, 1997), 567. For the taxi conversation, see Tim Chester, *Awakening to a World of Need: The Recovery of Evangelical Social Concern* (Leicester, England: InterVarsity Press, 1993), 27.

44. Carl F. H. Henry and W. Stanley Mooneyham, eds., *One Race, One Gospel, One Task: World Congress on Evangelism Berlin 1966: Official Reference Volumes: Papers and Reports*, 2 vols. (Minneapolis: World Wide Publications, 1967), 5. See also Brian Stanley, *The World Missionary Conference, Edinburgh 1910* (Grand Rapids, MI: Eerdmans, 2009), 18.

45. Billy Graham Center Archives, "World Congress on Evangelism, Berlin, West Germany, 1966," http://www2.wheaton.edu/bgc/archives/berlin66.htm.

46. Henry and Mooneyham, *One Race*, 5.

47. John Stott, "The Great Commission," in *One Race, One Gospel, One Task: World Congress on Evangelism, Berlin 1966*, Vol. I, ed. Carl F. H. Henry and W. Stanley Mooneyham (Minneapolis: World Wide Publications, 1967), 37.

48. Ibid., 50.

49. Ibid., 51.

50. Samuel Escobar, interview and translated by author, Valencia, October 21, 2013.

51. For a thorough account of the planning for Lausanne 1974, see Brian Stanley, *The Global Diffusion of Evangelicalism: The Age of Billy Graham and John Stott* (Downers Grove, IL: InterVarsity Press, 2013), 151–168.

52. David W. Bebbington, *Evangelicalism in Modern Britain: A History from the 1730s to the 1980s* (London: Routledge, 1993), 249. See Philip Crowe, ed., *Keele '67: The National Evangelical Anglican Congress Statement* (London: Falcon Books, 1967), 16.

53. See especially Andrew Atherstone, "The Keele Congress of 1967: A Paradigm Shift in Anglican Evangelical Attitudes," *Journal of Anglican Studies* 9, no. 2 (2011).

54. Crowe, ed., *Keele*, 23.

55. See Alister Chapman, *Godly Ambition: John Stott and the Evangelical Movement* (Oxford: Oxford University Press, 2012), 118–119. Chapman does not, however, credit Keele with completely changing Stott's mind. While it shook up his understanding, it was not until after the Lausanne Congress of 1974 that Stott wrote his redefinition of Christian mission in *Christian Mission in the Modern World* (Downers Grove, IL: InterVarsity Press, 1975).

56. Wacker, *America's Pastor*, 229. See also p. 244 for Graham's "awakening to the social implications of the gospel."

57. Mark A. Noll, *Turning Points: Decisive Moments in the History of Christianity* (Grand Rapids, MI: Baker Academic, 2012), 287.

58. BGCA, SC 46, Dain to Troutman, February 17, 1972. Cited in Brian Stanley, "'Lausanne 1974': The Challenge from the Majority World to Northern-Hemisphere Evangelicalism," *Journal of Ecclesiastical History* 64, no. 3 (2013): 535.

59. Ibid.

60. "A Challenge from Evangelicals," *Time*, August 5, 1974. See also Wacker, *America's Pastor*, 229. Wacker called the Lausanne Congress "extraordinarily influential."

61. C. René Padilla, "Evangelism and the World," in *Let the Earth Hear His Voice. International Congress on World Evangelization Lausanne, Switzerland: Official Reference Volume: Papers and Responses*, ed. J. D. Douglas (Minneapolis: World Wide Publications, 1975), 137.

62. Ibid., 311.

63. John Stott, "The Significance of Lausanne," *International Review of Mission* 64, no. 255 (July 1975): 289.

64. Ibid., 130.

65. World Council of Churches, *The Church for Others, and the Church for the World* (Geneva: World Council of Churches, 1967). For a discussion of the WCC's document *The Church for Others*, see Mark T. B. Laing, *From Crisis to Creation: Lesslie Newbigin and the Reinvention of Christian Mission* (Eugene, OR: Pickwick, 2012), 208–209. These trends were already

taking place in the 1950s, as well. See Yale Divinity School Archives, WSCF papers, SC 46, Box 284, Folder 2693, "Report on Leadership Training Course," Cochabamba, Bolivia, December 31, 1955, to January 15, 1956.

66. Samuel Escobar, interview and translated by author, Valencia, October 21, 2013.

67. See Chapter 7 for the appropriation of Latin American language by Americans in the Evangelical Left—especially Brian McLaren and Jim Wallis, along with conservative elder statesman John Stott. See pp. 141–166.

68. See, for example, BGCA, SC 111, Folder 10, Dain to Troutman, August 26, 1974.

69. See, for example, Swartz, *Moral Minority*.

Chapter 1

1. C. René Padilla, "Evangelism and the World," 130.

2. René Padilla, interview and translated by author, Buenos Aires, September 13, 2013.

3. Ibid.

4. Careful attention to private correspondence reveals that Graham ordered a report on reactions to Padilla and Escobar's plenary speeches, suggesting his concern. See BGCA, SC 580, Box 19, Folder 6, anonymous author to Billy Graham.

5. Researcher's note: this quote was spoken in English. René Padilla, interview by author, Buenos Aires, September 13, 2013.

6. See Kevin J. Vanhoozer, "'One Rule to Rule Them All?' Theological Method in an Era of World Christianity," in *Globalizing Theology: Belief and Practice in an Era of World Christianity*, ed. Craig Ott and Harold A. Netland (Grand Rapids, MI: Baker Academic, 2006), 92.

7. See, for example, Kwame Bediako, *Jesus and the Gospel in Africa: History and Experience* (New York: Orbis Books, 2004), 115; C. René Padilla, *The New Face of Evangelicalism: An International Symposium on the Lausanne Covenant* (Downers Grove, IL: InterVarsity Press, 1976), 140; Chris Sugden and Vinay Samuel, eds., *Sharing Jesus in the Two Thirds World: Evangelical Christologies from the Contexts of Poverty, Powerlessness, and Religious Pluralism: The Papers of the First Conference of Evangelical Mission Theologians from the Two Thirds World, Bangkok, Thailand, March 22–25, 1982* (Grand Rapids, MI: Eerdmans), 217.

8. Ruth Padilla DeBorst, "From Lausanne III to CLADE V," *Journal of Latin American Theology* 6, no. 1 (2011): 9; cf. Ruth Padilla DeBorst, Skype interview by author, December 4, 2014.

9. For more on its founding, see pp. 41–42.

10. Pete Lowman, *The Day of His Power: A History of the International Fellowship of Evangelical Students* (Downers Grove, IL: InterVarsity Press, 1988), 80–81.

11. Samuel Escobar Papers, Valencia, Escobar to Woods, August 2, 1972; BGCA, SC 49, Box 3, "Staff: 1971: E-Z & Misc. Correspondence," folder "Samuel Escobar: 1971," Woods to Escobar, October 13, 1971. For more, see BGCA, SC 46, Box 30, Folder 35.

12. BGCA, SC 49, Box 3, "Staff: 1971: E-Z & Misc. Correspondence," folder "Samuel Escobar: 1971," Woods to Escobar, August 22, 1972.

13. Ibid.

14. Samuel Escobar Papers, Valencia, Woods to IFES Staff, July 10, 1972.

15. BGCA, SC 49, Box 3, "Staff: 1971: E–Z & Misc. Correspondence," folder "Samuel Escobar: 1971," Woods to Escobar, August 2, 1972.

16. Stanley, *Global Diffusion*, 157.

17. Ibid.

18. BGCA, SC 49, Box 3, "Staff: 1971: E–Z & Misc. Correspondence," folder "Samuel Escobar: 1971," Escobar to Woods, August 2, 1972. For the invitation, see BGCA, SC 111, Box 32, Folder 17, Graham to Escobar, April 21, 1972.

19. BGCA, SC 49, Box 3, "Staff: 1971: E–Z & Misc. Correspondence," folder "Samuel Escobar: 1971," Woods to Escobar, August 2, 1972.

20. BGCA, SC 49, Box 3, "Staff: 1971: E–Z & Misc. Correspondence," folder "Samuel Escobar: 1971," Escobar to Woods, September 29, 1972.

21. See pp. 16–17.

22. Ibid.

23. Stanley, *Global Diffusion*, 54.

24. BGCA, SC 300, Box 139, Folder 35, Little Newsletter, June 1966. Little first met Padilla in 1966 working in a church called Pueblo Libre Church.

25. Lambeth Palace Library, John Stott Papers, John Stott Travel Diary, Mexico, January 9–14, 1974. See also Padilla's early description in *Certeza* magazine identifying him with Bruce. C. René Padilla, "Mensaje bíblico y revolución," *Certeza* 39 (1970). See also, for example, C. René Padilla, "God's Word and Man's Words," *Evangelical Quarterly* 53 (1981). Here, Padilla's bio begins with the description, "Dr. Padilla is a former student of Professor F. F. Bruce in the University of Manchester." See also Chris Sugden, phone interview by author, May 13, 2014.

26. Samuel Escobar, interview and translated by author, Valencia, October 21, 2013.

27. Billy Graham, "Why Lausanne?" in *Let the Earth Hear His Voice: Official Reference Volume, Papers and Responses*, ed. J. D. Douglas (Minneapolis: World Wide Publications, 1975), 28; cf. Graham, *Just as I Am*, 571.

28. Graham, "Why Lausanne?" 28.

29. V., 59, December 7, 1990. For online access, see the Official Website of the Holy See, http://w2.vatican.va/content/john-paul-ii/en/encyclicals/documents/hf_jp-ii_enc_07121990_redemptoris-missio.html. For example, Pope John Paul II wrote in *Redemptoris Missio*, "A new evangelization ought to create among the wealthy a realization that the time has arrived for them to become true brothers and sisters of the poor through the conversion of all to an 'integral development' open to the Absolute." Documents of the Third General Conference of Latin American Bishops, Puebla (1979), 3760 (1145). Quoted by Pope John Paul II in *Redemptoris Missio*.

30. C. René Padilla, "Evangelism and the World," 134.

31. See BGCA, SC 53, T7 and 74, for his Spanish presentation.

32. René Padilla, interview and translated by author, Buenos Aires, September 11, 2013. This conversation is indebted to Stanley, *Global Diffusion*, 22. Of Padilla's address in Spanish, Stanley wrote, "One suspects a political point was being made."

33. John Capon, "Let the Earth Hear Whose Voice?" *Crusade* 26 (1974): 6. If this was the case, it is unclear why the organizers would have made such a request.

34. Ibid.

35. C. René Padilla, "Evangelism and the World," 116.

36. Ibid., 130.

37. C. René Padilla, "Siervo de la palabra," in *Hacia una teología evangélica Latino-americana*, ed. C. René Padilla (San José: Editorial Caribe, 1984), 117. This translation was chosen in part due to Padilla continuing the "fire" metaphor with regard to Escobar's paper.

38. Escobar, "Evangelism and Man's Search for Freedom, Justice, and Fulfillment," in *Let the Earth Hear His Voice*, ed. J. D. Douglas (Minneapolis: World Wide Publications, 1975), 305–307

39. Ibid.

40. Orlando Costas, "Depth in Evangelism—An Interpretation of 'In-Depth Evangelism' Around the World," in J. D. Douglas, ed., *Let the Earth Hear His Voice* (Minneapolis: World Wide Publications), 675–697.

41. Ibid., 675. For more, see Allen Yeh, "Se hace camino al andar: Periphery and Center in the Missiology of Orlando E. Costas" (DPhil thesis, University of Oxford, 2008), 181ff.

42. Capon, "Let the Earth Hear Whose Voice?" 6.

43. "A Challenge from Evangelicals," *Time*, August 5, 1974; cf. Stanley, *Global Diffusion*, 165.

44. Capon, "Let the Earth Hear Whose Voice?" 6. See John R. W. Stott, "Significance of Lausanne," *International Review of Mission* 64, no. 255 (1975): 289. *Contra* David O. Moberg, *The Great Reversal: Evangelism Versus Social Concern* (Philadelphia: Lippincott, 1972), 73, Stott did not include Padilla in this description.

45. Chris Sugden, "Evangelicals and Wholistic Evangelism," in *Proclaiming Christ in Christ's Way: Studies in Integral Evangelism*, ed. Vinay Samuel and Albrecht Hauser (Oxford: Regnum Books, 1989), 30.

46. René Padilla, interview and translated by author, Buenos Aires, September 13, 2013.

47. Samuel Escobar, interview and translated by author, Valencia, October 21, 2013; René Padilla, interview and translated by author, Buenos Aires, September 13, 2013; BGCA, SC 580, Box 19, Folder 6, anonymous author to Billy Graham.

48. BGCA, SC 580, Box 19, Folder 6, anonymous author to Billy Graham.

49. For more on Padilla's view of the Lausanne Covenant, see C. René Padilla, "El pacto de Lausana," *Boletín Teológico* 13 (1975).

50. Andrew Kirk, Skype interview by author, December 1, 2014; René Padilla, interview and translated by author, Buenos Aires, September 13, 2013.

51. BGCA, SC 53, T180.

52. BGCA, SC 53, T180. This call for a political "third way" reflected critical continuity with liberation theologians such as Juan Segundo, *Liberation of Theology* (New York: Orbis, 1975).

53. See, for example, the later article by Juan Luis Segundo, "Capitalism vs. Socialism: Crux Theologica," in *Frontiers of Theology in Latin America*, ed. Rosino Gibellini (Maryknoll, NY: Orbis Books, 1990).

54. See also p. 217. C. René Padilla, "The Church and Political Ambiguity," *Christianity Today* July 26, 1974. See also C. René Padilla, "What Kind of Democracy?" *Transformation* 7, no. 4 (1990): 9-10.

55. BGCA, SC 236, Box 11, Folder 8, Woods to Fenton, January 25, 1966.

56. BGCA, SC 236, Box 11, Folder 8, Fenton to Woods, February 1, 1966; BGCA, CN 236, Box 11, Folder 8, Padilla to Troutman, October 12, 1966.

57. Stanley, *Global Diffusion*, 172–173.

58. BGCA, SC 53, T180.

59. BGCA, SC 53, T181.

60. Ibid.

61. Swartz, *Moral Minority*, 165; Daniel Salinas, *Latin American Evangelical Theology in the 1970's: The Golden Decade* (Leiden: Brill, 2009), 137.

62. Samuel Escobar, interview and translated by author, Valencia, October 22, 2013.

63. Chester, *Awakening to a World of Need*, 80–82.

64. John Howard Yoder, "Revolución y ética evangélica," *Certeza* 11, no. 44 (1971).

65. C. René Padilla, "My Theological Pilgrimage," 105–106. Swartz makes a convincing case for the Anabaptist roots of this later evangelical emphasis. See Swartz, *Moral Minority*, 164–165.

66. C. René Padilla, "Evangelismo y la responsabilidad social: De Wheaton '66 a Wheaton '83," *Misión* 4, no. 3 (1985). For Padilla's discussion of this, see Douglas, *Let the Earth Hear His Voice*, 1294.

67. Stanley, *Global Diffusion*, 169–173.

68. Ibid., 155.

69. Swartz, *Moral Minority*, 164–165.

70. C. René Padilla, "El pacto de Lausana," 6; cf. C. René Padilla, *New Face of Evangelicalism*. Padilla repeated this assertion in the second edition of *Mission Between the Times*. C. René Padilla, "From Lausanne I to Lausanne III," *Journal of Latin American Theology* 5, no. 2 (2010): 6.

71. C. René Padilla, "From Lausanne I to Lausanne III," 25.

72. Graham, "Why Lausanne?" 34; cf. on the perfect balance, see Steuernagel, "The Theology of Missions in Its Relation to Social Responsibility Within the Lausanne Movement" (PhD diss., Lutheran School of Theology, 1988), 156.

73. Stanley, *Global Diffusion*, 171; cf. Steuernagel, "The Theology of Missions," 156.

74. C. René Padilla, "El pacto de Lausana," 5.

75. Samuel Escobar, "A Movement Divided: Three Approaches to World Evangelisation Stand in Tension with One Another," *Transformation* 8, no. 4 (1991): 8.

76. Carl F. H. Henry, "Gospel and Society," *Christianity Today*, September 13, 1974, 67.

77. For more on opposition to Lausanne social elements, see Steuernagel, "The Theology of Missions," 151–156; Hedlund, *Roots of the Great Debate*, 294–299; C. René Padilla, "Evangelism and Social Responsibility: From Wheaton '66 to Wheaton '83," *Transformation* 2, no. 3 (1985): 29. For Stott's response to Johnston, see Arthur P. Johnston, *The Battle for World Evangelism* (Wheaton, IL: Tyndale House). Stott expanded on this in John R. W. Stott, "The

Battle for World Evangelism: An Open Response to Arthur Johnston," *Christianity Today*, January 5, 1979.

78. John R. W. Stott, "The Biblical Scope of Mission: We See in Scripture the Reflections of Our Own Prejudice Rather Than the Disturbing Message," *Christianity Today*, January 4, 1980.

79. BGCA, SC 111, Folder 10, Dain to Troutman, August 26, 1974.

80. Ibid.

81. BGCA Paul Little Collection, Box 18, Folder 17, Norman B. Rohrer to Paul Little, November 29, 1974.

82. IFES papers, Oxford, Box "International Student Movements: The Americas 1960–1983," Folder "South America," Barclay to Padilla, September 25, 1974.

83. Ibid.

84. Lambeth Palace Library, John Stott Papers, John Stott Travel Diary, Mexico, January 9–14, 1974.

85. For more on Graham's view of social transformation as an *implication* of evangelism, see his speech at the Berlin Congress of 1966. C. Peter Wagner, "Lausanne Twelve Months Later," *Christianity Today*, July 4, 1975, 963.

86. Chapman, *Godly Ambition*, 143.

87. Lambeth Palace Library, John Stott Papers, John Stott Travel Diary, Mexico, January 9–14, 1974.

88. Wagner was the associate general director of the Andes Evangelical Mission in Latin America and will appear later in our narrative.

89. BGCA, SC 46, Box 21, Folder 2, "Minutes of the Continuation Committee," January 13–20, 1975, 1975. For more on this, see Chester, *Awakening to a World of Need*, 85; Stanley, *Global Diffusion*, 173.

90. Wagner, "Lausanne Twelve Months Later," 963. Cited in Johnston, *The Battle for World Evangelism*, 344–345.

91. BGCA, SC 46, Folder 5, Box 30, Escobar to Dain, July 29, 1975.

92. Lambeth Palace Library, John Stott Papers, John Stott Travel Diary, Mexico, January 9–14, 1974. Stott and Graham remained close until Stott's death in 2011. Graham released a statement after Stott's death saying, "The evangelical world has lost one of its greatest spokesmen . . . and I have lost one of my close personal friends and advisers. I look forward to seeing him again when I go to heaven." Wolfgang Saxon, "Rev. John Stott, Major Evangelical Figure, Dies at 90," *New York Times*, July 28, 2011.

93. Steuernagel, "The Theology of Missions," 174–175.

94. I am indebted to a conversation with David Westlake of TearFund for this insight.

95. Brian Stanley, "'Lausanne 1974': The Challenge from the Majority World to Northern-Hemisphere Evangelicalism," *Journal of Ecclesiastical History* 64, no. 3 (2013): 534; cf. Stanley, *Global Diffusion*, 155.

96. See Swartz, *Moral Minority*, 4–6, 24, 133–135, 178–84, and 192–202 for extensive discussion on this workshop and its significance.

97. Marjorie Hyer, "Social and Political Activism Is Aim of Evangelical Group," *Washington Post*, November 30, 1973, D17. Cited in Swartz, *Moral Minority*, 1.

Chapter 2

1. Samuel Escobar, *La chispa y la llama: Breve historia de la comunidad internacional de estudiantes evangélicos en América Latina* (Buenos Aires: Ediciones Certeza, 1978), 86.

2. C. René Padilla, *Mission Between the Times: Essays on the Kingdom* (Grand Rapids, MI: Eerdmans, 1985), 109. He may have been echoing Gutiérrez here. See Gustavo Gutiérrez, *A Theology of Liberation: History, Politics, and Salvation* (Maryknoll, NY: Orbis Books, 1973), 89.

3. Camilo Torres Restrepo, "Message to Students," in *Latin American Radicalism: A Documentary Report on Left and Nationalist Movements*, ed. Josué De Castro, Irving Louis Horowitz, and John Gerassi (London: Random House, 1968), 496.

4. Ibid. This article originally appeared in the Spanish newspaper *La Gaceta*, no. 13, Bogotá, March–April 1965. Translated by Morton Marks.

5. Torres Restrepo, "Message to Students," 497–498.

6. David Tombs, *Latin American Liberation Theology* (Boston: Brill, 2002), 81.

7. Samuel Escobar, "Diálogo entre Cristo y Marx," *Certeza* 7, no. 25 (1966): 4–8. Magazine found in Padilla Papers, Buenos Aires, Kairos Centre.

8. C. René Padilla, "El testimonio Cristiano en la universidad Latinoamericana," *Pensamiento Cristiano* 14, no. 55 (September 1967): 176–183. Also appeared in English in *Journal of the IFES*, no. 2 (1966): 13–22.

9. Pedro Arana, Skype interview and translated by author, March 11, 2014; cf. Gutiérrez, *A Theology of Liberation*, xi.

10. Pedro Arana, Skype interview and translated by author, March 11, 2014.

11. Samuel Escobar, interview and translated by author, Valencia, October 22, 2013.

12. Ibid.

13. See David C. Kirkpatrick, "C. René Padilla and the Origins of Integral Mission in Post-War Latin America," *Journal of Ecclesiastical History* 67, no. 1 (January 2016): 351–371.

14. Argentina, Bolivia, Brazil, Chile, Colombia, Ecuador, El Salvador, Guatemala, Honduras, Nicaragua, Panama, Paraguay, Peru, and Venezuela (Uruguay 1981–1985).

15. See Erika Helgen, "Holy Wars: Protestants, Catholics, and the struggle for Brazilian National Identity, 1916–1945," (PhD diss., Yale University, 2015), 161, 188.

16. C. René Padilla, "My Theological Pilgrimage," in *Shaping a Global Theological Mind*, ed. Darren C. Marks (Burlington, VA: Ashgate, 2008), 2008; cf. C. René Padilla, "My Theological Pilgrimage," *Journal of Latin American Theology* 4, no. 2 (2009). Hereafter, I will reference the latter publication. See also Billy Graham Center Archives, Wheaton College, interview of René Padilla by Paul Ericksen, Collection 361, T1, March 12, 1987.

17. David Bushnell, *The Making of Modern Colombia: A Nation in Spite of Itself* (Berkeley: University of California Press, 1993), 186.

18. M. Epstein, ed., *Statesman's Yearbook, 1945* (London: Macmillan, 1945). See also ibid. I will further explore this in Chapter 2, pp. 43–44.

19. BGCA, Wheaton College, interview of René Padilla by Paul Ericksen, Collection 361, T1, March 12, 1987.

20. Ibid.

21. C. René Padilla, "My Theological Pilgrimage," 92–93. See Kirkpatrick, "Origins of Integral Mission."

22. René Padilla, interview and translated by author, Buenos Aires, September 13, 2013.

23. For more on the sociopolitical tumult in Colombia post-1930, see Herbert Braun, *The Assassination of Gaitán: Public Life and Urban Violence in Colombia* (Madison: University of Wisconsin Press, 2003). Wider archival records confirm the presence of both organized campaigns of violence and widespread, spontaneous acts against Protestants. See, for example, the Evangelical Foreign Missions Association papers, Wheaton College. See also Yale Divinity School Archives, World Christian Student Federation Papers.

24. For more on anti-Protestant violence in Colombia, see James E. Goff, "The Persecution of Protestant Christians in Colombia, 1948–1958, with an Investigation of Its Background and Causes" (PhD thesis, Centro Intercultural de Documentación, Cuernavaca, Mexico, 1968).

25. John Stott Papers, Lambeth Palace Library, London, England, "Stott 6/1/15 Travel Diaries 1977"; cf. C. René Padilla, "My Theological Pilgrimage," 93.

26. René Padilla, interview and translated by author, Buenos Aires, September 10, 2013.

27. Billy Graham Center Archives, Wheaton College, interview of René Padilla by Paul Ericksen, Collection 361, T1, March 12, 1987.

28. C. René Padilla, "My Theological Pilgrimage," 94.

29. Ibid., 94–95.

30. Samuel Escobar, "My Theological Pilgrimage," *International Bulletin of Missionary Research* 36, no. 4 (October 2012): 206.

31. Samuel Escobar, interview and translated by author, October 22, 2013.

32. Ibid. See also Escobar, "My Theological Pilgrimage," 206.

33. EUSA Papers, Centre for the Study of World Christianity, University of Edinburgh. At Edinburgh 1910, Western missionaries to Latin America were told that their region was officially *evangelized* and off the table for discussion; the designation was meant to appease Anglo-Catholics yet spurred backlash among evangelically minded missionaries.

34. Escobar noted this reality in personal interviews.

35. Samuel Escobar, interview and translated by author, Valencia, October 22, 2013.

36. Ibid.

37. Orlando Costas, "Teologo en la encrucijada," in *Hacia una teología evangélica Latinoamericana*, ed. C. René Padilla (San José: Editorial Caribe, 1984), 13.

38. Orlando Costas, *The Church and Its Mission* (Wheaton, IL: Tyndale House, 1974), 12.

39. For Padilla's praise of Wheaton, see C. René Padilla, "Siervo de la palabra," 114.

40. This discussion will be expanded in Chapter 5. See pp. 100–115.

41. C. René Padilla, "My Theological Pilgrimage," 97–98.

42. See ibid., 98. René Padilla, interview and translated by author, Buenos Aires, September 13, 2013.

43. Costas, "Teologo en la encrucijada," 17.

44. See also pp. 114–115.

45. C. René Padilla, "My Theological Pilgrimage," 97; cf. C. René Padilla, "Siervo de la palabra," 115. See also C. René Padilla Papers, Buenos Aires, Argentina, "Breve apreciación sobre la obra estudiantil en América Latina," 1965, where Padilla hinted at discontent with methods of evangelism.

46. Samuel Escobar, interview and translated by author, Valencia, October 22, 2013.

47. Orlando Costas, "Conversion as a Complex Experience—A Personal Case Study," in *Down to Earth: Studies in Christianity and Culture*, ed. John R. W. Stott and Robert Coote (Grand Rapids, MI: Eerdmans, 1980), 181; cited in Yeh, "Se hace camino al andar: Periphery and Center in the Missiology of Orlando E. Costas" (DPhil thesis, University of Oxford, 2008), 40.

48. Samuel Escobar, interview and translated by author, Valencia, October 22, 2013.

49. Pete Lowman, *The Day of His Power*, 79; MacLeod, *C. Stacey Woods and the Evangelical Rediscovery of the University* (Downers Grove, IL: InterVarsity Press Academic, 2007), 251. For more on the founding of IFES, see C. Stacey Woods, *The Growth of a Work of God: The Story of the Early Days of the Inter-Varsity Christian Fellowship of the United States of America as Told by Its First General Secretary* (Downers Grove, IL: InterVarsity Press, 1978), 137–141.

50. The SCM and IVF were both national movements within their larger parent organizations WSCF and IFES.

51. For more on Lloyd-Jones and his role in postwar evangelicalism, see Stanley, *Global Diffusion*, 48–52.

52. Ibid., 48. See also Risto Lehtonen, *Story of a Storm: The Ecumenical Student Movement in the Turmoil of Revolution, 1968 to 1973* (Grand Rapids, MI: Eerdmans, 1998), 122; Robin Boyd, *The Witness of the Student Christian Movement: Church Ahead of the Church* (London: SPCK, 2007), 112–116.

53. For an SCM perspective on the meeting, see Boyd, *The Witness of the Student Christian Movement*, 84–85. For an IFES perspective on the "death" of the SCM, see Lowman, *The Day of His Power*, 31–45. For more on the erosion of evangelical consensus in Britain, see Stanley, *Global Diffusion*, 44–52.

54. Stanley, *Global Diffusion*, 158; MacLeod, *C. Stacey Woods and the Evangelical Rediscovery of the University*.

55. Woods, *Growth of a Work of God*, 32–33.

56. Ibid.; Lowman, *Day of His Power*, 73.

57. Escobar, *La chispa y la llama*, 52. Campus-in-the-Woods was an evangelical camp run by IVCF Canada near the U.S.-Canadian border. Up until the late 1960s, it was co-operated by the American and Canadian chapters. See Escobar, *La chispa y la llama*, 117. See also MacLeod, *C. Stacey Woods and the Evangelical Rediscovery of the University*, 91, 109, 149, 212–213.

58. René Padilla, interview and translated by author, Buenos Aires, September 10, 2013.

59. *His*, 1948, June–September, 47. Cited in Escobar, *La chispa y la llama*, 51.

60. David Ruesga, "Acusan a gobernación de dejar a los protestantes en completo desamparo," *El Popular* (Mexico), September 28, 1948. Cited in Hartch, *Rebirth of Latin American Christianity*, 25–27.

61. See, for example, Yale Divinity School Archives, World Christian Student Federation Papers, SC 46, Box 284, Folder 2500.

62. Yale Divinity School Archives, World Christian Student Federation Papers, SC 46, Box 284, Folder 2500.

63. M. Epstein, ed., *Statesman's Yearbook, 1933* (London: Macmillan, 1933), 1193.

64. Epstein, ed., *Statesman's Yearbook, 1945*, 1176.

65. S. H. Steinberg, ed., *Statesman's Yearbook, 1955* (London: Macmillan, 1955), 1302.

66. Gabriel A. Almond and James Smoot Coleman, *The Politics of the Developing Areas* (Princeton, NJ: Princeton University Press, 1960), cited in *Latin American Radicalism*, 148.

67. "La UNAM en números," September 30, 2013, http://www.estadistica.unam.mx /numeralia/.

68. Cf. C. René Padilla, "Student Witness in Latin America Today," *I.F.E.S. Journal* 19, no. 2 (1966): 13.

69. M. Epstein, ed., *Statesman's Yearbook, 1930* (London: Macmillan, 1930), 1195; S. H. Steinberg, ed., *Statesman's Yearbook, 1950* (London: Macmillan, 1950) 1303; Steinberg, ed., *Statesman's Yearbook, 1955*, 1322.

70. Bushnell, *The Making of Modern Colombia*, 186.

71. C. René Padilla, "Student Witness in Latin America Today"; C. René Padilla, "El testimonio Cristiano en la universidad Latinoamericana," *Pensamiento Cristiano* 14, no. 55 (1967); C. René Padilla, "La universidad: Lo social, lo spiritual," *Certeza* 8, no. 31 (1968). The latter article can be found in the C. René Padilla Papers, Buenos Aires, Argentina.

72. C. René Padilla, "La universidad.".

73. Ibid., 205.

74. C. René Padilla, "Student Witness in Latin America Today," 12–13. See Kirkpatrick, "Origins of Integral Mission."

75. Irving Louis Horowitz, "The Socioeconomic Pivot," in *Latin American Radicalism*, 148.

76. Ibid., 145.

77. C. René Padilla, "La universidad," 206; C. René Padilla, "Student Witness in Latin America Today," 13; C. René Padilla, "El testimonio Cristiano en la universidad Latinoamericana," 178.

78. C. René Padilla, "Student Witness in Latin America Today," 12. See also C. René Padilla Papers, Buenos Aires, Argentina, "Breve apreciación sobre la obra estudiantil en América Latina," 1965. Here, Padilla names communism as the main ingredient that is fermenting discontent among young people.

79. Lehtonen, *Story of a Storm*, 42.

80. Tombs, *Latin American Liberation Theology*, 68.

81. Hartch, *Rebirth of Latin American Christianity*, 12.

82. The Spanish acronym of WSCF is FUMEC—Federación Universal de Movimientos Estudiantiles Cristianos. The SCM is known as MEC—Movimiento Estudiantil Cristiano.

83. Pedro Arana, *Providencia y revolución* (Lima: El Estandarte de la Verdad, 1970), 13.

84. Alan P. Neely, "Protestant Antecedents of the Latin American Theology of Liberation" (PhD diss., American University, 1977), 253. Cited in Christian Smith, *The Emergence of Liberation Theology: Radical Religion and Social Movement Theory* (Chicago: University of Chicago Press, 1991), 253. Christian Smith's work is published from his 1990 Harvard University

thesis under the same title. See also Neely, "Liberation Theology in Latin America: Anteced-ents and Autochthony," *Missiology: An International Review* 6, no. 3 (1978): 362.

85. Richard Shaull, *Encounter with Revolution* (New York: Association Press, 1955).

86. For more on Shaull's theological contribution within student movements in Latin America, see Angel Daniel Santiago-Vendrell, *Contextual Theology and Revolutionary Transformation in Latin America: The Missiology of M. Richard Shaull* (Eugene, OR: Pick-wick Publications, 2010), 67–76. For more on his theological influence on the WCC and lib-eration theology, see pp. 74–107.

87. Julio de Santa Ana was another influential early Protestant liberation theologian from the Methodist tradition. Smith, *The Emergence of Liberation Theology*, 117.

88. Paul Davies, *Faith Seeking Effectiveness: The Missionary Theology of José Míguez Bonino* (Zoetermeer: Boekencentrum, 2006), 18. For more on the SCM, see Robin Boyd, *The Witness of the Student Christian Movement: Church Ahead of the Church* (London: SPCK, 2007).

89. Neely, "Protestant Antecedents of the Latin American Theology of Liberation," 155–156; Smith, *The Emergence of Liberation Theology*, 254.

90. Smith, *The Emergence of Liberation Theology*, 116; Neely, "Protestant Antecedents of the Latin American Theology of Liberation," 189. See also Neely, "Liberation Theology in Latin America," 363.

91. Iglesia y Sociedad en América Latina (ISAL), *Social Justice and the Latin Churches* (Richmond, VA: John Knox Press, 1969). Cited in Neely, "Liberation Theology in Latin Amer-ica," 363.

92. World Council of Churches, *The Church for Others, and the Church for the World*. For a discussion of the WCC's document *The Church for Others*, see Laing, *From Crisis to Cre-ation*, 208–209. These trends were already taking place in the 1950s, as well. See Yale Divinity School Archives, WSCF papers, SC 46, Box 284, Folder 2693, "Report on Leadership Training Course Cochabamba, Bolivia. Dec. 31, 1955 to Jan. 15, 1956."

93. Bosch, *Transforming Mission*, 382.

94. Laing, *From Crisis to Creation*, xiii.

95. Santiago-Vendrell, *Contextual Theology and Revolutionary Transformation*, 88.

96. René Padilla, interview and translated by author, Buenos Aires, September 10, 2013.

97. Ibid.

98. Ibid.

99. Paulo Freire, *Pedagogy of the Oppressed*, ed. and trans. Myra Bergman Ramos and Donaldo P. Macedo (New York: Continuum, 2012), 35.

100. Ibid., 47, 59, 63–64.

101. Ibid.

102. Smith, *Emergence of Liberation Theology*, 115.

103. Ibid.

104. See, for example, C. René Padilla, "Siervo de la palabra," 116; Escobar Papers, Esco-bar to Woods, December 14, 1968.

105. René Padilla, e-mail message to author, translated by author, October 8, 2013.

106. C. René Padilla, "Evangelio y responsibilidad social," *Certeza* 7, no. 52 (1973).

107. C. René Padilla, "La teología en Latinoamerica," *Boletín Teológico* 2 (1972): 7.

108. C. René Padilla, "Church and World: A Study of the Relation Between the Church and the World in the Teaching of the Apostle Paul" (PhD diss., University of Manchester, 1965), 245.

109. Ibid., 252. See also pp. 114–116.

110. BGCA, Latin America Mission Papers, SC 236, Box 11, Folder 8, J. W. Voelkel to Ruben Lores, March 19, 1966.

111. Escobar, *La chispa y la llama*, 81. On the Roman Catholic Church, see especially Tombs, *Latin American Liberation Theology*, 85–86, 96–97.

112. Escobar, *La chispa y la llama*, 80. See footnote 1 in Lowman, *Day of His Power*, 201–202. See also Stanley, *Global Diffusion*, 158–159.

113. Escobar, *La chispa y la llama*, 81.

114. Samuel Escobar, interview and translated by author, Valencia, October 22, 2013; René Padilla, e-mail message to author, translated by author, October 8, 2013.

Chapter 3

1. René Padilla Papers, Buenos Aires, Argentina, Henry, "Evangelical Leader Reports on Religion in Latin America," August 21, 1973.

2. It is worth noting that Henry reluctantly accepted the task of examining SBL's evangelical credentials. He did so as a favor to Harold Lindsell, his former FTS colleague and veteran of the fundamentalist-modernist controversies. Henry privately regretted the controversy but stood by the claims made in his article. SBL Archives, San José, Costa Rica, Lindsell to Lores, July 13, 1973.

3. SBL Archive, San José, Lores to Rohrer, cc. Carl F. H. Henry, September 21, 1973.

4. René Padilla Papers, Buenos Aires, "SBL Faculty Open Letter," September 26, 1973.

5. Ibid.

6. René Padilla Papers, Buenos Aires, Samuel Escobar, "Evangelical Theology in Latin America," letter to the editor, EP News Service, October 6, 1973.

7. Orlando Costas, "En el camino hacia un seminario autóctono notas de viaje: 1970," SBL Archives, San José, Costa Rica, 4, 15.

8. C. René Padilla, "CLADE III: Un <<hito>> en la historia de la Iglesia," in *Discipulado y misión: Compromiso con el reino de Dios* (Buenos Aires: Ediciones Kairós, 1997), 118.

9. For a helpful discussion of development theories, see Neely, "Liberation Theology in Latin America," 348–350.

10. W. W. Rostow, *The Stages of Economic Growth, A Non-Communist Manifesto* (Cambridge: Cambridge University Press, 1960). For the global consensus, see David Ekbladh, *The Great American Mission: Modernization and the Construction of an American World Order* (Princeton, NJ: Princeton University Press, 2010), 4.

11. German economist Hans Singer also championed this theory at the same time. See also Alan P. Neely, "Protestant Antecedents of the Latin American Theology of Liberation" (PhD diss., American University, 1977). For its appropriation in the United States, see F. H. Cardoso, "The Consumption of Dependency Theory in the United States," *Latin American Research Review* 12, no. 3 (1977): 7–24.

12. Ekbladh, *Great American Mission*, 2, 8.

13. Ibid., 3.

14. Ibid., 2.

15. Brian Stanley, *The Bible and the Flag: Protestant Missions and British Imperialism in the Nineteenth and Twentieth Centuries* (Leicester, England: Apollos, 1990), 21–26.

16. Ibid.

17. See I.26. It also promoted "integral development"; see I.14. For a helpful synopsis of *Populorum progressio*, see Tombs, *Latin American Liberation Theology*, 100–101.

18. "Second General Conference of Latin American Bishops: The Church in the Present-Day Transformation of Latin America in Light of the Council," in *Liberation Theology: A Documentary History*, ed. Alfred T. Hennelly (Maryknoll, NY: Orbis Books, 1990), 101.

19. Ibid., 103. For more on these documents and dependency, see Hartch, *Rebirth of Latin American Christianity*, 62–63.

20. Smith, *Emergence of Liberation Theology*, 176.

21. Gutiérrez, *A Theology of Liberation*, 36; see also pp. 82–88. For interaction with Freire's theories of education, see pp. 91–92, 213.

22. Ibid., 85.

23. For personal correspondence, planning, and general papers from CLADE I, see BGCA, SC 324.

24. Andrew Kirk, Skype interview by author, December 1, 2014.

25. Padilla presented a paper titled "El debate contemporáneo sobre Mateo 16:17–19" (The Contemporary Debate over Matthew 16:17–19), which sought to articulate a Latin American ecclesiology in the midst of what is arguably the foremost Roman Catholic text. The Bonilla quotation in this paragraph is from Asociación Teológica Evangélica, "Actividades Asociación Teológica," *Pensamiento Cristiano* 16, no. 62 (1969): 231.

26. CLADE, *Acción en Cristo para un continente en crisis*. Personal correspondence, planning, and general papers from CLADE I can be found in collection 324 at BGCA.

27. Carlos Lastra, "Plan para América Latina," in *Acción en Cristo para un continente en crisis* (San José, Costa Rica: Editorial Caribe, 1970), 72–73.

28. C. René Padilla, "CLADE III," 118.

29. Salinas, *Golden Decade*, 76.

30. Anticommunism was widespread among conservative evangelical leaders, including in student organizations such as Campus Crusade for Christ. See John G. Turner, *Bill Bright & Campus Crusade for Christ: The Renewal of Evangelicalism in Postwar America* (Chapel Hill: University of North Carolina Press, 2008), 108. See also Gasaway, *Progressive Evangelicals*, 9.

31. For more on Padilla's response, see pp. 62, 147.

32. Samuel Escobar, interview and translated by author, Valencia, October 22, 2013.

33. Peter Wagner, *Latin American Theology: Radical or Evangelical? The Struggle for the Faith in a Young Church* (Grand Rapids, MI: Eerdmans, 1970), 9.

34. Ibid., 10.

35. Ibid. Quotation from Jorge Pantelís, "La dimensión de la iglesia," *Avance*, March–April, 1968, 2. Pantelís went on to complete his PhD at Union Theological Seminary in 1975. Jorge Pantelís, "Reino de Dios e iglesia en el proceso histórico de liberación: Perspectivas Latinoamericanas" (Kingdom of God and Church in the Historical Process of Liberation: Latin

American Perspectives) (PhD diss., Union Theological Seminary, 1976). Perhaps the most accessible example of liberation themes in Pantelís's work is Jorge Pantelís, "Implications of the Theologies of Liberation for the Theological Training of the Pastoral Ministry in Latin America," *International Review of Mission* 66, no. 261 (1977): 14–21.

36. Wagner, *Latin American Theology*, 10.

37. Ibid., 21.

38. Ibid., 27.

39. Ibid., 28.

40. Orlando Costas, "Teólogo en la encrucijada," in *Hacia una teología evangélica Latinoamericana: Ensayos en honor de Pedro Savage*, ed. C. René Padilla (Miami: Editorial Caribe, 1984), 26.

41. Ibid. C. René Padilla, "Teología Latinoamericana: ¿Izquierdista o evangélica?" *Pensamiento Cristiano* 17, no. 66 (1970).

42. Samuel Escobar, "Responsabilidad social de la iglesia," in *Acción en Cristo para un continente en crisis* (San José, Costa Rica: Editorial Caribe, 1970), 35.

43. Ibid.

44. Ibid., 34.

45. Ibid., 38.

46. Samuel Escobar, interview and translated by author, October 22, 2013.

47. C. René Padilla, "My Theological Pilgrimage," 103.

48. BGCA, SC 324, Box 2, Folder 3, Gerber to Escobar, December 4, 1969.

49. See George Marsden, *Reforming Fundamentalism: Fuller Seminary and the New Evangelicalism* (Grand Rapids, MI: Eerdmans, 1987).

50. Samuel Escobar, "Orlando Costas: In Memoriam," *Transformation* 5, no. 3 (July 1, 1988): 1.

51. Samuel Escobar Papers, Valencia, Escobar to Woods, December 19, 1969. The context of the letter seems to imply that Escobar was most likely using "famous" to imply "infamous."

52. Yeh, "*Se hace camino al andar*," 195.

53. Samuel Escobar, interview and translated by author, Valencia, October 22, 2013.

54. C. René Padilla, "My Theological Pilgrimage," 103. See also Padilla, "La Fraternidad Teológica Latinoamericana y la responsibilidad social de la iglesia," *Boletín Teológico* 59–60 (1995): 100; cf. Stoll, *Is Latin America Turning Protestant? The Politics of Evangelical Growth* (Berkeley: University of California Press, 1990), 131.

55. BGCA SC 46, Box 30, Folder 3, Troutman to Dain, February 28, 1972. See also Troutman to Bürki, February 11, 1974.

56. BGCA, John Stott Papers, Stott to Graham, 1972.

57. See, for example, BGCA, SC 473, T4, interview of Mike Berg, July 23, 2001. Lores attended CLADE.

58. B. W. Robbins, "Contextualization in Costa Rican Theological Education Today: A History of the Seminario Biblico Latinoamericano, San José, Costa Rica, 1922–1990" (PhD diss., Southern Methodist University, 1991), 101.

59. I am indebted to Dr. Bruce Robbins for access to key Costa Rican, SBL archival material.

60. Billy Graham Center Archives, Collection 473, T4, interview of Mike Berg, July 23, 2001.

61. Ibid.

62. Orlando Costas, "En el camino hacia un seminario autóctono notas de viaje: 1970," SBL Archives, San José, Costa Rica, p. 4.

63. Ibid., 15.

64. Ibid., 8. See also Plutarco Bonilla, "From the Rector," SBL Archives, San José, November, 1970.

65. Scott Nyborg, interview by Paul Ericksen, January 15, 1993, BGCA, SC 475, Tape 1.

Chapter 4

1. John Howard Yoder, "Revolución y ética evangélica," *Certeza* 44, no. 3 (1971): 104. Copy found in René Padilla Papers, Buenos Aires.

2. Ibid., 110.

3. John Howard Yoder, *The Politics of Jesus: Vicit agnus noster* (Grand Rapids, MI: Eerdmans, 1972).

4. "Books of the Century," *Christianity Today*, April 24, 2000.

5. Of course, social Christian ideas have longstanding roots in Anabaptist thinking—Yoder's ideas certainly did not originate with Latin American evangelicals.

6. BGCA, SC 358, Box 7, Folder 7, Peter Savage to Clyde Taylor, February 15, 1970.

7. See Padilla Papers, Buenos Aires, Argentina, "Administrator: Consulta Teológica—Outline of Duties (D. Smith)," November 4, 1970.

8. BGCA, SC 358, Box 7, Folder 7, FTL Memo, June 23, 1970.

9. BGCA, SC 358, Box 8, Folder 1, Clyde W. Taylor to Peter Savage, February 18, 1970. See also Savage to Taylor, January 27, 1972.

10. BGCA, SC 358, Box 8, Folder 1, Clyde W. Taylor to Peter Savage, February 18, 1970.

11. Ibid.

12. Gary J. Dorrien, *The Remaking of Evangelical Theology* (Louisville, KY: Westminster John Knox Press, 1998), 113.

13. Ibid.

14. BGCA, SC 358, Box 8, Folder 2, Wagner to Taylor, January 27, 1972.

15. Ibid.

16. BGCA, SC 358, Box 7, Folder 7, Savage to Clyde Taylor and Peter Wagner, January 27, 1972.

17. BGCA, SC 358, Box 7, Folder 7, Savage to Clyde Taylor, Vergil Gerber, C. P. Wagner, R. Sturz, E. L. Frizen. It is worth noting that Salinas cut off this illuminating final sentence. See Salinas, *Golden Decade*, 92–93.

18. Samuel Escobar, interview and translated by author, Valencia, October 22, 2013.

19. BGCA, SC 358, Box 7, Folder 7, Wagner to Savage, July 15, 1970.

20. Sharon E. Heaney, *Contextual Theology for Latin America: Liberation Themes in Evangelical Perspective* (Milton Keynes: Paternoster, 2008), 61. Both Padilla and Escobar confirmed this in personal interviews.

21. Anthony Christopher Smith, "The Essentials of Missiology from the Evangelical Perspective of 'the Latin American Theological Fraternity'" (PhD diss., Southern Baptist Theologi-

cal Seminary, 1983), 317–318. For Padilla's indebtedness to Savage's insistence on writing FTL essays, see C. René Padilla, "Siervo de la palabra," 117.

22. The following section builds on David C. Kirkpatrick, "Parachurch Competition in the Latin American Religious Marketplace," in *Relocating World Christianity: Interdisciplinary Studies in Universal and Local Expressions of the Christian Faith*, ed. Joel Cabrita, David Maxwell, and Emma Wild-Wood (Leiden: Brill, 2017), 93–114. Reference in text from Douglas A. Sweeney, *The American Evangelical Story: A History of the Movement* (Grand Rapids, MI: Baker Academic, 2005), 155–180.

23. See, for example, Ronald Youngblood, ed., *Evangelicals and Inerrancy: Selections from the Evangelical Theological Society* (Nashville, TN: Thomas Nelson, 1984).

24. Padilla Papers, Buenos Aires, "Primera consulta del FTL," December 12–18, 1970.

25. Costas, "Teólogo en la encrucijada," 25.

26. Wagner's paper is listed at Padilla Papers, Buenos Aires, "Primera consulta del FTL," December 12–18, 1970, but mention of Wagner's paper is scrubbed from later discussions such as in the published volume and later FTL press release.

27. Andrew Kirk, Skype interview by author, December 1, 2014.

28. Samuel Escobar, interview and translated by author, Valencia, October 22, 2013.

29. Samuel Escobar, "Una teología evangélica para Ibéroamerica," in *El debate contemporáneo sobre la Biblia*, ed. Peter Savage (Barcelona: Ediciones Evangélicas Europeas, 1972). For an English translation of Escobar's paper, see Samuel Escobar, "Biblical Content and Anglo-Saxon Trappings in Latin American Theology," *Occasional Bulletin of the Latin American Theological Fraternity* 1, no. 3 (1972).

30. Pedro Arana, "The Revelation of God," in *El debate contemporáneo sobre la Biblia*, ed. Pedro Savage (Barcelona: Ediciones Evangélicas Europeas, 1972), 31.

31. Ibid., 37–78.

32. Ibid., 70.

33. Padilla was identified as "Brethren" at FTL I. See Horacio Bojorge, "El debate contemporaneo sobre la Biblia," *Boletín Teológico* 1, no. 12 (1975): 24. The delay in publishing the review here reflects the delayed publication of the conference volume itself. See also C. René Padilla, "La autoridad de la Biblia en la teología Latinoamericana," in *El debate contemporáneo sobre la Biblia*, ed. Pedro Savage (Barcelona: Ediciones Evangélicas Europeas, 1972), 123.

34. C. René Padilla, "La autoridad de la Biblia en la teología Latinoamericana," 123.

35. Ibid. For more on Ramm's understanding of Word and Spirit, see Gary J. Dorrien, *The Remaking of Evangelical Theology* (Louisville, KY: Westminster John Knox Press, 1998), 123ff.

36. C. René Padilla, "Autoridad de la Biblia," 123. These included *The Pattern of Religious Authority* (1958), *The Witness of the Spirit: An Essay on the Contemporary Relevance of the Internal Witness of the Holy Spirit* (1959), and *Special Revelation and the Word of God* (1961). See Dorrien, *The Remaking of Evangelical Theology*, 123.

37. Ramm took an entire year's sabbatical leave from his teaching post at American Baptist Seminary of the West in Covina, California, to reexamine his theological methodology. Ibid., 124.

38. Bernard L. Ramm, *After Fundamentalism: The Future of Evangelical Theology* (San Francisco: Harper & Row, 1983), 27–28, 30–31.

39. C. René Padilla, "Autoridad de la Biblia."

40. Ibid., 129.

41. C. René Padilla, "La teología en Latinoamerica," 128–129; C. René Padilla, "Autoridad de la Biblia."

42. Savage, *El debate contemporáneo sobre la biblia*, 227.

43. Bojorge, "El debate contemporaneo sobre la Biblia," 24.

44. For a British example, see Padilla's discussion with IVF General Secretary Oliver Barclay, IFES Papers, Oxford, Barclay to Padilla, February 15, 1972.

45. Samuel Escobar, interview and translated by author, Valencia, October 22, 2013.

46. Ibid.; René Padilla, interview and translated by author, Buenos Aires, Argentina, p. 45 of field notes. See also Orlando E. Costas, *The Church and Its Mission* (Wheaton, IL: Tyndale House, 1974), 214–217.

47. Samuel Escobar, interview and translated by author, Valencia, October 22, 2013.

48. C. Peter Wagner, "My Pilgrimage in Mission," *International Bulletin of Missionary Research*, October 1999, 164.

49. Samuel Escobar, interview and translated by author, October 10, 2013.

50. C. Peter Wagner, "High Theology in the Andes," *Christianity Today*, January 15, 1971, 28.

51. Ibid.

52. Ibid.

53. Samuel Escobar, interview and translated by author, Valencia, October 22, 2013.

54. BGCA 358, Box 8, Folder 1, Padilla to Savage, April 14, 1971. See also Woods to Padilla, March 4, 1971.

55. Padilla Papers, Buenos Aires, Woods to Kathleen Camache, March 4, 1971.

56. Padilla Papers, Buenos Aires, Woods to Padilla, March 4, 1971.

57. Ibid.

58. Padilla Papers, Buenos Aires, Woods to Arana, Escobar and Padilla, March 5, 1971.

59. Padilla Papers, Buenos Aires, Padilla to Woods, March 15, 1971.

60. Padilla Papers, Buenos Aires, C. Peter Wagner, "Carta abierta a Rene Padilla para 'Noticiero de la Fraternidad,'" June 15, 1971.

61. BGCA, SC 358, Box 8, Folder 1, Wagner to Padilla, May 13, 1971. For more correspondence regarding this controversy, see BGCA, SC 358, Box 8, Folder 1, Wagner to Savage, June 1, 1971; BGCA, SC 358, Box 8, Folder 1, Wagner to Padilla, March 31, 1971. For more on Wagner, FTS, and his later involvement in the Vineyard Movement, see Jon Bialecki, "The Kingdom and Its Subjects: Charisms, Language, Economy, and the Birth of a Progressive Politics in the Vineyard" (PhD diss., University of California, San Diego, 2009).

62. BGCA, SC 358, Box 8, Folder 1, Padilla to Harold Lindsell, February 9, 1971.

63. Padilla Papers, Buenos Aires, Padilla to Woods, March 15, 1971.

64. Ibid.

65. C. René Padilla, "La teología en Latinoamerica," 129. "*Quien demanda una precisión absoluta en detalles mínimos de geografía, historia, ciencias naturales, etc., como requisito indispensable para la aceptación de la autoridad bíblica, la demanda porque.*"

66. C. René Padilla, "Autoridad de la Biblia," 127. Padilla Papers, Buenos Aires, Argentina, Padilla to Woods, March 15, 1971.

67. BGCA, SC 358, Box 8, Folder 1, Padilla to Savage, April 14, 1971.

68. Padilla Papers, Buenos Aires, Padilla to Woods, March 15, 1971.

69. Samuel Escobar, "Realidad y promesa de la Fraternidad Teologica Latinoamericana," *Boletín Teológico* 1, no. 2 (1977): 25. Escobar's article placed the FTL in conversation with Lausanne.

70. Samuel Escobar, interview and translated by author, Valencia, October 22, 2013. For more on Escobar's opinion on the Wagner controversy, see Samuel Escobar, "Doing Evangelical Theology at a Time of Turmoil," in *Mission in Context: Explorations Inspired by J. Andrew Kirk*, ed. John Corrie and Cathy Ross (Surrey, England: Ashgate, 2012), 38.

71. Samuel Escobar, "Heredero de la reforma radical," in *Hacia una teología evangélica Latinoamericana: Ensayos en honor de Pedro Savage*, ed. C. René Padilla (Miami: Editorial Caribe, 1984), 66.

72. Salinas, *Golden Decade*, 99. See footnote 88. See also p. 102.

73. BGCA, SC 358, Box 8, Folder 1, Alec Clifford to Peter Wagner, June 19, 1971.

74. BGCA, SC 49, Box "I.F.E.S. Minutes," Folder "General Committee (9th) 8/20–9/1/75," "Minutes of the Meeting of the Ninth General Committee, 20 August–1 September 1975," p. 13. Special thanks to IFES General Secretary Dr. Daniel Bourdanné for access to this restricted file.

75. René Padilla Papers, Buenos Aires, "Evangelical Leader Reports on Religion in Latin America," Religious New Service, August 21, 1973.

76. See also Padilla Papers, Buenos Aires, Oliver Barclay to Padilla, cc. Stacey Woods and Chua Wee Hian, February 15, 1972.

77. Padilla Papers, Buenos Aires, Argentina, "Declaración evangélica de Cochabamba," December 18, 1970. For an English translation of the Cochabamba Declaration, see Salinas, *Golden Decade*, 199–201.

78. Wagner, "High Theology in the Andes," 29.

79. C. René Padilla, "La Fraternidad Teológica Latinoamericana: Una evaluación crítica," *Misión* 7 (1983); C. René Padilla, "La Fraternidad Teológica Latinoamericana en tela de juicio," *Misión* 9 (1984). The latter engaged one of the first doctoral dissertations on the Latin American Theological Fraternity.

80. Escobar Papers, Woods to Escobar, December 17, 1969.

81. This must be inferred from the tone of Escobar's letter. See IFES Papers, Oxford, Escobar to Woods, January 24, 1972.

82. IFES Papers, Oxford, Escobar to Woods, January 24, 1972; Escobar Papers, Valencia, Padilla to Escobar, January 29, 1972. For the FTL announcement and farewell, see FTL, "Notas del momento," *Boletín Teológico* 2 (1972).

83. International Fellowship of Evangelical Students papers, Oxford, Box "International Student Movements: The Americas 1960–1983," Folder "South America," "Ediciones Certeza, Announcement of New Director," no date given.

84. Papers from the consultation can be found in C. René Padilla, ed., *Fe Cristiana y Latinoamérica hoy* (Buenos Aires: Certeza, 1974). The publishing date was delayed due to lack

of funds. The book announcement appeared alongside a farewell to Samuel Escobar. See FTL, "Notas del momento."

85. Samuel Escobar, e-mail message to author, translated by author, December 20, 2013.

86. Escobar Papers, Valencia, Padilla to Escobar, January 29, 1972.

87. Smith, "Essentials of Missiology," 29; Stoll, *Is Latin America Turning Protestant?* 131.

88. Smith, "Essentials of Missiology," 29–30.

89. C. René Padilla, *Fe Cristiana y Latinoamérica hoy*; C. René Padilla, "My Theological Pilgrimage," 104.

90. See especially Chapter 2, pp. 46–47.

91. Samuel Escobar, e-mail correspondence with author, translated by author, December 20, 2013. This will be expanded in Chapter 6, especially pp. **000–000**.

92. Samuel Escobar, interview and translated by author, Valencia, October 22, 2013.

93. Samuel Escobar, e-mail message to author, translated by author, December 20, 2013.

94. C. René Padilla, ed., *El reino de Dios y América Latina* (El Paso, TX: Casa Bautista de Publicaciones, 1975), 7.

95. René Padilla, interview and translated by author, Buenos Aires, September 10, 2013.

96. Samuel Escobar, e-mail message to author, translated by author, December 20, 2013.

97. Ibid.

98. C. René Padilla, *El reino de Dios y América Latina*, 7.

99. Ibid., 9.

100. For more on Nuñez, see Emilio Antonio Nuñez C., "Testigo de un nuevo amanecer," in *Hacia una teología evangélica Latinoamericana: Ensayos en honor de Pedro Savage*, ed. C. René Padilla (Miami: Editorial Caribe, 1984).

101. Smith, "Essentials of Missiology," 313; Escobar interview.

102. Samuel Escobar, e-mail message to author, translated by author, December 20, 2013.

103. Emilio Antonio Nuñez C., "La naturaleza del reino de Dios," in *El reino de Dios y América Latina*, ed. C. René Padilla (El Paso, TX: Casa Bautista Publicaciones, 1975), 32.

104. Ibid., 32.

105. C. René Padilla, "El reino de Dios y la iglesia," in *El reino de Dios y América Latina*, ed. C. René Padilla (El Paso, TX: Casa Bautista Publicaciones, 1975), 44.

106. Ibid., 57.

107. Ibid., 61.

108. Ibid.

109. See 123–127.

110. John Howard Yoder, "El reino de Dios y la iglesia," in *El reino de Dios y América Latina*, ed. C. René Padilla (El Paso, TX: Casa Bautista Publicaciones, 1975), 108.

111. Ibid., 118.

112. C. René Padilla, *El reino de Dios y América Latina*, 7.

113. C. René Padilla, "My Theological Pilgrimage," 104.

114. Other prominent examples include the second consultation of the Commission on the Life and Mission of the Church, held in Buenos Aires, from March 13 to 20, 1976, where all five thinkers presented.

115. C. René Padilla, *El reino de Dios y América Latina*, 10.

116. Ibid.

117. C. René Padilla, "My Theological Pilgrimage," 104.

118. C. René Padilla, "Global Partnership and Integral Mission," in *Mission in Context: Explorations Inspired by J. Andrew Kirk,* eds. John Corrie and Cathy Ross (Burlington, VA: Ashgate, 2012), 56.

119. Ibid.

Chapter 5

1. Name Withheld, "Why Some Latin Americans Dislike American Missionaries," *HIS*, November 1959, 9. For more on *HIS* magazine, see A. Donald MacLeod, *C. Stacey Woods and the Evangelical Rediscovery of the University* (Downers Grove, IL: Intervarsity Press Academic, 2007), 85, 121–127.

2. Name Withheld, "Why Some Latin Americans Dislike American Missionaries," 9.

3. Ibid., 15.

4. Paul Little was a staff worker with InterVarsity-USA and later associate professor at Trinity Evangelical Divinity School and Program Director of Lausanne 1974. BGCA, Collection 300, Box 139, Folder 36, Paul Little Diary, June 4, 1959.

5. Tim Grass, *Gathering to His Name: The Story of the Open Brethren in Britain and Ireland* (Milton Keynes: Paternoster, 2006), 3. The movement divided in the late 1840s, giving rise to two streams known since as "Open" and "Exclusive" Brethren. Due to space and coherence, this chapter refers to the Open Brethren simply as Brethren.

6. See David C. Kirkpatrick, "'Freedom from Fundamentalism': Christian Brethrenism and the Rise of Latin American Social Christianity," *Journal of World Christianity* 7, no. 2 (2017): 211–233.

7. Padilla DeBorst, "Catharine Feser Padilla: Bible, Bed and Bread: A Matter of Distance," in *Mission as Transformation: Learning from Catalysts*, ed. David Cranston and Ruth Padilla DeBorst (Eugene, OR: Wipf & Stock, 2014), 34.

8. See Samuel Escobar, "My Pilgrimage in Mission," *International Bulletin of Missionary Research* 19 (1995): 206.

9. Ibid., 206.

10. Samuel Escobar, interview and translated by author, Valencia, October 21, 2013.

11. Joel A. Carpenter, *Revive Us Again: The Reawakening of American Fundamentalism* (New York: Oxford University Press, 1997), 244–245.

12. Stanley, *Global Diffusion*, 93.

13. For more on the Scottish missionary diaspora, see Andrew F. Walls, *The Cross-Cultural Process in Christian History: Studies in the Transmission and Appropriation of Faith* (Maryknoll, NY: Orbis Books, 2002), 259–272.

14. Mackay studied at the University of Aberdeen, where he earned an honors degree in 1913. The definitive biography of Mackay was written by his grandson. John Mackay Metzger, *The Hand and the Road: The Life and Times of John A. Mackay* (Louisville, KY: Westminster John Knox Press, 2010). See Samuel Escobar, "The Legacy of John Alexander Mackay," *International Bulletin of Missionary Research* 16, no. 3 (1992): 116–117.

15. R. Wilson Stanton, "Studies in the Life and Work of an Ecumenical Churchman" (ThM thesis, Princeton Theological Seminary, 1958), 13; Escobar, "The Legacy of John Alexander Mackay," 116.

16. Gerald W. Gillette and John A. Mackay, "John A. Mackay: Influences on My Life," *Journal of Presbyterian History* 56, no. 1 (1978): 29.

17. Ibid., 29.

18. John Alexander Mackay, *The Other Spanish Christ: A Study in the Spiritual History of Spain and South America* (London: SCM Press, 1932), 95.

19. Ibid., 262.

20. Ibid., 210.

21. Samuel Escobar, interview and translated by author, Valencia, October 22, 2013.

22. Ibid.

23. Ibid.

24. Escobar, "The Legacy of John Alexander Mackay," 116. For another mention of Mackay's influence on Padilla, see Yeh, "Se hace camino al andar," 78, 81. For Escobar, see especially Escobar, "The Legacy of John Alexander Mackay." See also Escobar, "Doing Theology on Christ's Road," 71, and Escobar, "Heredero de la reforma radical," 53ff.

25. Pedro Arana, Skype interview and translated by author, March 11, 2014.

26. Ruth Padilla DeBorst, Skype interview by author, December 4, 2014.

27. Ruth Padilla DeBorst, "Liberate My People," *Christianity Today* 51, no. 8 (2007).

28. C. René Padilla, "My Theological Pilgrimage," *Journal of Latin American Theology* 4, no. 2 (2009): 94–95.

29. C. René Padilla, "Student Witness in Latin America Today," 21.

30. C. René Padilla, "Evangelical Theology in Latin American Contexts," in *The Cambridge Companion to Evangelical Theology*, ed. Timothy Larsen and Daniel J. Treier (Cambridge: Cambridge University Press, 2007), 261.

31. C. René Padilla, "A Steep Climb Ahead for Theology in Latin America," *Evangelical Missions Quarterly* 7, no. 2 (1971): 41.

32. While Escobar noted in "My Theological Pilgrimage" that he met Padilla at the congress, they actually met prior to the congress with Wayne Bragg and Benton Melbourne. They were on an exploration to possibly start an evangelical university. Padilla, Bragg, and Melbourne were acquainted through Wheaton and included Escobar. Samuel Escobar, interview and translated by author, October 21, 2013.

33. Ibid., 203.

34. David Bebbington, "The Place of the Brethren Movement in International Evangelicalism," in *The Growth of the Brethren Movement: National and International Experiences*, ed. Neil Dickson, Tim Grass, and Harold Hamlyn Rowdon (Milton Keynes: Paternoster, 2006), 246–247.

35. A. Pulleng, "Opportunities Today in Central America and in South America," *Echoes Quarterly Review* 25, no. 1 (January–March 1973): 19–20; W. T. Stunt, *Turning the World Upside Down: A Century of Missionary Endeavour* (Eastbourne: Upperton Press, 1972), 225; Frederick A. Tatford and John Heading, *Dawn over Latin America*, 10 vols., vol. 2 (Bath: Echoes of Service, 1983), 66–67. Many of the early publications of *El sendero del creyente* are digitally preserved in Carlos A. Bisio, comp., *Congregados en su Nombre: 125 Años en Argentina* (Pilar: Echoes of Service, 2007).

36. Bebbington, "The Place of the Brethren Movement," 259.

37. Ibid., 257.

38. Billy Graham Center Archives (BGCA) at Wheaton College, SC 49, Box 162, Folder "Correspondence: Literature Committee Association General Secretary for Literature."

39. BGCA, SC 49, Box 162, "Correspondence: Literature Committee Association General Secretary for Literature." Special thanks to Dr. Daniel Bourdanné for access to this restricted file.

40. Others included *Pensamiento Cristiano* of the Latin America Mission (LAM), which was also founded by Clifford in 1953. Tatford and Heading, *Dawn over Latin America*, 2, 67.

41. International Fellowship of Evangelical Students Papers, Oxford, England, "IFES Information Sheet 1974."

42. Ibid.

43. BGCA, SC 49, Box 162, "Correspondence: Literature Committee Association General Secretary for Literature."

44. See especially Kirkpatrick, "Origins of Integral Mission," 1–21.

45. Escobar, "Heredero de la reforma radical," 58.

46. Ibid., 59.

47. Samuel Escobar, interview and translated by author, Valencia, October 22, 2013.

48. C. René Padilla, "Student Witness in Latin America Today," *I.F.E.S. Journal* 19, no. 2 (1966): 20.

49. Ibid.

50. I am indebted to a conversation with Dana Robert for inspiring this section.

51. Turner, *Bill Bright & Campus Crusade for Christ*, 3–12, 208–216. See also Wuthnow, *The Restructuring of American Religion: Society and Faith Since World War II* (Princeton, NJ: Princeton University Press, 1988), 114.

52. Margaret Lamberts Bendroth, *Fundamentalism & Gender, 1875 to the Present* (New Haven, CT: Yale University Press, 1993), 86.

53. Ibid.

54. Craig M. Miller, associate registrar of Eastern Baptist Theological Seminary, e-mail correspondence with author, May 16, 2014.

55. Scott Alexander, Registrar's Office Manager, Transcript Officer, Eastern University, e-mail correspondence with author, June 16, 2014.

56. Craig M. Miller, associate registrar of Eastern Baptist Theological Seminary, e-mail correspondence with author, May 16, 2014. In a 2013 interview, René said Catharine's father

had earned a PhD but, according to Miller, EBTS never awarded the PhD degree and did not begin awarding the doctor of ministry until the late 1980s. EBTS's affiliate, Eastern University, also only began awarding the PhD in 2012, according to Alexander. Scott Alexander, Registrar's Office Manager, Transcript Officer, Eastern University, e-mail correspondence with author, June 16, 2014.

57. "Misión: Special Report from the Latin American Mission, 1982," unpublished paper provided by Wheaton College, Office of the Registrar, June 12, 2014.

58. Donna Rourke, Wheaton College Office of the Registrar, e-mail correspondence with author, July 12, 2014. Christopher J. H. Wright and Jonathan Lamb, eds., *Understanding and Using the Bible*, SPCK International Study Guides (London: Society for Promoting Christian Knowledge, 2009), viii.

59. John Woodbridge, interview by author, Trinity Evangelical Divinity School, Deerfield, IL, April 22, 2014.

60. Billy Graham Center Archives, Wheaton College, interview of René Padilla by Paul Ericksen, Collection 361, T1, March 12, 1987. Padilla was deeply influenced by Puerto Rican and Mexican immigrants at this church. See Padilla, "Siervo de la palabra," 114.

61. René Padilla, interview and translated by author, Buenos Aires, September 12, 2013. See also Ruth Padilla DeBorst, "Catharine Feser Padilla: Bible, Bed and Bread," 34.

62. "Misión: Special Report from the Latin America Mission, 1982," unpublished paper provided by Wheaton's Registrar Office; BGCA, interview of René Padilla by Paul Ericksen, Collection 361, T1, March 12, 1987.

63. Bendroth, *Fundamentalism & Gender*, 75.

64. For Feser Padilla's focus on teaching the Bible, see Catharine Feser Padilla, "Using the Bible in Groups," in *Understanding and Using the Bible*, ed. Christopher J. H. Wright and Jonathan Lamb (London: Society for Promoting Christian Knowledge, 2009).

65. "Offerings Go Many Places," *Delaware County Daily Times*, February 15, 1964, 23.

66. "Misión: Special Report from the Latin America Mission," unpublished paper provided by Wheaton College Office of the Registrar, June 12, 2014.

67. Instituto Bíblico Buenos Aires was founded in 1946 through C&MA missionaries Samuel and Vera Barnes.

68. Catharine F. and C. René Padilla, *Mujer y hombre en la misión de Dios* (Buenos Aires: Ediciones Kairos, 1994). Catharine F. Padilla and Elsa Tamez, *La relación hombre-mujer en perspectiva Cristiana: El testimonio evangélico hacia el tercer milenio: Palabra, espíritu y misión* (Buenos Aires: Ediciones Kairos, 2002). See also Feser Padilla's presentation at ASIT Consultation in Santa Cruz, Bolivia, Catharine F. Padilla, "El ministerio de la mujer en la iglesia," *Encuentro y diálogo* 8 (1991). Catharine F. Padilla, "Los 'laicos' en la misión en el Nuevo Testamento," in *Bases bíblicas de la misión: Perspectivas Latinoamericanas*, ed. C. René Padilla (Buenos Aires: Eerdmans, 1998).

69. C. René Padilla, "My Theological Pilgrimage," 96. For more on this connection to Padilla, see Chapter 4, p. **000**; Padilla, "Siervo de la palabra," 114; Billy Graham Center Archives, Wheaton College, interview of René Padilla by Paul Ericksen, Collection 361, T1, March 12, 1987.

70. The present researcher viewed Padilla's Wheaton transcripts at the Kairos Center, Pacheco, Buenos Aires, September 12, 2013.

71. BGCA, interview of René Padilla by Paul Ericksen, Collection 361, T1, March 12, 1987.

72. BGCA, interview of René Padilla by Paul Ericksen, Collection 361, T2, March 12, 1987.

73. Ruth Padilla DeBorst, "Twin Peaks: From the Padilla-DeBorsts," unpublished support letter (2009).

74. René Padilla, interview and translated by author, Buenos Aires, September 11, 2013.

75. Pedro Arana, Skype interview and translated by author, March 11, 2014.

76. International Fellowship of Evangelical Students Papers, Oxford, England, Box "International Student Movements: The Americas 1960–1983," Folder "South America," Samuel Escobar to C. Stacey Woods, cc. Barclay, Chua Wee Hian, and Padilla, January 24, 1972.

77. Dannette Costas, "Missiology: From the Underside of History," an interview with Orlando Costas. See David Traverzo Galarza, "The Emergence of a Latino Radical Evangelical Social Ethic in the Work and Thought of Orlando E. Costas: An Ethico-Theological Discourse from the Underside of History" (PhD diss., Drew University, 1992), Appendix B.

78. Wee Hian was general secretary of IFES from 1972 to 1991. Interview of René Padilla by author, translated by author, Buenos Aires, Argentina, September 12, 2013.

79. Interview of René Padilla by author, translated by author, Buenos Aires, Argentina, September 12, 2013.

80. Ibid.

81. René has since remarried.

82. Interview of René Padilla by author, translated by author, Buenos Aires, Argentina, September 10, 2013.

83. René Padilla, interview and translated by author, Buenos Aires, September 12, 2013.

84. Ibid.

85. Dana Lee Robert, *American Women in Mission: A Social History of Their Thought and Practice* (Macon, GA: Mercer University Press, 1996), 17–24.

86. Ibid., 21.

87. Ruth Padilla DeBorst, "'Unlikely Partnerships': Global Discipleship in the Twenty-First Century," *Transformation* 28, no. 4 (2011): 242.

88. Catharine and René settled in Bogotá in 1961, where Padilla had lived as a child. See also Chapter 2, pp. 36–37. René Padilla, interview and translated by author, Buenos Aires, September 12, 2013. See also C. René Padilla, "My Theological Pilgrimage," Yale Divinity School Archives, World Christian Student Federation Papers, SC 46, Box 284, Folder 2500.

89. Escobar, *La chispa y la llama*, 70.

90. Lambeth Palace Library, London, England, John R. W. Stott Papers, "Argentina 4–10 July 1977." Special thanks to archivist Adele Allen for providing access to Stott's papers while they were being catalogued.

91. Lambeth Palace Library, London, John R. W. Stott Papers, "Travel Diary 1980."

92. Emily J. Manktelow, *Missionary Families: Race, Gender and Generation on the Spiritual Frontier* (Manchester: Manchester University Press, 2013), 78–81.

93. Escobar, *La chispa y la llama*, 71.

94. Lambeth Palace Library, London, John R. W. Stott Papers, "Galapagos 24 June to 1 July 1977."

95. René Padilla, interview and translated by author, Buenos Aires, September 11, 2013.

96. Ibid.

97. Elisa Padilla, "Ojalá pudiera darte otro abrazo y decirte cuánto, cuánto te quiero," *Revista Kairos* Informe especial en memoria de Catalina F. Padilla (2009): 32. See also C. René Padilla, "Dios me la dio, Dios me la quitó. ¡Bendito sea el nombre de Dios!" *Revista Kairos* Informe especial en memoria de Catalina F. Padilla (2009): 29, https://revistakairos.files .wordpress.com/2011/07/25-artc2a1culo3.pdf.

98. Gladys Amador, "No hablaba mucho, pero decía mucho con sus acciones," *Revista Kairos* Informe especial en memoria de Catalina F. Padilla (2009): 32.

99. Padilla Papers, Buenos Aires, "Encuentro y diálogo, ASIT, number 8, 1991."

100. C. René Padilla, "La Relación Hombre-Mujer en la Biblia," in *Fundamentos bíblicos teológicos de matrimonio y la familia*, ed. Jorge Maldonado (Buenos Aires: Nueva Creación, 1995).

101. Catharine F. Padilla, *La palabra de Dios para el pueblo de Dios: Una introducción al estudio de la Biblia* (Buenos Aires: Ediciones Kairos, 2007). For more on this work, see Padilla DeBorst, "Catharine Feser Padilla: Bible, Bed and Bread," 36.

102. René Padilla, interview and translated by author, Buenos Aires, September 9, 2013. See a similar account in Padilla DeBorst, "Catharine Feser Padilla: Bible, Bed and Bread."

103. Robert, *American Women in Mission*, xviii–xix.

104. Ibid.

105. Padilla DeBorst, "Catharine Feser Padilla: Bible, Bed and Bread."

106. Catharine F. Padilla, Global Connections' "Thinking Mission" Forum, October 8, 2008. This can be found online at http://www.globalconnections.org.uk/sites/newgc.localhost /files/papers/Reading%20the%20Bible%20with%20the%20People%20%28paper%29%20 -%20Catharine%20Padillas%20-%20Oct%2008.pdf.

107. This conviction also permeated her work as one of the primary curriculum writers for the Center for Interdisciplinary Theological Studies or CETI, whose courses are taught widely throughout Latin American churches.

108. Padilla DeBorst, "Twin Peaks: From the Padilla-DeBorsts" (unpublished support letter), 2.

109. Ibid.

110. For example, C. René Padilla, "Hombre y mujer, coherederos del reino," in *Discipulado y misión: Compromiso con el reino de Dios* (Buenos Aires: Ediciones Kairos, 1997), 197; C. René Padilla, "Amor y sexo," *Certeza* 59 (1975); C. René Padilla, "La mujer: Un ser humano," *Certeza* 57 (1975).

111. René Padilla, interview and translated by author, Buenos Aires, September 9, 2013.

112. Pedro Arana, Skype interview and translated by author, March 11, 2014.

113. Dana Lee Robert, *Christian Mission: How Christianity Became a World Religion* (Chichester: Wiley-Blackwell, 2009), 118; Robert, *American Women in Mission*; Manktelow, *Missionary Families*; Jane Hunter, *The Gospel of Gentility: American Women Missionaries in*

Turn-of-the-Century China (New Haven, CT: Yale University Press, 1984); Eva Jane Price, *China Journal 1889–1900: An American Missionary Family During the Boxer Rebellion* (New York: Scribner, 1989).

114. Skype interview of Pedro Arana by author, translated by author, March 11, 2014.

Chapter 6

1. Lambeth Palace Library, London, John R. W. Stott Papers, "Stott 6/1/15 Travel Diaries 1977."

2. Davies, *Faith Seeking Effectiveness*, 31; cf. Heaney, *Contextual Theology for Latin America*, 4.

3. Mario I. Aguilar, *The History and Politics of Latin American Theology*, 3 vols., vol. 1 (London: SCM Press, 2007), 56.

4. See his early interpretation of the Council: José Míguez Bonino, *Concilio abierto: Una interpretación Protestante del Concilio Vaticano II* (Buenos Aires: Editorial La Aurora, 1967).

5. Tom Quigley, "The Great North-South Embrace," *America* 201, no. 18 (2009), http://americamagazine.org/issue/718/article/great-north-south-embrace.

6. Davies, *Faith Seeking Effectiveness*, 22.

7. This is further discussed on pp. 46–47.

8. Smith, *Emergence of Liberation Theology*. The rise of ISAL and Protestant theologies of liberation are explored further below.

9. Davies, *Faith Seeking Effectiveness*, 3.

10. Ibid.

11. Costas, "Teólogo en la encrucijada," 25.

12. Ibid.

13. José Míguez Bonino, "Fundamentos teológicos de la responsabilidad social de la iglesia," in *La responsabilidad social del Cristiano*, ed. Rodolfo Obermüller (Buenos Aires: Montevideo, 1964).

14. C. René Padilla, *El reino de Dios y América Latina*, 10.

15. José Míguez Bonino, "El reino de Dios y la historia," in *El reino de Dios y América Latina*, ed. C. René Padilla (El Paso: Casa Bautista de Publicaciones, 1975), 75.

16. Ibid., 86–87; cf. José Míguez Bonino, "Historical Praxis and Christian Identity," in *Frontiers of Theology in Latin America*, ed. Rosino Gibellini (Maryknoll, NY: Orbis Books, 1979), 276.

17. Ibid.

18. Brian Stanley, *Christianity in the Twentieth Century: A World History* (Princeton, NJ: Princeton University Press, 2018).

19. Ibid., 76.

20. Ibid., 82; Míguez Bonino says something similar in Míguez Bonino, "Historical Praxis and Christian Identity," 282.

21. C. René Padilla, "El reino de Dios y la iglesia," 46ff.

22. Míguez Bonino, "El reino de Dios y la historia," 82; Míguez Bonino, "Historical Praxis and Christian Identity," 271–272.

23. Gibellini, *Frontiers of Theology in Latin America*. Míguez Bonino's FTL paper was later published in the conference volume and elsewhere. José Míguez Bonino, "Reino de Dios e historia: Reflexiones para una discusión del tema," *Acción Pastoral Ecuménica* 2, no. 2 (1974); Mario Aguilar called this book Míguez Bonino's "seminal work." Aguilar, *The History and Politics of Latin American Theology*, 1, 61. The title *Revolutionary Theology Comes of Age* reflects the U.K. title.

24. See, for example, José Míguez Bonino, *Doing Theology in a Revolutionary Situation* (Philadelphia: Fortress Press, 1975), 134–135; Míguez Bonino, "El reino de Dios y la historia," 77–79.

25. See, for example, Míguez Bonino, *Doing Theology in a Revolutionary Situation*, x.

26. René Padilla, interview and translated by author, Buenos Aires, September 10, 2013.

27. Davies, *Faith Seeking Effectiveness*, 106–107.

28. For the conference papers, see *El Cristianismo Evangélico en la América Latina: Informes y resoluciones de la Primera Conferencia Evangélica Latinoamericana* (Buenos Aires: La Auora, 1949). For more on CELA, see Salinas, *Golden Decade*, 52ff; Mondragón, *Like Leaven in the Dough*, 73–74, 108; Heaney, *Contextual Theology for Latin America*, 53.

29. José Míguez Bonino, *Faces of Latin American Protestantism: 1993 Carnahan Lectures* (Grand Rapids, MI: Eerdmans, 1997), 44.

30. Escobar, "Heredero de la reforma radical," 63.

31. Salinas, *Golden Decade*, 56.

32. Asamblea de Iglesias Cristianas Consejo Latinoamericano de Iglesias, *Oaxtepec 1978: Unidad y misión en América Latina* (San José, Costa Rica: Comité Editorial del CLAI, 1980).

33. Raimundo C. Barreto Jr., "Facing the Poor in Brazil: Towards an Evangélico Progressive Social Ethics" (PhD diss., Princeton Theological Seminary, 2006), 191.

34. René Padilla, interview and translated by author, Buenos Aires, September 10, 2013; Samuel Escobar, interview and translated by author, Valencia, October 22, 2013.

35. Castro was director of the WCC's Commission of World Mission and Evangelism (CWME) from 1973 to 1983 and president of the World Council of Churches (WCC) from 1985 to 1992.

36. René Padilla, interview and translated by author, Buenos Aires, September 10, 2013.

37. Emilio Castro, "Editorial," *International Review of Mission* 40, no. 1 (1988): 3.

38. René Padilla, interview and translated by author, Buenos Aires, September 10, 2013.

39. [Unknown author], "In Tribute: Friends, Colleagues Recall Dean Costas," *Today's Ministry: A Report from Andover Newton* 5, no. 2 (Winter 1988), cited in Yeh, "Se hace camino al andar," 74.

40. Ibid.

41. Orlando Costas, *Liberating News: A Theology of Contextual Evangelization* (Grand Rapids, MI: Eerdmans, 1989).

42. René Padilla Papers, Buenos Aires, FTL, "Notas del momento," 11.

43. Davies, *Faith Seeking Effectiveness*, 23.

44. C. René Padilla, "La teología en Latinoamerica," 5.

45. C. René Padilla, "Iglesia y Sociedad en América Latina," in *Fe Cristiana y Latinoamérica hoy*, ed. C. René Padilla (Buenos Aires: Ediciones Certeza, 1974), 126.

46. Ibid.

47. José Míguez Bonino, "El camino del teólogo Protestante Latinoamericano," *Cuadernos de Marcha* 29 (1969): 64.

48. Ibid., 62.

49. Míguez Bonino, *Faces of Latin American Protestantism*, 24–25.

50. Quoted in Míguez Bonino, *Doing Theology in a Revolutionary Situation*, 87.

51. Ibid.

52. C. René Padilla, "Iglesia y Sociedad en América Latina," 146. See also C. René Padilla, "La teología en Latinoamerica," 7.

53. C. René Padilla, "La teología en Latinoamerica," 4.

54. C. René Padilla, "Theology of Liberation," 70.

55. Ibid.

56. C. René Padilla, "La Teología en Latinoamerica," 7.

57. For example, José Míguez Bonino, "Comments 'Unity of the Church—Unity of Mankind,'" *Ecumenical Review* 24, no. 1 (1972); José Míguez Bonino, "Unidad cristiana y reconciliación social: Coincidencia y tensión," *Cuadernos de Teología* 2, no. 2 (1972); José Míguez Bonino, "Christian Unity and Social Reconciliation: Consonance and Tension," *Study Encounter* 9, no. 1 (1973); José Míguez Bonino, "A Latin American Attempt to Locate the Question of Unity," *Ecumenical Review* 26, no. 2 (1974); José Míguez Bonino, "El ecumenismo en 1975," *Acualidad Pastoral* 9, no. 95/96 (1976).

58. René Padilla, interview and translated by author, Buenos Aires, September 10, 2013. See also below the discussion of CLADE III.

59. Míguez Bonino, *Faces of Latin American Protestantism*, 48.

60. Ibid.

61. Ibid., 49.

62. Ibid.

63. Ibid., 49–50.

64. Samuel Escobar, interview and translated by author, Valencia, October 22, 2013. Costas himself gave credit to Míguez Bonino for influencing him in this realm. See Costas, *Theology of the Crossroads*, 254ff.

65. Míguez Bonino, "A Latin American Attempt to Locate the Question of Unity"; Costas, *Theology of the Crossroads*, 264–265.

66. Costas, *Theology of the Crossroads*, 265.

67. Ibid.

68. José Míguez Bonino, *Christians and Marxists: The Mutual Challenge to Revolution* (Grand Rapids, MI: Eerdmans, 1976).

69. C. René Padilla, "Unidad y misión," *Misión* 4, nos. 4–5 (1985); C. René Padilla, "Misión integral: Evangélica y ecuménica," in *Discipulado y misión* (Buenos Aires: Ediciones Kairós, 1997). See also C. René Padilla, "Wholistic Mission: Evangelical and Ecumenical," *International Review of Mission* 81 (1992); C. René Padilla, "Prológo: Evangélico y ecuménico," in *Crónicas de aparecida: Un pastor Evangélico en la V Conferencia General del Episcopado Latinoamericano y del Caribe*, ed. Harold Segura (Buenos Aires: Ediciones Kairós, 2008).

70. René Padilla, interview and translated by author, Buenos Aires, September 10, 2013.

71. Ibid.

72. C. René Padilla, "CLADE III."

73. Samuel Escobar, "The Whole Gospel for the Whole World from Latin America," *Transformation* 10, no. 1 (1993): 30.

74. Míguez Bonino, *Faces of Latin American Protestantism*, 50–51.

75. José Míguez Bonino, "CLADE III como reunión ecuménica," *Boletín Teológico* 25, no. 51 (1993): 161.

76. Ibid.

77. Ibid., 163.

78. Escobar, "The Whole Gospel," 30.

79. René Padilla, interview and translated by author, Buenos Aires, September 10, 2013.

80. Ibid.

81. Ibid.

82. Samuel Escobar, interview and translated by author, Valencia, October 22, 2013.

83. Mackay made the metaphorical distinction between theology from the balcony (*el balcón*) and that made on the path (*el camino*). John Alexander Mackay, *Prefacio a la teología Cristiana* (1945; México: Casa Unida de Publicaciones, 1984), 38.

Chapter 7

1. The present researcher observed these stations at the conference in 2011.

2. Ibid.

3. Giglio eventually rejected the invitation—widely seen as the result of pressure from LGBT activists and the White House regarding his traditional stance on sexual ethics.

4. Jordan Hultine, "College Students Raise Funds to Fight Slavery," CNN Belief Blog, http://religion.blogs.cnn.com/2013/01/06/college-students-raise-funds-to-fight-slavery; Sheryl Gay Stolberg, "Pastor Chosen for Inauguration Was Criticized as AntiGay," *New York Times*, January 10, 2013; Sheryl Gay Stolberg, "Minister Backs Out of Speech at Inaugural," *New York Times*, January 11, 2013.

5. This quote was found by the present researcher on the wall of the sex trafficking booth at the Passion Conference.

6. Richard Stearns, *A Hole in the Gospel: What Does God Require of Us? The Answer That Changed My Life and Might Just Change the World* (Nashville, TN: Thomas Nelson, 2010), 2, 201.

7. Piper was especially impacted by Ralph Winter's Lausanne presentation and his "unreached people groups" emphasis. John Piper, "John Piper's Personal Tribute to the Late Ralph Winter," May 21, 2009, https://www.desiringgod.org/articles/john-pipers-personal -tribute-to-the-late-ralph-winter.

8. Vinay Samuel, phone interview by author, May 13, 2014.

9. "Globe at a Glance," *World Vision*, March 1971.

10. Vinay Samuel and Chris Sugden, eds., *The Church in Response to Human Need* (Grand Rapids, MI: Eerdmans), ix.

11. David Brooks, "Who Is John Stott," *New York Times*, November 30, 2004.

12. Timothy Dudley-Smith, *John Stott: A Global Ministry* (Downers Grove, IL: Inter-Varsity Press, 2001), back cover.

13. Wolfgang Saxon, "Rev. John Stott, Major Evangelical Figure, Dies at 90," *New York Times*, July 28, 2011, A27.

14. See especially Chapman, *Godly Ambition*.

15. Ibid., 133.

16. René Padilla, interview by author, Buenos Aires, September 10, 2013.

17. Samuel Escobar, interview and translated by author, Valencia, October 22, 2013.

18. René Padilla, interview and translated by author, Buenos Aires, September 10, 2013. This is expanded from the discussion in the Introduction, pp. **000–000**.

19. C. René Padilla, "From Lausanne I to Lausanne III," 25.

20. Ibid., 50.

21. See also pp. 9–10.

22. Stott, "The Great Commission," 51.

23. Ibid., 37.

24. Lambeth Palace Library, John Stott Papers, John Stott Travel Diary, "Southern Chile January 24–31 1974."

25. Ibid.

26. René Padilla, interview and translated by author, Buenos Aires, September 10, 2013.

27. Stott, *Christian Mission in the Modern World*, 23.

28. Ibid.

29. Ibid. For more on Stott's conversion to social dimensions of the gospel, see Chapman, *Godly Ambition*, 113–132.

30. I discuss this briefly in Kirkpatrick, "Origins of Integral Mission," 351–371.

31. Ibid.

32. John R. W. Stott, *Making Christ Known: Historic Mission Documents from the Lausanne Movement, 1974–1989* (Exeter: Paternoster, 1996). For more on the article, see pp. 99–101 and pp. 155, 185.

33. René Padilla, interview and translated by author, Buenos Aires, September 10, 2013.

34. Lausanne Movement YouTube Channel, "Plenary 3: Lausanne and Latin America—Samuel Escobar and Rene Padilla—Cape Town 2010," YouTube, https://www.youtube.com/watch?v=nqWsFL1pOoA.

35. Lambeth Palace Library, John Stott Papers, John Stott Travel Diary.

36. Samuel Escobar, "On the Road with John Stott," in *Portraits of a Radical Disciple*, ed. Christopher J. H. Wright (Downers Grove, IL: InterVarsity Press, 2011), 137.

37. Ibid.

38. Chapman, *Godly Ambition*, 118–119; cf. Andrew Kirk, Skype interview by author, December 1, 2014. For the discussion of Keele, see pp. 27–28.

39. Atherstone, "The Keele Congress of 1967," 186.

40. Marjorie Hyer, "Social and Political Activism Is Aim of Evangelical Group," *Washington Post*, November 30, 1973, D17. Cited in Swartz, *Moral Minority*, 1.

41. Eastern Baptist is now called Palmer Theological Seminary. Escobar, "My Pilgrimage in Mission," 209.

42. Ibid.

43. For faculty photographs, see http://tmcdaniel.palmerseminary.edu/archives/Peru .html.

44. See pp. 98, 105–108.

45. Swartz, *Moral Minority*, 153. Swartz expanded "Ron Sider and his fellow Anabaptists helped a new evangelical left coalesce around issues of global justice and simple living," 154. Sider's book, *Rich Christians in an Age of Hunger: A Biblical Study* (Downers Grove, IL: Inter-Varsity Press, 1977), was distributed widely in evangelical circles, including conservative organizations such as Campus Crusade for Christ and more progressive ones such as Padilla's IFES.

46. See, for example, the emphasis on simple lifestyle in Doris Janzen Longacre, *More-with-Less Cookbook* (Scottdale, PA: Herald Press, 1976). For more on this book, see Swartz, *Moral Minority*, 161–163. See also Arthur G. Gish, *The New Left and Christian Radicalism* (Grand Rapids, MI: Eerdmans, 1970); Arthur G. Gish, *Beyond the Rat Race* (Scottdale, PA: Herald Press, 1973).

47. Ronald J. Sider, *Christian Century*, March 19, 1980, 314. For more on an "evangelical liberation theology," see Gasaway, *Progressive Evangelicals*, 203–210.

48. C. René Padilla, "Theology of Liberation," *Christianity Today*, November 9, 1973, 70.

49. Ronald J. Sider, "Words and Deeds," *Journal of Theology for Southern Africa* no. 29 (December 1979): 47.

50. "Rev. Orlando Costas, 45; Protestant Theologian," obituary in the *New York Times*, November 8, 1987, 52.

51. "An Open Letter to North American Christians," *Vanguard* (January–February 1977): 4–5. Cited in Swartz, *Moral Minority*, 129.

52. Swartz, *Moral Minority*, 129.

53. See ibid., 129–130.

54. Shane Claiborne, *Irresistible Revolution: Living as an Ordinary Radical* (Grand Rapids, MI: Zondervan, 2006). See John Leland, "Rebels with a Cross," *New York Times*, March 2, 2006, https://www.nytimes.com/2006/03/02/fashion/thursdaystyles/rebels-with -a-cross.html.

55. See especially Gasaway's extensive discussion of Campolo in *Progressive Evangelicals*, 11–14, etc.

56. Swartz, *Moral Minority*, p. 130.

57. Samuel Escobar, interview and translated by author, Valencia, October 22, 2013.

58. Donald McGavran, *Understanding Church Growth* (Grand Rapids, MI: Eerdmans, 1970), 198.

59. Martin Luther King Jr., "Meet the Press," April 17, 1960.

60. Ibid., 139. Progressive evangelical activist Jim Wallis spoke positively of Padilla's discussion in his work, *Agenda for Biblical People* (New York: Harper & Row, 1976), 13.

61. C. René Padilla, "Evangelism and the World," 137. Padilla later expanded his argument against the Homogeneous Unit Principle in his paper "The Unity of the Church and the

Homogeneous Unit Principle," *International Bulletin of Missionary Research* 6, no. 1 (January 1, 1982): 23–30.

62. C. René Padilla, "Teología Latinoamericana," 136–137.

63. Padilla Papers, Buenos Aires, McGavran to Padilla, May 24, 1971.

64. René Padilla, interview and translated by author, Buenos Aires, September 10, 2013. McGavran also wrote to Paul Little, asking him to forward one of his articles to Padilla, "The Theological Meaning of the Growing Interest in Church Growth in Asia," and to ask him to stop his criticism. Little did send on the article but without McGavran's suggested comment. See SC 426, Box 1, Folder E, McGavran to Little, August 22, 1974.

65. BGCA, SC 49, Box 3, Folder "Staff: 1971: E-Z & Misc. Correspondence," Woods to Escobar, October 23, 1972.

66. Steuernagel, "The Theology of Missions," 177; C. René Padilla, "The Unity of the Church and the Homogeneous Unit Principle," *International Bulletin of Missionary Research* VI, no. 1 (1982); C. René Padilla, "La unidad de la iglesia y el principio de unidades homogéneas," in *Misión integral* (Grand Rapids, MI: Nueva Creación, Eerdmans, 1986); C. René Padilla, "The Unity of the Church and the Homogeneous Unit Principle," in *Landmark Essays in Mission and World Christianity*, ed. Robert L. Gallagher and Paul Hertig (Maryknoll, MD: Orbis Books, 2009); C. René Padilla, "The Unity of the Church and the Homogeneous Unit Principle," in *Exploring Church Growth*, ed. Wilbert R. Shenk (Grand Rapids, MI: Eerdmans, 1983).

67. The proceedings can be found online at https://www.lausanne.org/content/lop/lop-1.

68. René Padilla, interview and translated by author, Buenos Aires, September 10, 2013. The present researcher asked, "Tell me about your relationship with John Stott."

69. Lambeth Palace Library, John Stott Papers, John Stott Travel Diary, Stott 6/1/15, "Travel Diaries 1977," 156ff.

70. Padilla's paper at the HUP consultation was titled "The Unity of the Church and the Homogeneous Unit Principle," which later largely comprised a chapter in his work *Mission Between the Times*. It also appeared in the *International Bulletin of Missionary Research* and Wilbert R. Shenk, ed., *Exploring Church Growth* (Grand Rapids, MI: Eerdmans, 1983).

71. These four are similar to those raised by Padilla in C. René Padilla, "Siervo de la palabra," 118; cf. C. René Padilla, "From Lausanne I to Lausanne III," 7.

72. Escobar, "Realidad y Promesa de la Fraternidad Teológica Latinoamericana," 26. For plenary speech titles, see Mae Rooy, "Una reflexion Latinoamericana sobre 'el pueblo de Dios,'" *Boletín Teológico* 1, no. 2 (1977). See also Escobar, "Heredero de la reforma radical," 69.

73. Samuel Escobar, "Missionary Dynamism in Search of Missiological Discernment," *Evangelical Review of Theology* 23, no. 1 (1999).

74. Other examples within *Boletín Teológico* include Samuel Escobar, "Lausana II y el peregrinaje de la misiología Evangélica," *Boletín Teológico* 36 (1989). Elsewhere, Escobar interacts with these themes in English: Samuel Escobar, "A Movement Divided: Three Approaches to World Evangelisation Stand in Tension with One Another," *Transformation* 8, no. 4 (1991).

75. Escobar, "Realidad y Promesa de la Fraternidad Teologica Latinoamericana," 23.

76. Ibid. Escobar's paper "La formación del pueblo de Dios en las grandes urbes" can be found in Rooy, "Una reflexión Latinoamericana sobre 'El pueblo de Dios,'" 13–17.

77. Samuel Escobar, interview and translated by author, Valencia, October 22, 2013.

78. Samuel Escobar, interview and translated by author, Valencia, October 22, 2013.

79. For Padilla's agreement, see C. René Padilla, "From Lausanne I to Lausanne III," 8.

80. H. Richard Niebuhr, *Christ and Culture* (New York: Harper, 1951).

81. Orlando Costas, "Proclaiming Christ in the Two Thirds World," in *Sharing Jesus in the Two Thirds World: Evangelical Christologies from the Contexts of Poverty, Powerlessness, and Religious Pluralism*, ed. Sugden Chris and Vinay Samuel (Grand Rapids, MI: Eerdmans, 1982), 3.

82. Ruth Padilla DeBorst, Skype interview by author, December 4, 2014.

83. The Lausanne Movement, "The Thailand Statement," http://www.lausanne.org /content/statement/thailand-statement; cf. Costas, "Proclaiming Christ in the Two Thirds World," 4, 5.

84. C. René Padilla, "From Lausanne I to Lausanne III," 9.

85. Vinay Samuel, phone interview by author, May 13, 2014.

86. Bosch, *Transforming Mission*, 405–406.

87. Sugden and Samuel, *Sharing Jesus in the Two Thirds World*.

88. Ibid., preface.

89. BGCA, SC 49, I.F.E.S. Minutes, Gen. Com. II AB I + Executive Committee, Folder General Committee (9th), August 20 to September 1, 1975.

90. INFEMIT, "The Declaration of Osijek 'Freedom and Justice in Church State Relationships,'" *Transformation* 8, no. 3 (1991): 6. For more on the OCMS, see INFEMIT, "News of the International Fellowship of Evangelical Mission Theologians," *Transformation* 8, no. 3 (1991).

91. Vinay Samuel, phone interview by author, May 13, 2014; cf. Al Tizon, *Transformation After Lausanne: Radical Evangelical Mission in Global-Local Perspective* (Eugene, OR: Wipf & Stock, 2008), 76–78.

92. Vinay Samuel, phone interview by author, May 13, 2014.

93. Ibid. For more on the relationship between WEF and Lausanne, see "An Open Letter to WEF and Lausanne Committee," *Transformation* 4, no. 1 (1987): 1–7.

94. Ruth Padilla DeBorst, Skype interview by author, December 4, 2014.

95. Compassion International, "Financial Integrity," http://www.compassion.com/about /financial.htm.

96. David Westlake, interview by author, Edinburgh, November 11, 2014.

97. Padilla Papers, Buenos Aires, "Micah Network Oxford Consultation, 2001."

98. Vinay Samuel and Chris Sugden, eds., *The Church in Response to Human Need* (Grand Rapids, MI: Eerdmans, Regnum, 1987), 260.

99. Bosch, *Transforming Mission*, 407.

100. Christopher Wright, ed., *Cape Town Commitment* (Peabody, MA: Hendrickson Publishers, 2011), part I, 10b.

101. Lausanne Movement YouTube Channel, "Plenary 3: Lausanne and Latin America—Samuel Escobar and Rene Padilla—Cape Town 2010," YouTube, https://www.youtube.com/watch?v=nqWsFL1pOoA. Padilla expanded on these three concerns in C. René Padilla, "From Lausanne I to Lausanne III," 20–25.

102. I am grateful to Michael Clawson and a 2013 conversation, which put me on the trail of this integral mission–Brian McLaren connection.

103. Time Staff, "The 25 Most Influential Evangelicals in America," *Time,* January 20, 2005.

104. Skype interview with Brian McLaren, November 20, 2014. For example, in Peralta, Dominican Republic, McLaren met a young Pentecostal pastor named Franciso Sanchez Roso. For McLaren, this church was "one of the most inspiring churches I ever met." Roso told McLaren, "Everything he had done in his church . . . had just flowed out of reading [Padilla's book *Local Church: Agent of Transformation*]."

105. Michael Clawson, "Misión Integral and Progressive Evangelicalism: The Latin American Influence on the North American Emerging Church," *Religions* 3, no. 3 (2012).

106. McLaren, interview.

107. Ibid. McLaren expanded on these ideas in Brian D. McLaren, *A New Kind of Christianity: Ten Questions That Are Transforming the Faith* (New York: HarperOne, 2010).

108. McLaren, interview.

109. Swartz, *Moral Minority*, 8.

110. Samuel Escobar, *The New Global Mission: The Gospel from Everywhere to Everyone* (Downers Grove, IL: InterVarsity Press, 2003).

Conclusion

1. The Henry Center for Theological Understanding, Trinity Evangelical Divinity School, Deerfield, Illinois, http://henrycenter.tiu.edu/trinity-debates/previous-debates/.

2. Brian McLaren, Skype interview by author, November 20, 2014.

3. Jim Wallis, Public Lecture and Question and Answer Session at St. John's Episcopal Church, Edinburgh, Scotland, August 29, 2013.

4. Sider, *Rich Christians in an Age of Hunger*, 158.

5. Andrew Preston, *Sword of the Spirit, Shield of Faith: Religion in American War and Diplomacy* (New York: Knopf, 2012).

6. Ibid.

7. Andrew Preston, "Evangelical Internationalism: A Conservative Worldview for the Age of Globalization," in *The Right Side of the Sixties: Reexamining Conservatism's Decade of Transformation*, ed. Laura Jane Gifford and Daniel K. Williams (New York: Palgrave Macmillan, 2012), 232.

8. Robert Wuthnow, *Boundless Faith: The Global Outreach of American Churches* (Berkeley: University of California Press, 2010), 6. See also Mark Noll, *The New Shape of World Christianity: How American Experience Reflects Global Faith* (Downers Grove, IL: IVP Academic, 2013).

9. For more on global student protests, see Lehtonen, *Story of a Storm*, 43–44. See also E. R. Norman, *Christianity and World Order* (Oxford: Oxford University Press, 1979), 52. For more on the rise of Third World theologies and its impact on the missionary movement, see Stanley, *Global Diffusion*, 25.

10. Stanley, "'Lausanne 1974,'" 534. See also Stanley, *Global Diffusion*, 155.

11. Marsden, *Reforming Fundamentalism*, 81, 94; see also 135, 204, 211. See also Stanley, "Evangelical Social and Political Ethics: An Historical Perspective," especially 33ff.

12. Pew Research Forum on Religion and Public Life, "Global Christianity," December 2011, http://www.pewforum.org/files/2011/12/Christianity-fullreport-web.pdf.

BIBLIOGRAPHY

Primary Source Materials

Manuscript Collections

United Kingdom
>*Edinburgh*
>>Archives, Centre for the Study of World Christianity, School of Divinity, University of Edinburgh
>>Evangelical Union of South America Papers
>*London*
>>Archives, Lambeth Palace Library
>>The John Stott Papers
>*Oxford*
>>The International Fellowship of Evangelical Students Headquarters
>>>Box: "International Student Movements: The Americas 1960–1983"
>>>>Folder: "South America"

Argentina
>*Buenos Aires*
>>The René Padilla Papers (uncatalogued)

Spain
>*Valencia*
>>The Samuel Escobar Papers (uncatalogued)

Costa Rica
>*San José*
>>Archives of Seminario Bíblico Latinoamericano (uncatalogued)

United States
>*Deerfield, IL*
>>The Archives of Trinity Evangelical Divinity School
>>>Carl F. H. Henry Papers

Milwaukee, WI

The Juan Alvarez Cuauhtémoc Photographic Collection of El Movimiento in Milwaukee's Latino Community, UW–Milwaukee Library Archives

Wheaton, IL

Billy Graham Center Archives, Wheaton College:

Collection 046 Lausanne Committee on World Evangelism

096 Interview of Wayne G. Bragg

111 Charles Henry Troutman Papers

236 Latin America Mission Records

300 InterVarsity Christian Fellowship Records

324 Primer Congreso Latinoamericano de Evangelización (CLADE)

358 C. Peter Wagner Papers

361 Carlos René Padilla Papers

426 The Paul Little Papers

475 W. Scott Nyberg Interview

521 Nancy Duarte-Gomez Interview (tape 3)

580 Billy Graham Evangelistic Association: Montreat Office

590 John R. W. Stott Collection

New Haven, CT

Special Collections, Yale Divinity School Library

World Student Christian Federation Papers, Collection 46

Spanish Primary Sources

Costas, Orlando. "Teólogo en la encrucijada." In *Hacia una teología evangélica Latinoamericana: Ensayos en honor de Pedro Savage*, edited by C. René Padilla. Miami: Editorial Caribe, 1984.

Escobar, Samuel. *La chispa y la llama: Breve historia de la comunidad internacional de estudiantes evangélicos en América Latina*. Buenos Aires: Ediciones Certeza, 1978.

———. "Heredero de la reforma radical." In *Hacia una teología Evangélica Latinoamericana: Ensayos en honor de Pedro Savage*, edited by C. René Padilla, 51–72. Miami: Editorial Caribe, 1984.

———. "Lausana II y el peregrinaje de la misiología evangélica." *Boletín Teológico* 36 (1989): 321–333.

———. "Realidad y promesa de la Fraternidad Teologica Latinoamericana." *Boletín Teológico* 1, no. 2 (1977): 23–31.

———. "Responsabilidad social de la iglesia." In *Acción en Cristo para un continente en crisis*, 32–39. San José: Editorial Caribe, 1970.

Lastra, Carlos. "Plan para América Latina." In *Acción en Cristo para un continente en crisis*. San José: Editorial Caribe, 1970.

Míguez Bonino, José. "Ante un viaje fecundo, algunas valiosas observaciones sobre la vida de las iglesias Europeas y Estadounidenses: Declaraciones de José Míguez Bonino." *Estandarte Evangélico* 71, no. 3–4 (1954): 7–9.

———. "El camino del teólogo Protestante Latinoamericano." *Cuadernos de Marcha* 29 (1969): 59–67.

———. "CLADE III como reunión ecuménica." *Boletín Teológico* 25, no. 51 (1993): 161–164.

———. *Concilio abierto: Una interpretación Protestante del Concilio Vaticano II.* Buenos Aires: Editorial La Aurora, 1967.

———. "Cristología y misión en los dos-terceros mundos." *Boletín Teológico* 8 (1982): 39–60.

———. "Fundamentos teológicos de la responsibilidad social de la iglesia." In *La responsibilidad social del Cristiano*, edited by Rodolfo Obermüller. Buenos Aires: Montevideo, 1964.

———. "¿Para qué sirve la teología?" *Certeza* 12, no. 45 (1971): 6–9.

———. "Reino de Dios e historia, reflexiones para una discusión del tema." *Acción Pastoral Ecuménica* 2, no. 2 (1974): 4–16.

———. "Unidad Cristiana y reconciliación social: Coincidencia y tensión." *Cuadernos de Teología* 2, no. 2 (1972): 109–123.

Padilla, C. René. "Amor y sexo." *Certeza* 59 (1975): 74–78.

———. "La autoridad de la Biblia en la teología Latinoamericana." In *El debate contemporáneo sobre la Biblia,* edited by Pedro Savage, 121–154. Barcelona: Ediciones Evangélicas Europeas, 1972.

———. "La Biblia hoy." *Certeza* 42 (1971): 56–59.

———. "Ciencias sociales y compromiso Cristiano." *Boletín Teológico* 31 (1988): 247–51.

———. "El círculo hermenéutico." In *Hacia una hermenéutica evangélica Tomo II*, edited by C. René Padilla, Mervin Breneman, Sidney H. Rooy, B. Melano Couch, Eugene Nida, Elsa R. Powell, and Samuel Escobar, 1–4. Buenos Aires: Ediciones Kairós, 1977.

———. "CLADE II: Un <<hito>> en la historia de la iglesia." In *Discipulado y misión: Compromiso con el reino de Dios.* Buenos Aires: Ediciones Kairós, 1997.

———. "¿El Congreso de Lausana diez años después?" *Misión* 3 (September 1983): 110–111.

———. "Cuatro tesis de Leonardo Boff sobre la iglesia." *Misión* 14 (1985): 94–96.

———, ed. *De la marginación al compromise: Los Evangélicos y la política en América Latina.* Buenos Aires: Fraternidad Teológica Latinoamericana, 1991.

———. *Los derechos humanos y el reino de Dios.* Lima: Concilio Nacional Evangélico de Peru—PROMIES, 1992.

———. "Desafíos para la próxima década." *Apuntes Pastorales* 17, no. 2 (2000): 34–39.

———. "Dios me la dio, Dios me la quitó. ¡Bendito sea el nombre de Dios!" *Revista Kairos,* Informe especial en memoria de Catalina F. Padilla, July 25, 2011.

———. *Discipulado, compromiso y misión.* San José: Visión Mundial, 1994.

———. *Discipulado y misión: Compromiso con el reino de Dios.* Buenos Aires: Ediciones Kairós, 1997.

———. "Una eclesiología para la misión integral." In *La iglesia local como agente de transformación: Una eclesiología para la misión integral*, edited by C. René Padilla and Tetsunao Yamamori, 13–45. Buenos Aires: Ediciones Kairós, 2003.

———. *Economía humana y economía del reino de Dios.* Buenos Aires: Ediciones Kairós, 2002.

———. "El Espíritu Santo y la misión integral de la iglesia." In *El trino Dios y la misión integral*, Pedro Arana Quiroz, Samuel Escobar and C. René Padilla, 115–147. Buenos Aires: Ediciones Kairós, 2003.

———. "El estado desde una perspectiva bíblica." In *Los Evangélicos y el poder político en América Latina*, edited by Pablo A. Deiros, 23–40. Buenos Aires: Nueva Creación, 1986.

———. "Los evangélicos." In *De la marginación al compromiso: Los evangélicos y la política en América Latina*, edited by C. René Padilla and Víctor Arroyo, 5–19. Buenos Aires: Fraternidad Teologica Latinoamericana, 1991.

———. *El evangelio hoy*. Buenos Aires: Certeza, 1975.

———. "Evangelismo y la responsabilidad social: De Wheaton '66 a Wheaton '83." *Misión* 4, no. 3 (September 1985): 82–90.

———. "La explosión teológica en el tercer mundo." *Misión* 2 (January–March 1983): 30–31.

———, ed. *Fe Cristiana y Latinoamérica hoy*. Buenos Aires: Certeza, 1974.

———. "La Fraternidad Teológica Latinoamericana en tela de juicio." *Misión* 9 (1984): 62–64.

———. "La Fraternidad Teológica Latinoamericana: Una evaluación crítica." *Misión* 7 (1983): 28–30.

———. "La Fraternidad Teológica Latinoamericana y la responsabilidad social de la iglesia." *Boletín Teológico* 59/60 (1995): 98–114.

———, ed. *La fuerza del Espíritu en la evangelización*. Buenos Aires: Kairós, 2006.

———. "El futuro del cristianismo en América Latina: Perspectivas y desafíos misionológicos." In *Iglesia, ética y poder*, edited by John H. Yoder, Lilia Solano, and C. René Padilla, 62–87. Buenos Aires: Ediciones Kairós, 1998.

———. "Hacia una cristología evangélica contextual." *Boletín Teológico* 30 (1988): 87–101.

———. "Hacia una definición de la misión integral." In *El proyecto de Dios y las necesidades humanas: Más modelos de ministerio integral en América Latina*, edited by C. René Padilla and Tetsunao Yamamori, 19–34. Buenos Aires: Ediciones Kairós, 2000.

———. "Hacia una ética política Evangélica." *Boletín Teológico* 44 (1991): 261–274.

———. "Hacia una evaluación teológica del ministerio integral." In *Servir con los pobres en América Latina*, edited by Gregorio Rake, C. René Padilla, and Tetsunao Yamamori, 29–52. Buenos Aires: Ediciones Kairós, 1997.

———. "Hacia una hermenéutica contextual." *Encuentro y diálogo* 1 (1984): 1–23.

———, ed. *Hacia una teología evangélica Latinoamericana: Ensayos en honor de Pedro Savage*. San José: Editorial Caribe, 1984.

———. "¿Hay lugar para Dios en la política?" *Misión* 6 (March 1987): 4–5.

———. "Hombre y mujer, coherederos del reino." In *Discipulado y misión: Compromiso con el reino de Dios*, 196–198. Buenos Aires, Argentina: Ediciones Kairos, 1997.

———. "Iglesia y Estado." *Misión* 5 (December 1986): 92–93.

———. "Iglesia y Sociedad en América Latina." In *Fe Cristiana y Latinoamérica hoy*, edited by C. René Padilla, 119–147. Buenos Aires: Ediciones Certeza, 1974.

———. "Itinerario de la misión integral: De CLADE I a CLADE IV." *Iglesia y misión* 74 (2000): 4–15.

———. "Jesús y los pobres." *Certeza* 77 (1980): 151–156.

———. "Justicia y paz." *Misión* 11 (1984): 140–143.

———. "Kairós: Formar al pueblo de Dios para la misión integral." *Orientación Cristiana* (October–December 1996): 1–2.

———. "Un largo aprendizaje." In *La aventura de escribir: Testimonio de catorce escritores Cristianos*, edited by Adriana Powell, 139–148. Lima: Ediciones Certeza, 1974.

———. "Lo de Dios y lo de César." *Certeza* 41 (1970): 2–3.

———. "La lucha por la paz." *Misión* 5 (December 1986): 92–93.

———. "El lugar de la revelación en la epistemología." In *Hacia una hermenéutica Evangélica Tomo II*, edited by C. René Padilla, Mervin Breneman, Sidney H. Rooy, B. Melano Couch, Eugene Nida, Elsa R. Powell, and Samuel Escobar, 1–4. Buenos Aires: Ediciones Kairós, 1977.

———. "Luz del mundo, sal de la tierra." *Misión* 8, no. 2 (1989): editorial.

———. "La mayordomía de los bienes materiales: Una exploración en la ética reformada." *Iglesia y Misión* 53 (1995): 6–11.

———. "Mensaje bíblico y revolución." *Certeza* 39 (1970): 200.

———. "Mensaje inaugural: Todo el evangelio para todos los pueblos desde América Latina." In *Congreso Latinoamericano de Evangelización (CLADE), III, 24 de agosto a 4 de septiembre de 1992, Quito: Todo el Evangelio para todos los pueblos desde América Latina*, 6–11. Quito: Fraternidad Teológica Latinoamericana, 1993.

———. "La misión Cristiana en las Américas: Una perspectiva Latinoamericana." In *Misión en el camino: Ensayos en homenaje a Orlando E. Costas*, edited by Samuel Escobar, Sidney Rooy, Valdir Steurernagel, C. René Padilla, Guillermo Cook, Beatriz Melano Couch, Edesio Sanchez Cetina, and Daniel Schipani, 67–94. Buenos Aires: Fraternidad Teológica Latinoamericana, 1992.

———. "La misión de la iglesia a la luz del reino de Dios." *Misión* 5 (December 1986): 122–129.

———. "La misión en la década de los años noventa." *Boletín Teológico* 34 (1989): 159–166.

———. *Misión integral: Ensayos sobre el Reino y la iglesia*. Grand Rapids, MI: Eerdmans, 1986.

———. "Misión integral: Evangélica y ecuménica." In *Discipulado y misión*, 73–75. Buenos Aires: Ediciones Kairós, 1997.

———. "Misión integral y evangelización." *Iglesia y misión* 71–72 (2000): 34–39.

———. "Misión y prosperidad." *Textos para la acción* 4, no. 6 (1996): no page numbers given.

———. "La mujer: Un ser humano." *Certeza* 57 (1975): 20–23.

———. "La nueva eclesiología en América Latina." *Boletín Teológico* 24 (1986): 201–229.

———. "Una nueva manera de hacer teología." *Misión* 1, no. 1 (1982): 20–23.

———. "Nuevas alternativas de educación teológica." *Boletín Teológico* 19 (1985): 4–20.

———, ed. *Nuevas alternativas de educación teológica*. Buenos Aires: Nueva Creación, 1986.

———. "¿Un nuevo Gustavo Gutiérrez?" *Misión* 21 (April–June 1983): 21.

———. "¡Nunca más!" *Misión* (June 1985): 51–53.

———. "El pacto de Lausana." *Boletín Teológico* 13 (1975): 4–8.

———. "La palabra de Dios y las palabras humanas." *Pensamiento Cristiano* 100 (1984): 31–32.

———. "La palabra interpretada: Reflexiones sobre hermenéutica contextual." *Boletín Teológico*, 2nd ser., no. 1 (1981): 1–8.

———. *La palabra interpretada: Reflexiones sobre hermenéutica contextual*. Lima: Asociación de Grupos Evangélicos, 1989.

———. "¿Para qué sirve la teología?" *Misión* 4, no. 4 (December 1985): 116–117.

——. "Pentecostés y la iglesia." *Encuentro y Fe* 35 (1995): 10–13.

——. "Pobreza y mayordomía." *Boletín Teológico* 42/43 (1991): 93–101.

——. "La política de Jesús." *Certeza* 53 (1974): 152–155.

——. "Politización y acción Cristiana." *Certeza* 52 (October–December 1973): 96–97.

——. "Por qué Leonardo Boff ha sido silenciado." *Cuadernos de Teología* VI, no. 4 (1985): 107–112.

——. "Prológo: Evangélico y ecuménico." In *Crónicas de aparecida: Un pastor Evangélico en la v conferencia general del episcopado Latinoamericano y del Caribe*, edited by Harold Segura, 5–23. Buenos Aires: Ediciones Kairós, 2008.

——. "El propósito de la Biblia." *Certeza* 10 (1962): 95.

——. "Proyecto para una ética social Evangélica." In *Fe Cristiana y Latinoamérica hoy*, edited by C. René Padilla, 209–214. Buenos Aires: Ediciones Certeza, 1974.

——, ed. *El reino de Dios y América Latina*. El Paso, TX: Casa Bautista de Publicacionces, 1975.

——. "El reino de Dios y la historia en la teología Latinoamericana." *Cuadernos de Teología* 7, no. 1 (1985): 5–12.

——. "El reino de Dios y la iglesia." In *El reino de Dios y América Latina*, edited by C. René Padilla, 43–68. El Paso, TX: Casa Bautista de Publicaciones, 1975.

——. "La relación hombre-mujer en la biblia." In *Fundamentos bíblicos teológicos de matrimonio y la familia*, edited by Jorge Maldonado, 47–51. Buenos Aires: Nueva Creación, 1995.

——. "La Segunda Consulta de la FTL en Lima." *Boletín Teológico* 4 (1973): no page numbers given.

——. "Ser prójimo." *Certeza* 69 (1978): 147–150.

——. "Ser prójimo." *Iglesia y misión* 74 (2000): 40–44.

——. "Siervo de la palabra." In *Hacia una teología evangélica Latinoamericana*, edited by C. René Padilla, 113–120. San José: Editorial Caribe, 1984.

——. "La sociedad de consumo en perspectiva bíblica." *Revista Certeza* 61 (1976): 148–150.

——. "La teología de la liberación: Una evaluación crítica." *Misión* 1, no. 2 (1982): 16–21.

——. "La teología en Latinoamerica." *Boletín Teológico* 2 (July 1972): 1–8.

——. "Teología Latinoamericana: ¿Izquierdista o evangélica?" *Pensamiento Cristiano* 17, no. 66 (1970): 133–140.

——. "El testimonio Cristiano en la universidad Latinoamericana." *Pensamiento Cristiano* 14, no. 55 (1967): 176–183.

——. "La unidad de la iglesia y el principio de unidades homogéneas." In *Misión integral*. Grand Rapids, MI: Nueva Creación, Eerdmans, 1986.

——. "Unidad y misión." *Misión* 4 (1985): 4–5.

——. "La universidad: Lo social, lo spiritual." *Certeza* 8, no. 31 (1968).

——. "El uso de la Biblia en el púlpito." *Misión* 7 (1983): 21–23.

——. "Vigencia del Jubileo en el mundo actual (Levítico 25)." *Boletín Teológico* 63 (1996): 71–88.

——. "Viñetas de una iglesia sierva." *Iglesia y Misión* 62 (1997): 6–11.

———. "La violencia en el Nuevo Testamento." *Boletín Teológico* 39 (1990): 197–207.

———. "Voces para nuestro tiempo: F. F. Bruce." *Certeza* 13, no. 49 (1973): 10–12.

Padilla, C. René, Mervin Breneman, Sidney H. Rooy, B. Melano Couch, Eugene Nida, Elsa R. Powell, and Samuel Escobar, eds. *Hacia una hermenéutica evangélica Tomo II*. Buenos Aires: Ediciones Kairós, 1977.

Padilla, C. René, Claudia Lorena Juárez, and Juan José Barreda Toscano. *¿Qué es la mision integral?* Buenos Aires: Ediciones Kairós, 2006.

Padilla, C. René, and Tetsunao Yamamori, eds. *La iglesia local como agente de transformación: Una eclesiología para la misión integral*. Buenos Aires: Ediciones Kairós, 2003.

———, eds. *El proyecto de Dios y las necesidades humanas*. Buenos Aires: Ediciones Kairós, 2000.

Padilla DeBorst, Ruth, Zac Niringiye, and C. René Padilla, eds. *Semillas de nueva creación: Pistas bíblicas para una vida ecologicamente justa*. Buenos Aires: Ediciones Kairós, 2010.

Yoder, John Howard. "Revolución y ética evangélica." *Certeza* año 11, num. 44, no. 3. (1971): 104–111.

English Primary Sources

Costas, Orlando. *Christ Outside the Gate: Mission Beyond Christendom*. Maryknoll, NY: Orbis Books, 1982.

———. *The Church and Its Mission*. Wheaton, IL: Tyndale House, 1974.

———. "Conversion as a Complex Experience—A Personal Case Study." In *Down to Earth: Studies in Christianity and Culture*, edited by John R. W. Stott and Robert Coote. Grand Rapids, MI: Eerdmans, 1980.

———. "Depth in Evangelism—An Interpretation of 'In-Depth Evangelism' Around the World." In *Let the Earth Hear His Voice*, edited by J. D. Douglas, 675–697. Minneapolis, MN: World Wide Publications.

———. *The Integrity of Mission: The Inner Life and Outreach of the Church*. San Francisco: Harper & Row, 1979.

———. "Proclaiming Christ in the Two Thirds World." In *Sharing Jesus in the Two Thirds World: Evangelical Christologies from the Contexts of Poverty, Powerlessness, and Religious Pluralism*, edited by Chris Sugden and Samuel Vinay, 1–15. Grand Rapids, MI: Eerdmans, 1982.

———. *Theology of the Crossroads in Contemporary Latin America: Missiology in Mainline Protestantism, 1969–1974*. Amsterdam: Rodopi, 1976.

Escobar, Samuel. "Biblical Content and Anglo-Saxon Trappings in Latin American Theology." *Occasional Bulletin of the Latin American Theological Fraternity* 1, no. 3 (1972): 1–11.

———. "Doing Evangelical Theology at a Time of Turmoil." In *Mission in Context: Explorations Inspired by J. Andrew Kirk*, edited by John Corrie and Cathy Ross, 35–44. Surrey: Ashgate, 2012.

———. "Doing Theology on Christ's Road." In *Global Theology in Evangelical Perspective: Exploring the Contextual Nature of Theology and Mission*, edited by Jeffrey P. Greenman and Gene L. Green, 67–85. Downers Grove, IL: IVP Academic, 2012.

———. "The Legacy of John Alexander Mackay." *International Bulletin of Missionary Research* 16, no. 3 (1992): 116–122.

———. "Missionary Dynamism in Search of Missiological Discernment." *Evangelical Review of Theology* 23, no. 1 (1999): 70–91.

———. "A Movement Divided: Three Approaches to World Evangelisation Stand in Tension with One Another." *Transformation* 8, no. 4 (1991): 7–13.

———. "My Pilgrimage in Mission." *International Bulletin of Missionary Research* 36, no. 4 (2012): 206–211.

———. *The New Global Mission: The Gospel from Everywhere to Everyone.* Downers Grove, IL: InterVarsity Press, 2003.

———. "The Whole Gospel for the Whole World from Latin America." *Transformation* 10, no. 1 (1993): 30–32.

Míguez Bonino, José. *Christians and Marxists: The Mutual Challenge to Revolution.* Grand Rapids, MI: Eerdmans, 1976.

———. "Christian Unity and Social Reconciliation: Consonance and Tension." *Study Encounter* 9, no. 1 (1973): 1–8.

———. "Comments 'Unity of the Church—Unity of Mankind.'" *Ecumenical Review* 24, no. 1 (1972): 47–50.

———. "The Condition and Prospects of Christianity in Latin America." In *The New Face of the Church in Latin America*, edited by Guillermo Cook, 259–267. Maryknoll, NY: Orbis Books, 1994.

———. *Doing Theology in a Revolutionary Situation.* Philadelphia: Fortress Press, 1975.

———. *Faces of Latin American Protestantism: 1993 Carnahan Lectures.* Grand Rapids, MI: Eerdmans, 1997.

———. "Historical Praxis and Christian Identity." In *Frontiers of Theology in Latin America*, edited by Rosino Gibellini, 260–283. Maryknoll, NY: Orbis Books, 1979.

———. "A Latin American Attempt to Locate the Question of Unity." *Ecumenical Review* 26, no. 2 (1974): 210–221.

Padilla, C. René "Being God's Church in Latin America: CLADE II Affirms Evangelical Convictions in the Context of Violence, Exploitation, and Corruption." *Christianity Today*, March 21, 1980.

———. "Bible Studies." *Missiology* 10 (July 1982): 319–338.

———. "The Biblical Basis for Social Ethics." In *Transforming the World? The Gospel and Social Responsibility*, edited by Jamie A. Grant and Dewi Arwel Hughes, 187–204. Nottingham: Apollos, 2009.

———. "Biblical Foundations: A Latin American Study." *Evangelical Review of Theology* 7, no. 1 (1983): 79–88.

———. "CELAM III: A Gospel of Freedom and Justice." *Christianity Today*, June 8, 1979.

———. "Christianity American-Style." *Christianity Today*, October 10, 1975.

———. "Christology and Mission in the Two Thirds World." In *Sharing Jesus in the Two Thirds World*, edited by Vinay Samuel and Chris Sugden, 17–47. Grand Rapids, MI: Eerdmans, 1983.

———. "The Church and Political Ambiguity." *Christianity Today*, July 26, 1974.

——. "The Church and the Third World." *Right On* 7, no. 3 (October 1975).

——. "The Contextualization of the Gospel." *Journal of Theology for Southern Africa* 24 (September 1978): 12–30.

——. "Current Religious Thought." *Christianity Today*, November 9, 1973.

——. "Evangelicals and Politics in Latin America." *Transformation* 9 (1992): 2–33.

——. "Evangelical Theology in Latin American Contexts." In *The Cambridge Companion to Evangelical Theology*, edited by Timothy Larsen and Daniel J. Treier, 259–274. Cambridge: Cambridge University Press, 2007.

——. "Evangelism and Social Responsibility from Wheaton '66 to Wheaton '83." In *How Evangelicals Endorsed Social Responsibility*, edited by C. René Padilla and Chris Sugden, 4–17. Nottingham: Grove Books, 1985.

——. "Evangelism and Social Responsibility: From Wheaton '66 to Wheaton '83." *Transformation* 2, no. 3 (1985): 27–33.

——. "Evangelism and the World." In *Let the Earth Hear His Voice: International Congress on World Evangelization Lausanne, Switzerland*, edited by J. D. Douglas, 116–146. Minneapolis, MN: World Wide Publications, 1974.

——. "From Lausanne I to Lausanne III." In *Mission Between the Times*, 1–25. Carlisle: UK: Langham Monographs, 2010.

——. "From Lausanne I to Lausanne III." *Journal of Latin American Theology* 5, no. 2 (2010): 19–50.

——. "The Fruit of Justice Will Be Peace." *Transformation* 2 (January/March 1985): 2–4.

——. "The Fullness of Mission." *Occasional Bulletin of Missionary Research* 3, no. 1 (1979): 6–11.

——. "Globalization, Ecology and Poverty." In *Creation in Crisis: Christian Perspectives on Sustainability*, edited by R. S. White. London: SPCK, 2009.

——. *Global Poverty and Integral Mission*. Oxford: Church Mission Society, 2008.

——. "God's Call to Do Justice." In *The Justice Project*, edited by Brian D. McLaren, Elisa Padilla, and Ashley Bunting Seeber, 23–30. Grand Rapids, MI: Baker Books, 2009.

——. "God's Word and Man's Myth." *Themelios* 3, no. 1 (1977): 3–9.

——. "God's Word and Man's Words." *Evangelical Quarterly* 53 (1981): 216–226.

——. "Hermeneutics and Culture—A Theological Perspective." In *Down to Earth: Studies in Christianity and Culture*, edited by John R. W. Stott and Robert Coote, 63–87. Grand Rapids, MI: Eerdmans, 1980.

——. "Integral Mission and Its Historical Development." In *Justice, Mercy and Humility: The Papers of the Micah Network International Consultation on Integral Mission and the Poor (2001)*, edited by Tim Chester, 42–58. Milton Keynes, UK: Paternoster, 2002.

——. "Integral Mission Today." In *Justice, Mercy and Humility: The Papers of the Micah Network International Consultation on Integral Mission and the Poor (2001)*, edited by Tim Chester, 59–64. Milton Keynes: Paternoster, 2002.

——. "The Interpreted Word: Reflections on Contextual Hermeneutics." *Themelios* 7 (September 1981): 18–23.

——. "The Kingdom of God and the Church." *Theological Fraternity Bulletin* 1–2 (1976): 1–23.

———. "Latin America: Cooperate to Evangelize?" *Christianity Today*, January 17, 1975.

———. "Latin American Evangelicals Enter the Public Square." *Transformation* 9, no. 3 (1995): 2–7.

———. "Liberation Theology (I)." *Reformed Journal* 33, no. 6 (June 1983): 21–23.

———. "Liberation Theology (II)." *Reformed Journal* 33, no. 7 (July 1983): 14–18.

———. "Liberation Theology: An Appraisal." In *Freedom and Discipleship*, edited by Daniel S. Schipani, 34–51. Maryknoll, MD: Orbis Books, 1989.

———. "Liberation Theology Is Remarkably Protestant." *Christianity Today*, May 15, 1987.

———. "Meditation on the Love of God." *Transformation* 6, no. 1 (January/March 1989): 15–18.

———. "A Message for the Whole Person." *Transformation* 10, no. 3 (July/September 1993): 1–4.

———. *Mission Between the Times: Essays on the Kingdom*. Grand Rapids, MI: Eerdmans, 1985.

———. "Mission Is Compassion." *Missiology: An International Review* 10, no. 3 (1982): 319–338.

———. "My Theological Pilgrimage." In *Shaping a Global Theological Mind*, edited by Darren C. Marks, 127–137. Burlington, VA: Ashgate, 2008.

———. "My Theological Pilgrimage." *Journal of Latin American Theology* 4, no. 2 (January 1, 2009): 91–111.

———. "New Actors on the Political Scene." In *New Face of the Church in Latin America*, edited by Guillermo Cook, 82–95. Maryknoll, MD: Orbis Books, 1994.

———, ed. *New Alternatives in Theological Education*. Oxford: Regnum, 1988.

———. "A New Ecclesiology in Latin America." *International Bulletin of Missionary Research* 11, no. 4 (1987): 156–164.

———, ed. *The New Face of Evangelicalism: An International Symposium on the Lausanne Covenant*. Downers Grove, IL: InterVarsity Press, 1976.

———. "Padilla Replies." In *Conflict and Context: Hermeneutics in the Americas*, edited by Mark Lau Branson and C. René Padilla, 103–105. Grand Rapids, MI: Eerdmans, 1986.

———. "Partnership in Mission." *Theological Fraternity Bulletin* no. 3 (1978): 1–18.

———. "Peru: Evangelicals Under Attack." *Christianity Today*, April 11, 1975.

———. "The Politics of the Kingdom of God and the Political Mission of the Church." In *Mission as Transformation: A Theology for the Whole* Gospel, edited by Vinay Samuel and Chris Sugden, 438–455. Oxford: Regnum, 1999.

———. "The Politics of the Kingdom of God and the Political Mission of the Church." In *Proclaiming Christ in Christ's Way*, edited by Vinay Samuel and Albrecht Hauser, 180–198. Oxford: Regnum, 1989.

———. "Religious Identity and the Gospel of Reconciliation: A Response to Prof. Miklós Tomka." *Mission Studies* 26, no. 1 (2009): 45–48.

———. "Rome and the Bible." *Christianity Today*, October 25, 1974.

———. "A Steep Climb Ahead for Theology in Latin America." *Evangelical Missions Quarterly* 7, no. 2 (1971): 37–43.

———. "Student Witness in Latin America Today." *I.F.E.S. Journal* 19, no. 2 (1966): 11–22.

———. "Theology in the Making." *Christianity Today*, May 10, 1974.

———. "Theology of Liberation." *Christianity Today*, November 9, 1973.

———. "Towards a Contextual Christology from Latin America." In *Conflict and Context: Hermeneutics in the Americas*, edited by Mark Lau Branson and C. René Padilla, 81–91. Grand Rapids, MI: Eerdmans, 1986.

———. "The Unity of the Church and the Homogenous Unit Principle." In *Exploring Church Growth*, edited by William R. Shenk, 285–303. Grand Rapids, MI: Eerdmans, 1983.

———. "The Unity of the Church and the Homogeneous Unit Principle." In *Landmark Essays in Mission and World Christianity*, edited by Robert L. Gallagher and Paul Hertig, 73–94. Maryknoll, NY: Orbis Books, 2009.

———. "The Unity of the Church and the Homogeneous Unit Principle." *International Bulletin of Missionary Research* 6, no. 1 (1982): 23–30.

———. "The WCC 7th Assembly." *Transformation* 8 (October 1991): 1–6.

———. "What Is the Gospel." *Christianity Today*, July 20, 1973.

———. "What Is the Gospel?" In *The Gospel Today: Working Papers for Discussion and Application*. Paper presented at the IFES General Committee, 1975.

———. "What Kind of Democracy?" *Transformation* 7 (October–December 1990): 9–10.

———. "Wholistic Mission: Evangelical and Ecumenical." *International Review of Mission* 81 (1992): 381–382.

———. "With Love from Argentina." *Third Way* (October 1982): 28–29.

Padilla, C. René, and Mark L. Branson, eds. *Conflict and Context: Hermeneutics in the Americas*. Grand Rapids, MI: Eerdmans, 1986.

Padilla, C. René, and Lindy Scott. *Terrorism and the War in Iraq: A Christian Word from Latin America*. Buenos Aires: Kairos Ediciones, 2004.

Padilla, C. René, and Chris Sugden, eds. *Texts on Evangelical Social Ethics, 1974–1983 (I–III)*. Nottingham: Grove Books, 1985.

Padilla, C. René, Tetsunao Yamamori, and Steven M. Voth, eds. *The Local Church, Agent of Transformation: An Ecclesiology for Integral Mission*. Buenos Aires, Argentina: Ediciones Kairós, 2004.

Spanish Secondary Sources

Amador. "No hablaba mucho, pero decía mucho con sus acciones." *Revista Kairos*, Informe especial en memoria de Catalina F. Padilla, July 25, 2011: 32,

Asociación Teológica Evangélica. "Actividades asociación teológica." *Pensamiento Cristiano* 16, no. 62 (1969): 230–233.

Bojorge, Horacio. "El debate contemporáneo sobre la biblia." *Boletín Teológico* 1, no. 12 (1975): 23–26.

CLADE III. *Todo el evangelio para todos los pueblos: CLADE III: Documentos*. Lima: Ediciones Puma del Centro de Investigaciones y Publicaciones (CENIP), 1992.

Consejo Latinoamericano de Iglesias, Asamblea de Iglesias Cristianas. *Oaxtepec 1978: Unidad y misión en América Latina*. San José: Comité Editorial del CLAI, 1980.

FTL. "Notas del momento." *Boletín Teológico* 2 (1972): 8–11.

———. "Novedad y promesa: La tercera consulta de la Fraternidad Teologica Latinoamericana." *Boletín Teológico* 1, no. 2 (1977): no page numbers given.

———. "Resumen del trabajo de la Fraternidad (1972–1977)." *Boletín Teológico* 1, no. 2 (1977): 22.

———. "Sentido y espíritu del CLADE II." *Boletín Teológico*, no. 1–2 (1979): no page numbers given.

Guevara, Ernesto Che. *La guerra de guerrillas*. Melbourne: Ocean Sur, 2006.

Gutiérrez, Gustavo. *Teología de la liberación*. Lima: CEP, 1971.

Kirk, Andrés. *Así confesamos la fe Cristiana*. Buenos Aires: La Aurora, 1976.

Lastra, Carlos. "Plan para america latina." In *Acción en cristo para un continente en crisis*. San José: Editorial Caribe, 1970.

León, Jorge. "Místico y racionalista." In *Hacia una teología evangélica latinoamericana: Ensayos en honor de pedro savage*, edited by C. René Padilla, 89–100. Miami: Editorial Caribe, 1984.

Nuñez, Emilio Antonio. "Testigo de un nuevo amanecer." In *Hacia una teología evangélica latinoamericana: Ensayos en honor de Pedro Savage*, edited by C. René Padilla, 101–111. Miami: Editorial Caribe, 1984.

Padilla, Catharine Feser. "Los 'laicos' en la misión en el Nuevo Testamento." In *Bases bíblicas de la misión: Perspectivas Latinoamericanas*, edited by C. René Padilla. Buenos Aires: Nueva Creacion, Eerdmans, 1998.

———. "El ministerio de la mujer en la iglesia." *Encuentro y Diálogo* 8 (1991).

———. *La palabra de Dios para el pueblo de Dios: Una introducción al estudio de la Biblia*. Buenos Aires: Ediciones Kairos, 2007.

Padilla, Catharine Feser, and C. René Padilla. *Mujer y hombre en la misión de Dios*. Buenos Aires: Ediciones Kairos, 1994.

Padilla, Catharine Feser, and Elsa Tamez. *La relación hombre-mujer en perspectiva Cristiana: El testimonio Evangélico hacia el Tercer Milenio: Palabra, espíritu y misión*. Buenos Aires: Ediciones Kairos, 2002.

Padilla, Elisa. "Ojalá pudiera darte otro abrazo y decirte cuánto, cuánto te quiero." *Revista Kairos*, Informe especial en memoria de Catalina F. Padilla, July 25, 2011

Pantelís, Jorge. "Reino de Dios e iglesia en el proceso histórico de liberación: Perspectivas latinoamericanas (Kingdom of God and Church in the Historical Process of Liberation: Latin American Perspectives)." PhD diss., Union Theological Seminary, 1976.

Rooy, Mae. "Una reflexión Latinoamericana sobre 'el pueblo de Dios.'" *Boletín Teológico* 1, no. 2 (1977): 4–21.

Savage, Pedro, and Rolando Gutiérrez, eds. *América Latina y la evangelización en los años 80*. México: Fraternidad Teológica Latinoamericana, 1980.

Savage, Peter, ed. *El debate contemporáneo sobre la biblia*. Barcelona: Ediciones Evangélicas Europeas, 1972.

English Secondary Sources

Aguilar, Mario I. *The History and Politics of Latin American Theology*. 3 vols. Vol. 1. London: SCM Press, 2007.

Almond, Gabriel A., and James Smoot Coleman. *The Politics of the Developing Areas*. Princeton, NJ: Princeton University Press, 1960.

Annis, Sheldon. *God and Production in a Guatemalan Town*. Austin: University of Texas Press, 1987.

Assmann, Hugo. *Theology for a Nomad Church*. Maryknoll, NY: Orbis Books, 1975.

Atherstone, Andrew. "The Keele Congress of 1967: A Paradigm Shift in Anglican Evangelical Attitudes." *Journal of Anglican Studies* 9, no. 2 (2011): 175–197.

Avila, Mariano. "Towards a Latin American Contextual Hermeneutics: A Critical Examination of the Contextual Hermeneutics of the Fraternidad Teológica Latinoamericana." PhD diss., Westminster Theological Seminary, 1996.

Barreto, Raimundo C., Jr. "Facing the Poor in Brazil: Towards an Evangélico Progressive Social Ethics." PhD diss., Princeton Theological Seminary, 2006.

Barro, Antonio Carlos. "Orlando Enrique Costas: Mission Theologian on the Way and at the Crossroads." PhD diss., Fuller Theological Seminary, School of World Mission, 1993.

Bebbington, David W. *Evangelicalism in Modern Britain: A History from the 1730s to the 1980s*. London: Routledge, 1993.

———. "Evangelicals and Reform: An Analysis of Social and Political Action." *Third Way*, May 1983, 10–13.

———. *The Nonconformist Conscience: Chapel and Politics, 1870–1914*. London: G. Allen & Unwin, 1982.

Bediako, Kwame. *Jesus and the Gospel in Africa: History and Experience*. New York: Orbis Books, 2004.

Bendroth, Margaret Lamberts. *Fundamentalism & Gender, 1875 to the Present*. New Haven, CT: Yale University Press, 1993.

Bialecki, Jon. "The Kingdom and Its Subjects: Charisms, Language, Economy, and the Birth of a Progressive Politics in the Vineyard." PhD diss., University of California, San Diego, 2009.

Boberg, John T., and James A. Scherer. *Mission in the 70's: What Direction?* Chicago: Chicago Cluster of Theological Schools, 1972.

Bosch, David J. *Transforming Mission: Paradigm Shifts in Theology of Mission*. Maryknoll, NY: Orbis Books, 1991.

Boyd, Robin. *The Witness of the Student Christian Movement: Church Ahead of the Church*. London: SPCK, 2007.

Branson, Mark, and C. René Padilla, eds. *Conflict and Context: Hermeneutics in the Americas: A Report on the Context and Hermeneutics in the Americas Conference*. Grand Rapids, MI: Eerdmans, 1986.

Braun, Herbert. *The Assassination of Gaitán: Public Life and Urban Violence in Colombia*. Madison: University of Wisconsin Press 2003.

Brown, Harold O. J. "A Theology of Liberation: History, Politics, and Salvation." *Christianity Today*, June 22, 1973.

Brown, Stewart J. *Providence and Empire: Religion, Politics and Society in the United Kingdom, 1815–1914*. Harlow: Pearson Education, 2008.

Bushnell, David. *The Making of Modern Colombia: A Nation in Spite of Itself.* Berkeley: University of California Press, 1993.

Capon, John. "Let the Earth Hear Whose Voice?" *Crusade* 26 (September 1974): 3–12.

Cardoso, F. H. "The Consumption of Dependency Theory in the United States." *Latin American Research Review* 12, no. 3 (1977): 7–24.

Carey, Elaine. *Plaza of Sacrifices: Gender, Power, and Terror in 1968 Mexico*. Albuquerque: University of New Mexico Press, 2005.

Carpenter, Joel A. *Revive Us Again: The Reawakening of American Fundamentalism*. New York: Oxford University Press, 1997.

Castro, Emilio. "Editorial." *International Review of Mission* 40, no. 1 (1988): 1–3.

CELAM. "Second General Conference of Latin American Bishops: The Church in the Present-Day Transformation of Latin America in Light of the Council." In *Liberation Theology: A Documentary History*, edited by Alfred T. Hennelly, 89–119. Maryknoll, NY: Orbis Books, 1990.

"A Challenge from Evangelicals." *Time*, August 5, 1974, 54.

Chapman, Alister. *Godly Ambition: John Stott and the Evangelical Movement*. Oxford: Oxford University Press, 2012.

Chesnut, R. Andrew. *Born Again in Brazil: The Pentecostal Boom and the Pathogens of Poverty*. New Brunswick, NJ: Rutgers University Press, 1997.

———. *Competitive Spirits: Latin America's New Religious Economy*. Oxford: Oxford University Press, 2003.

Chester, Tim. *Awakening to a World of Need: The Recovery of Evangelical Social Concern*. Leicester, England: Inter-Varsity Press, 1993.

Christopher, J. H. Wright, and Jonathan Lamb, eds. *Understanding and Using the Bible*. Edited by Emma Wild-Wood. SPCK International Study Guides. London: Society for Promoting Christian Knowledge, 2009.

Cleary, Edward L. *How Latin America Saved the Soul of the Catholic Church*. New York: Paulist Press, 2009.

Crowe, Philip, ed. *Keele '67: The National Evangelical Anglican Congress Statement*. London: Church Pastoral-Aid Society, Falcon Books, 1967.

Davies, Paul. *Faith Seeking Effectiveness: The Missionary Theology of José Míguez Bonino*. Zoetermeer: Boekencentrum, 2006.

del Salto, David. "The Promise of a Trinitarian Christology for the Latin American Evangelical Church." PhD diss., Lutheran School of Theology at Chicago, 2008.

D'Elia, John A. *A Place at the Table: George Eldon Ladd and the Rehabilitation of Evangelical Scholarship in America*. Oxford: Oxford University Press, 2008.

Dorrien, Gary J. *The Remaking of Evangelical Theology*. Louisville, KY: Westminster John Knox Press, 1998.

Douglas, James Dixon. *Let the Earth Hear His Voice: International Congress on World Evangelization, Lausanne, Switzerland, Official Reference Volume, Papers and Responses*. Minneapolis, MN: World Wide Publications, 1975.

Dussel, Enrique D. *History and the Theology of Liberation: A Latin American Perspective*. Maryknoll, NY: Orbis Books, 1976.

———. *A History of the Church in Latin America: Colonialism to Liberation (1492–1979)*. Translated by Alan Neely. Grand Rapids, MI: Eerdmans, 1981.

Ekbladh, David. *The Great American Mission: Modernization and the Construction of an American World Order*. Princeton, NJ: Princeton University Press, 2010.

Feitlowitz, Marguerite. *A Lexicon of Terror: Argentina and the Legacies of Torture*. New York: Oxford University Press, 1998.

Freire, Paulo. *Pedagogy of the Oppressed*. Translated by Myra Bergman Ramos and Donaldo P. Macedo. New York: Continuum, 2012.

Gasaway, Brantley W. *Progressive Evangelicals and the Pursuit of Social Justice*. Chapel Hill: University of North Carolina Press, 2014.

George, Timothy, James Earl Massey, and Robert Smith Jr., eds. *Our Sufficiency Is of God: Essays on Preaching in Honor of Gardner C. Taylor*. Macon, GA: Mercer University Press, 2010.

Gibellini, Rosino, ed. *Frontiers of Theology in Latin America*. Maryknoll, NY: Orbis Books, 1979.

Gish, Arthur G. *Beyond the Rat Race*. Scottdale, PA: Herald Press, 1973.

———. *The New Left and Christian Radicalism*. Grand Rapids, MI: Eerdmans, 1970.

Goff, James E. "The Persecution of Protestant Christians in Colombia, 1948–1958, with an Investigation of Its Background and Causes." PhD diss., Centro Intercultural de Documentación, Cuernavaca, Mexico, 1968.

Goffin, Alvin M. *The Rise of Protestant Evangelism in Ecuador, 1895–1990*. Gainesville: University Press of Florida, 1994.

González, Ondina E., and Justo L. González. *Christianity in Latin America: A History*. Cambridge: Cambridge University Press, 2008.

Graham, Billy. *Just as I Am: The Autobiography of Billy Graham*. San Francisco: HarperSanFrancisco, 1997.

———. "Why Lausanne?" In *Let the Earth Hear His Voice: Official Reference Volume, Papers and Responses*, edited by J. D. Douglas, 22–36. Minneapolis, MN: World Wide Publications, 1975.

Grass, Tim. *F. F. Bruce: A Life*. Grand Rapids, MI: Eerdmans, 2012.

Gutiérrez, Gustavo. *A Theology of Liberation: History, Politics, and Salvation*. Maryknoll, NY: Orbis Books, 1973.

Gutmann, Matthew C. *The Romance of Democracy: Compliant Defiance in Contemporary Mexico*. Berkeley: University of California Press, 2002.

Harmer, Tanya. *Allende's Chile and the Inter-American Cold War*. Chapel Hill: University of North Carolina Press, 2011.

Harries, Jim. "'Material Provision' or Preaching the Gospel: Reconsidering 'Holistic' (Integral) Mission." *Evangelical Review of Theology* 32, no. 3 (2008): 257–270.

Hartch, Todd. *The Rebirth of Latin American Christianity.* Oxford Studies in World Christianity. Oxford: Oxford University Press, 2014.

Heaney, Sharon E. *Contextual Theology for Latin America: Liberation Themes in Evangelical Perspective.* Milton Keynes: Paternoster, 2008.

Heltzel, Peter. *Jesus and Justice: Evangelicals, Race, and American Politics.* New Haven, CT: Yale University Press, 2009.

Hennelly, Alfred T. *Liberation Theology: A Documentary History.* Maryknoll, NY: Orbis Books, 1990.

Henry, Carl F. H. "Gospel and Society." *Christianity Today,* September 13, 1974.

———. *The Uneasy Conscience of Modern Fundamentalism.* Grand Rapids, MI: Eerdmans, 1947.

Holmes, Arthur F. *Faith Seeks Understanding: A Christian Approach to Knowledge.* Grand Rapids, MI: Eerdmans, 1971.

Horowitz, Irving Louis. "The Socioeconomic Pivot." In *Latin American Radicalism: A Documentary Report on Left and Nationalist Movements,* edited by Irving Louis de Castro Horowitz and John Josué Gerassi, 140–176. New York: Random House, 1969.

Hunter, Jane. *The Gospel of Gentility: American Women Missionaries in Turn-of-the-Century China.* New Haven, CT: Yale University Press, 1984.

Iglesia y Sociedad en América Latina (ISAL). *Social Justice and the Latin Churches.* Richmond, VA: John Knox Press, 1969.

INFEMIT. "The Declaration of Osijek 'Freedom and Justice in Church State Relationships.'" *Transformation* 8, no. 3 (1991): 1–6.

———. "News of the International Fellowship of Evangelical Mission Theologians." *Transformation* 8, no. 3 (1991): 32.

International Council on Biblical Inerrancy. *The Chicago Statement on Biblical Inerrancy.* Oakland, CA: International Council on Biblical Inerrancy, 1978.

Johnston, Arthur P. *The Battle for World Evangelism.* Wheaton, IL: Tyndale House.

Kidd, Thomas S. *George Whitefield: America's Spiritual Founding Father.* New Haven, CT: Yale University Press, 2014.

Kirkpatrick, David C. "C. René Padilla and the Origins of Integral Mission in Post-War Latin America." *Journal of Ecclesiastical History* 67, no. 2 (April): 351–371.

———. "American Protestant Foreign Missions after World War II." In *Oxford Encyclopedia of Religion in America,* edited by John Corrigan, 25–37. New York: Oxford University Press, 2018.

———. "Freedom from Fundamentalism: The Surprising Influence of Christian Brethrenism on the Rise of Latin American Social Christianity." *Journal of World Christianity* 7, no. 2 (2017): 211–233.

———. "Parachurch Competition in the Latin American Religious Marketplace: Scriptural Inerrancy and the Reshaping of Global Protestant Evangelicalism." In *Relocating World Christianity: Interdisciplinary Studies in Universal and Local Expressions of Christianity,* edited by Joel Cabrita, David Maxwell, and Emma Wild-Wood, 93–112. Leiden: Brill, 2017.

Ladd, George Eldon. *Jesus and the Kingdom: The Eschatology of Biblical Realism.* New York: Harper & Row, 1964.

————. *The Presence of the Future: The Eschatology of Biblical Realism*. Grand Rapids, MI: Eerdmans, 1974.

Laing, Mark T. B. *From Crisis to Creation: Lesslie Newbigin and the Reinvention of Christian Mission*. Eugene, OR: Pickwick Publications, 2012.

Lehtonen, Risto. *Story of a Storm: The Ecumenical Student Movement in the Turmoil of Revolution, 1968 to 1973*. Grand Rapids, MI: Eerdmans, 1998.

Lewis, Paul H. *Guerrillas and Generals: The "Dirty War" in Argentina*. Westport, CT: Praeger, 2011.

Longacre, Doris Janzen. *More-with-Less Cookbook*. Scottdale, PA: Herald Press, 1976.

Lowman, Pete. *The Day of His Power: A History of the International Fellowship of Evangelical Students*. Downers Grove, IL: Inter-Varsity Press, 1988.

Mackay, Gerald W. Gillette, and John A. Mackay. "John A. Mackay: Influences on My Life." *Journal of Presbyterian History* 56, no. 1 (1978): 20–34.

Mackay, John A. *The Other Spanish Christ: A Study in the Spiritual History of Spain and South America*. London: SCM Press, 1932.

MacLeod, A. Donald. *C. Stacey Woods and the Evangelical Rediscovery of the University*. Downers Grove, IL: Intervarsity Press Academic, 2007.

Manktelow, Emily J. *Missionary Families: Race, Gender and Generation on the Spiritual Frontier*. Manchester: Manchester University Press, 2013.

Marsden, George M. *Fundamentalism and American Culture: The Shaping of Twentieth Century Evangelicalism, 1870–1925*. New York: Oxford University Press, 1980.

————. *Reforming Fundamentalism: Fuller Seminary and the New Evangelicalism*. Grand Rapids, MI: Eerdmans, 1987.

Martin, David. *Tongues of Fire: The Explosion of Protestantism in Latin America*. Oxford: Blackwell, 1990.

Martinez, Juan F. "Stepchildren of the Empire: The Formation and Reformation of the Latino Evangélico Identity." In *Evangelicals and Empire: Christian Alternatives to the Political Status Quo*, edited by Bruce Ellis Benson and Peter Heltzel, 141–151. Grand Rapids, MI: Brazos Press, 2008.

Mathew, C. V., and Saphir P. Athyal. *Integral Mission: The Way Forward: Essays in Honour of Dr. Saphir P. Athyal*. Tiruvalla: Christava Sahitya Samithi, 2006.

McGavran, Donald A., ed. *Eye of the Storm: The Great Debate in Mission*. Waco: Word Books, 1972.

Metzger, John Mackay. *The Hand and the Road: The Life and Times of John A. Mackay*. Louisville, KY: Westminster John Knox Press, 2010.

Miller, Donald Earl, and Tetsunao Yamamori. *Global Pentecostalism: The New Face of Christian Social Engagement*. Berkeley: University of California Press, 2007.

Moberg, David O. *The Great Reversal: Evangelism Versus Social Concern*. Philadelphia: Lippincott, 1972.

Moltmann, Jürgen. "On Latin American Liberation Theology: An Open Letter to José Miguez Bonino." *Christianity and Crisis* 36, no. 5 (1976): 57–63.

Mondragón, Carlos. *Like Leaven in the Dough: Protestant Social Thought in Latin America, 1920–1950*. Madison, NJ: Fairleigh Dickinson University Press, 2010.

Mooneyham, W. Stanley, and Carl F. H. Henry, eds. *One Race, One Gospel, One Task: World Congress on Evangelism Berlin 1966: Official Reference Volumes: Papers and Reports.* 2 vols. Minneapolis, MN: World Wide Publications, 1967.

Norman, E. R. *Christianity and World Order.* Oxford: Oxford University Press, 1979.

Neely, Alan P. "Liberation Theology in Latin America: Antecedents and Autochthony." *Missiology: An International Review* 6, no. 3 (1978): 343–367.

———. "Protestant Antecedents of the Latin American Theology of Liberation." PhD diss., American University, 1977.

Niebuhr, H. Richard. *Christ and Culture.* New York: Harper, 1951.

Noelliste, Diememme E. "The Church and Human Emancipation: A Critical Comparison of Liberation Theology and the Latin American Theological Fraternity." PhD diss., Northwestern University, 1987.

Noll, Mark A. *Turning Points: Decisive Moments in the History of Christianity.* Grand Rapids, MI: Baker Academic, 2012.

Nuñez, Kenneth Mullholand, and Emilio Antonio, eds. *The Contextualization of the Gospel: The Documents of CLADE II.* San José: LAECPS, 1980.

Padilla, Catharine Feser. "Using the Bible in Groups." In *Understanding and Using the Bible,* edited by Christopher J. H. Wright and Jonathan Lamb, 85–101. London: Society for Promoting Christian Knowledge, 2009.

Padilla DeBorst, Ruth. "Catharine Feser Padilla: Bible, Bed and Bread: A Matter of Distance." In *Mission as Transformation: Learning from Catalysts,* edited by David Cranston and Ruth Padilla DeBorst, 33–38. Eugene, OR: Wipf & Stock, 2014.

———. "From Lausanne III to CLADE V." *Journal of Latin American Theology* 6, no. 1 (2011): 7–13.

———. "Liberate My People." *Christianity Today,* August 1, 2007).

———. "Twin Peaks: From the Padilla-Deborsts (Unpublished Support Letter)." 2009.

———. "'Unlikely Partnerships': Global Discipleship in the Twenty-First Century." *Transformation* 28, no. 4 (2011): 241–252.

Pantelís, Jorge M. "Implications of the Theologies of Liberation for the Theological Training of the Pastoral Ministry in Latin America." *International Review of Mission* 66, no. 261 (1977): 14–21.

Price, Eva Jane. *China Journal 1889–1900: An American Missionary Family During the Boxer Rebellion.* New York: Scribner, 1989.

Quigley, Tom. "The Great North-South Embrace." *America* 201, no. 18 (2009): 17–20.

Ramm, Bernard L. *After Fundamentalism: The Future of Evangelical Theology.* San Francisco: Harper & Row, 1983.

———. *Protestant Biblical Interpretation: A Textbook of Hermeneutics.* Grand Rapids, MI: Baker, 1970.

Ratzinger, Joseph. "Liberation Theology." In *Liberation Theology: A Documentary History,* edited by Alfred T. Hennelly, 367–374. Maryknoll, NY: Orbis Books, 1990.

Regnerus, Mark D., and Christian Smith. "Selective Deprivatization Among American Religious Traditions: The Reversal of the Great Reversal." *Social Forces* 76, no. 4 (1998): 1347–1372.

Restrepo, Camilo Torres. "Message to Students." In *Latin American Radicalism: A Documentary Report on Left and Nationalist Movements*, edited by Josué De Castro, Irving Louis Horowitz, and John Gerassi, 496–498. London: Random House, 1968.

Robbins, B. W. "Contextualization in Costa Rican Theological Education Today: A History of the Seminario Biblico Latinoamericano, San José, Costa Rica, 1922–1990." PhD diss., Southern Methodist University, 1991.

Robert, Dana Lee. *American Women in Mission: A Social History of Their Thought and Practice*. Macon, GA: Mercer University Press, 1996.

———. *Christian Mission: How Christianity Became a World Religion*. Malden, MA: Wiley-Blackwell, 2009.

Roberts, W. Dayton. "Latin American Protestants: Which Way Will They Go?" *Christianity Today*, October 10, 1969.

———. "My Pilgrimage in Mission." *International Bulletin of Missionary Research* 19 (1995): 110–112.

Romero, Luis Alberto. *A History of Argentina in the Twentieth Century*. University Park: Pennsylvania State University Press, 2002.

Rostow, W. W. *The Stages of Economic Growth, a Non-Communist Manifesto*. Cambridge: Cambridge University Press, 1960.

Salinas, Daniel. *Latin American Evangelical Theology in the 1970's: The Golden Decade*. Leiden: Brill, 2009.

Samuel, Vinay, and Albrecht Hauser. *Proclaiming Christ in Christ's Way: Studies in Integral Evangelism: Essays Presented to Walter Arnold on the Occasion of His 60th Birthday*. Oxford: Regnum, 1989.

———. *Proclaiming Christ in Christ's Way: Studies in Integral Mission: Essays Presented to Walter Arnold on the Occasion of His 60th Birthday*. Eugene, OR: Wipf & Stock, 2007.

Santiago-Vendrell, Angel Daniel. *Contextual Theology and Revolutionary Transformation in Latin America: The Missiology of M. Richard Shaull*. Eugene, OR: Pickwick Publications, 2010.

Saxon, Wolfgang. "Rev. John Stott, Major Evangelical Figure, Dies at 90." *New York Times*, July 28, 2011, A27.

Scott, Lindy. *Salt of the Earth: A Socio-Political History of Mexico City Evangelical Protestants (1964–1991)*. Santo Domingo: Editorial Kyrios, 1991.

Sernett, Milton G. "Black Religion and the Question of Evangelical Identity." In *The Variety of American Evangelicalism*, edited by Donald W. Dayton and Robert K. Johnston, 135–147. Knoxville: University of Tennessee Press, 1991.

Shaull, Richard. *Encounter with Revolution*. New York: Association Press, 1955.

Smith, Anthony Christopher. "The Essentials of Missiology from the Evangelical Perspective of 'the Latin American Theological Fraternity.'" PhD diss., Southern Baptist Theological Seminary, 1983.

Smith, Christian. *The Emergence of Liberation Theology: Radical Religion and Social Movement Theory*. Chicago: University of Chicago Press, 1991.

Smith, Timothy L. "Popular Protestantism in Mid-Nineteenth Century America." PhD diss., Harvard University, 1955.

Stanley, Brian. *The Bible and the Flag: Protestant Missions and British Imperialism in the Nineteenth and Twentieth Centuries*. Leicester: Apollos, 1990.

———. "Evangelical Social and Political Ethics: An Historical Perspective." *Evangelical Quarterly* 62 (1990): 19–36.

———. *The Global Diffusion of Evangelicalism*. Nottingham: InterVarsity Press, 2013.

———. "'Lausanne 1974': The Challenge from the Majority World to Northern-Hemisphere Evangelicalism." *Journal of Ecclesiastical History* 64, no. 3 (2013): 533–551.

Stanton, R. Wilson. "Studies in the Life and Work of an Ecumenical Churchman." Master's thesis, Princeton Theological Seminary, 1958.

Steuernagel, Valdir. "The Theology of Missions in Its Relation to Social Responsibility Within the Lausanne Movement." PhD diss., Lutheran School of Theology, 1988.

Stoll, David. *Is Latin America Turning Protestant? The Politics of Evangelical Growth*. Berkeley: University of California Press, 1990.

Stott, John R. W. "The Battle for World Evangelism: An Open Response to Arthur Johnston." *Christianity Today*, January 5, 1979.

———. "The Biblical Scope of Mission: We See in Scripture the Reflections of Our Own Prejudice Rather Than the Disturbing Message." *Christianity Today*, January 4, 1980

———. *Christian Mission in the Modern World*. Downers Grove, IL: InterVarsity Press, 1975.

———. *Making Christ Known: Historic Mission Documents from the Lausanne Movement, 1974–1989*. Exeter: Paternoster, 1996.

———. "Significance of Lausanne." *International Review of Mission* 64, no. 255 (1975): 288–294.

Sugden, Chris. "Evangelicals and Wholistic Evangelism." In *Proclaiming Christ in Christ's Way: Studies in Integral Evangelism*, edited by Vinay Samuel and Albrecht Hauser, 29–51. Oxford: Regnum, 1989.

Sugden, Chris, and Vinay Samuel, eds. *The Church in Response to Human Need*. Grand Rapids, MI: Regnum, 1987.

Swanson, Jeffrey. *Echoes of the Call Identity and Ideology Among American Missionaries in Ecuador*. New York: Oxford University Press, 1995.

Swartz, David R. *Moral Minority: The Evangelical Left in an Age of Conservatism*. Philadelphia: University of Pennsylvania Press, 2012.

Sweeney, Douglas A. *The American Evangelical Story: A History of the Movement*. Grand Rapids, MI: Baker Academic, 2005.

Taylor, Gardner. "What Are You Doing Here? (John 13:34)," In *The Words of Gardner Taylor: NBC Radio Sermons, 1959–1970*, Vol. 1 of *The Words of Gardner Taylor*, 56–60. Valley Forge, PA: Judson, 2004.

Thomas, Gerald Lamont. *African American Preaching: The Contribution of Dr. Gardner C. Taylor*, Vol. 5 of *Martin Luther King, Jr. Memorial Studies in Religion, Culture, and Social Development*, ed. Mozella G. Mitchell. New York: Peter Lang, 2004.

Thompson, David. "John Clifford's Social Gospel." *Baptist Quarterly* 21, no. 5 (1986): 199–219.

Tippner, Jeffrey E. "The Third World Evangelical Missiology of Orlando E. Costas." PhD diss., University of St. Andrews, 2012.

Tizon, Al. *Transformation After Lausanne: Radical Evangelical Mission in Global-Local Perspective*. Eugene, OR: Wipf & Stock, 2008.

Tombs, David. *Latin American Liberation Theology*. Boston: Brill Academic, 2002.

Turner, John G. *Bill Bright & Campus Crusade for Christ: The Renewal of Evangelicalism in Postwar America*. Chapel Hill: University of North Carolina Press, 2008.

VanderPol, Gary F. "The Least of These: American Evangelical Parachurch Missions to the Poor, 1947–2005." ThD diss., Boston University, 2010.

Vinay, Samuel, and Chris Sugden, eds. *Sharing Jesus in the Two Thirds World: Evangelical Christologies from the Contexts of Poverty, Powerlessness, and Religious Pluralism: The Papers of the First Conference of Evangelical Mission Theologians from the Two Thirds World, Bangkok, Thailand, March 22–25, 1982*. Grand Rapids, MI: Eerdmans, 1983.

Wacker, Grant. *America's Pastor: Billy Graham and the Shaping of a Nation*. Cambridge, MA: Harvard University Press, 2014.

Wagner, C. Peter. *Church/Mission Tensions Today*. Chicago: Moody, 1972.

———. "High Theology in the Andes." *Christianity Today*, January 15, 1971.

———. *Latin American Theology: Radical or Evangelical? The Struggle for the Faith in a Young Church*. Grand Rapids, MI: Eerdmans, 1970.

———. "Lausanne Twelve Months Later." *Christianity Today*, July 4, 1975.

———. "My Pilgrimage in Mission." *International Bulletin of Missionary Research* 23, no. 4 (October 1999): 164–167.

Walls, Andrew F. *The Cross-Cultural Process in Christian History: Studies in the Transmission and Appropriation of Faith*. Maryknoll, NY: Orbis Books, 2002.

Westcott, B. F. *Social Aspects of Christianity*. London: Cambridge University Press, 1887.

"Why Some Latin Americans Dislike American Missionaries." *HIS*, November 1959, 7–16.

Woods, C. Stacey. *The Growth of a Work of God: The Story of the Early Days of the Inter-Varsity Christian Fellowship of the United States of America as Told by Its First General Secretary*. Downers Grove, IL: Inter-Varsity Press, 1978.

World Council of Churches. *The Church for Others, and the Church for the World*. Geneva: WCC, 1967.

Wuthnow, Robert. *The Restructuring of American Religion: Society and Faith Since World War II*. Princeton, NJ: Princeton University Press, 1988.

Yeh, Allen. "*Se hace camino al andar*: Periphery and Center in the Missiology of Orlando E. Costas." DPhil thesis, University of Oxford, 2008.

Yoder, John Howard. *The Politics of Jesus: Vicit Agnus Noster*. Grand Rapids, MI: Eerdmans, 1972.

Youngblood, Ronald, ed. *Evangelicals and Inerrancy: Selections from the Evangelical Theological Society*. Nashville, TN: Thomas Nelson, 1984.

INDEX

ACKNOWLEDGMENTS

I am grateful for encouragement and support from tremendous colleagues at James Madison University, Florida State University (FSU), and the University of Edinburgh. I am also grateful for generous funding from the Gannon Foundation at FSU and various funding sources at the University of Edinburgh, including the Global Research Scholar grant, the Yale-Edinburgh World Christianity Group, and New College School of Divinity.

I want to thank my wonderful editor Bob Lockhart at the University of Pennsylvania Press for his dedication and insight throughout this project. For printing earlier versions or portions of this project, I appreciate the *Journal of Ecclesiastical History*, *Oxford Encyclopedia of Religion in America*, Brill Publishers, and *Journal of World Christianity*.

I am grateful to a number of mentors who generously dedicated time and editorial wisdom throughout this book project. Brian Stanley, Naomi Haynes, and Doug Sweeney appear at the top of that list. Brian's patient and wise mentorship in particular has made me a better historian and person, and for him I am sincerely grateful. Many of the strongest insights in this book have Brian's fingerprints on them.

Historians could never practice our craft without the work of dedicated librarians and archivists. I am grateful to Adele Allen at Lambeth Palace Library in London (who allowed access to John Stott's personal papers while they were being catalogued); Kirsty Thorburn at the IFES in Oxford; Bob Shuster, Paul Ericksen, Katherine Graber, and the staff of the Billy Graham Center Archives in Wheaton, Illinois; Rob Krapohl at Trinity Evangelical Divinity School; Martha Smalley and Kevin Crawford of Yale Divinity School; Craig Miller at Palmer Theological Seminary; Diana S. H. Bacci and Joy Dlugosz at Eastern University; and Bruce Robbins with Seminario Bíblico Latinoamericano. Special thanks to Wheaton College President Philip Rykan and IFES General Secretary Daniel Bourdanné for providing access to restricted files.

I am grateful to a number of individuals who provided unrestricted access to personal papers and generous time for interviews. I want to especially thank René Padilla and Beatriz Vásquez in Buenos Aires, as well as Samuel Escobar and Lilly Artola de Escobar in Valencia, for access to personal papers and over a week of interviews. I am also grateful to the late Rose Costas, Pedro Arana, Elisa Padilla, Ruth Padilla DeBorst, Brian McLaren, Vinay Samuel, Chris Sugden, and Andrew Kirk for their generous help.

Many colleagues have been conversation partners in this process and provided critical insight at various points. The list is potentially endless, but I wish to highlight David Bebbington and Casey High, who read a full, early draft of the book. Key conversation partners also include Andrew Walls, Dana Robert, Mark Noll, Heath Carter, Amanda Porterfield, John Corrigan, Mike McVicar, Jamil Drake, Jason Bruner, Corey Williams, Deanna Womack, Peter Cha, Alex Chow, Jim Wallis, Kathryn Long, David Swartz, Aaron Griffith, Heather Curtis, David King, Brantley Gasaway, Tucker Adkins, and many others. I am grateful for all of their contributions.

I am deeply thankful for my family, for constant encouragement over the course of this project and across multiple continents. I continue to draw inspiration from all of you: Kelli, Ronaldo, Andy, Clare, Mom, and Dad.

Finally, I dedicate this book to my wife, Anna. Her persevering love, hope, belief, brilliance, and encouragement are daily gifts. Life with her is a joyous adventure and each day together is my new favorite day.